R

Sources Of
American Spirituality

William Ellery Channing

SELECTED WRITINGS

Edited by David Robinson

PAULIST PRESS
New York ◆ Mahwah

Library of Congress
Catalog Card Number: 84-62567

ISBN: 0-8091-0359-1

Published by Paulist Press
997 Macarthur Boulevard
Mahwah, N.J. 07430

Printed and bound in the United States of America

CONTENTS

To Gwendolyn, Elena, and Paul
with love

PREFACE

William Ellery Channing's voice is by no means lost to us now, almost a century and a half after his death. The totality of his message, however, is not well understood. It is my hope that this collection of his writings may help to change that situation. The problem arises in large part from Channing's medium. He was a preacher, one of America's most original masters of the sermon. But he held mastery over a form of address largely out of favor now with the modern reader. Only historical reconstruction and a determined intellectual sympathy can overcome that barrier, but the rewards of so doing are great. Fortunately, however, Channing has been rich in his biographers, from John White Chadwick's turn-of-the-century portrait to the modern studies of Jack Mendelsohn and Andrew Delbanco. These studies can help to bring out the complex personality behind these forceful utterances, but only a firsthand acquaintance with Channing's writings themselves can establish his stature for the reader. This collection attempts to present those texts, from the beginning to the end of his career, which brought Channing to prominence, gave him his greatest impact on his contemporaries, and have continued to sustain his reputation.

For helping to initiate this project, I am very grateful to David B. Parke, Carl Seaburg, and Conrad Wright. During my work on the project, I have had much valuable help from Conrad Wright, for which I am grateful. John Farina has also given me many helpful suggestions. I want to thank Doris Tilles and the staff of the Interlibrary Loan Department at the Oregon State University Library, and Alan Seaburg of the Andover-Harvard Theological Library for helping me in gathering materials for this project. I am grateful to the editors of the *Harvard Theological Review* for permission to reprint certain portions of my essay ''The Legacy of Channing: Culture as a

1

Religious Category in New England Thought,'' *Harvard Theological Review* 74 (1981): 221–39, copyright 1981 by the President and Fellows of Harvard College, reprinted by permission. Research for this project was supported by a fellowship from the American Council of Learned Societies, through a grant from the National Endowment for the Humanities, and a sabbatical leave from Oregon State University.

INTRODUCTION

I

William Ellery Channing "differed from the rest of us, not so much in severity of practice, as in spirituality of mind." So wrote Frederic Henry Hedge, one of the many New England liberals who looked to Channing as the source of their movement in theology.

> In that, he had no equal among all the men whom I have known. And that I conceive to be the characteristic thing in Channing,—Spirituality: living in the contemplation and pursuit of the highest; the habit of viewing all things in reference to the supreme good. All questions, movements, institutions, enterprises, all discoveries and inventions, he judged by this standard.[1]

Hedge's sense of Channing's characteristic "spirituality" was one of many attempts to account for the enormous influence of Channing, an influence felt most keenly by the generation of thinkers who not only secured the Unitarian movement in New England, but in many cases pushed beyond Unitarianism into the modernist radicalism of that day, Transcendentalism. Upon Channing's death in 1842, Theodore Parker, who was then emerging as a champion of Transcendentalism, made this sweeping claim: "It is speaking with moderation to say, that no man, of our century, who writes the English tongue, had so much weight with the wise and pious men who speak it."[2] The accumulated weight of tributes like these suggests the deep chord which Channing struck among his contemporaries. That influence is most readily seen in the formation of the Unitarian

3

movement from the liberal congregational churches in eastern Massachusetts. It was Channing who accepted the responsibility of articulating publicly the liberal position, and laying an intellectual groundwork for the denomination which emerged. And well into the twentieth century, the opposing camps of the Unitarian movement vied for Channing as their spiritual ancestor. "Dr. Channing, whilst he lived, was the star of the American Church," Ralph Waldo Emerson wrote, "and we then thought, if we do not still think, that he left no successor in the pulpit."[3]

Nor was Channing's influence restricted to New England's liberal movement in theology. He was not bound by a limited sense of his audience and his appeal has been universal. "He was of no sect in Religion," Parker wrote. "He loved Piety, and honored a Divine Life, wherever he saw their light, and did not think living water impure because it flowed into an urn of different form from his own. All denominations of Theology—there is but one of Religion—have been blessed by him."[4] Thus as one changes the focus from the specific milieu of Boston and begins to survey the development of American culture in general, Channing's prominence continues to be felt. As Emerson put it, "he was a kind of public *Conscience*."[5]

But how do we account for that influence? Even though Hedge spoke of Channing's remarkable force of character with grave respect, he did not attribute it to intellectual genius. He in fact almost denigrates Channing in his account of him:

> And curious it was how this man—without learning, without research, not a scholar, not a critic, without imagination or fancy, not a poet, not a word-painter, without humor or wit, without profundity of thought, without grace of elocution—could, from the spiritual height on which he stood, by mere dint of gravity (coming from such an elevation), send his word into the soul with more searching force than all the orators of his time.[6]

In how many instances in the history of criticism have a man's weaknesses been so paraded in an act of praise? What, indeed, was left to praise in Channing except the peculiar quality of spirituality which accounted for all his force? In Hedge's view, at least, Channing's impact has to be accounted for in terms of his rare and penetrating vision in spiritual matters. Of course we must not accept too literally Hedge's claim that Channing lacked learning, imagination, profundity and grace of elocution. The record of his writings proves the contrary. But if Hedge oversteps the strictest factual boundaries, he deserves to be heard on other grounds—that the ordinary means of assessment of a mind do not quite succeed in judging Channing. We get closer to a true sense of Channing's worth by attending not only to what intellectual positions he took, but how he arrived at them. The direction of his thinking is in many respects as important as the result.

Comment on Channing, if pressed far enough, inevitably exposes what Sydney Ahlstrom termed "the mystery of Channing," the as yet unexplicated "basis of Channing's claim on people." How do we account for the force of his impact on his contemporaries, and on broadening circles of readers here and abroad? Ahlstrom asked. It is a force strong enough not only to influence thinking, but to work "conversions."[7] Is Hedge's appeal to Channing's spirituality merely a way of begging the question of this mystery, or does it hint at a profitable direction of inquiry?

If we understand spirituality to be the living out of religious doctrine, if we see it as a term for the translation of theology into devotional practice and moral action, then it may indeed illumine Channing's impact. His significance was that he reconceived the model of the religious life which he inherited from New England theology, and did it so completely that it changed the intellectual landscape of early nineteenth-century America. He did not, of course, do it alone. He was part of a movement, Unitarianism, whose growing sense of mission was to remodel the spiritual life. But he was the unquestioned center of that movement, and no other liberal of his generation approached his power of expressing this new view. An essential step in this revolution was a redefinition of the spiritual capacities of human nature in opposition to the inherited doctrines of Calvinism, which made the self a repository of enormous potential spiritual energy. This complete rethinking of the nature of the self was inevitably more than a theological innovation, for a new sense of the self implied a new sense of all the relations of the self—moral, social and political. When Channing therefore came to define the religious life as a continual pursuit of self-culture, he offered a new way of living religiously, or a new spirituality. It is this turn to which the modern reader must direct his attention to understand Channing's significance.

It is, of course, risky to try to piece together the history of an inward, spiritual development from the remains of an external record. Channing himself, however, left his biographers some signposts which suggest that the growth of his religious outlook began early. His childhood in Newport, Rhode Island, was not happy in any conventional sense. In John White Chadwick's words, Channing's unhappiness was rooted in his parents' stern sense of duty: they "were not affable and friendly with him, gave him a stony formalism when he craved spontaneous affection, were of the opinion that he should be seen and not heard, and that he should know his place."[8] It is impossible to say how unusual this parental sternness was in late eighteenth-century New England. But Channing himself retained a reserve through life that was both a benefit and a burden to him, increasing the force of his impact on others while it lessened his intimacy with them. "He was made for the Public; he was the most unprofitable private companion," Emerson recalled.[9]

Chadwick also attributed part of Channing's early sadness to "the burden of the inherited theology and the cheerless piety of the New England Puritan" (See footnote 8). One well-known anecdote of Channing's boyhood illustrates his incipient rebellion. Taken one day by his father to hear a "famous preacher," he was introduced to the Calvinist vision of human depravity, of lost souls in a dark universe, in desperate need of "sovereign grace." The sombre terror of the sermon struck the sensitive boy deeply, and when his father later pronounced it "sound doctrine," young Channing was crushed: "It is all *true* then." But as the boy's anguish grew during the silent drive home, he was jarred when his father began to whistle. And when his father reached home and proceeded calmly to read his newspaper, the boy realized something: "No! his father did not believe it; people did not believe it! It was *not* true!"[10] While the anecdote tells us something of Channing's early resistance to orthodox versions of theology, it also suggests another trait of mind, a pragmatism that looked to action as the most important signpost of a theology. "From that time he constantly neglected what people *said*,"

Elizabeth Peabody tells us, "in the endeavor to divine by their actions what they really *meant*." [11]

We must not make the mistake, however, of using the anecdote as a measure of Channing's early rejection of Calvinism, for the case is a much more complicated one than that. In Channing's youth and early manhood the liberal movement in New England theology that became Unitarianism was still in its incipient stages. The original Puritan churches had not yet divided into Congregationalists and Unitarians, although serious disputes on theological issues were beginning to create distinct camps. [12] "The earliest religious influences on Channing were those of moderate Calvinism," Conrad Wright has noted, and the stress might well be put on the word moderate. [13] The liberals were, after all, those who accepted the body of orthodox Calvinist doctrine and moderated it on several key points—innate human depravity and election to grace, most notably. This process of moderation, or liberalization, could continue until Calvinism was no longer an appropriately descriptive term. At least we know that Channing "became familiar with a more liberal theology at Harvard" (1794–98) and possibly before. By 1806, correspondence with his grandfather, William Ellery, confirms that he felt himself part of the liberal movement. [14]

Perhaps the most important step in this early spiritual growth was Channing's development of a theory of "disinterestedness," or complete selflessness, as the defining characteristic of moral virtue and the spiritual life. The origin of this belief was as much emotional as intellectual, as Channing remembered it. One epiphanic experience occurred during his college years, while he was reading the works of the English moral philosopher Francis Hutcheson. "I longed to die," he recalled, "and felt as if heaven alone could give room for the exercise of such emotions." But resigning himself to life as a mere mortal, he poured out his emotions in a letter to the woman he would later marry, Ruth Gibbs. "But I never got the courage to send the letter, and have it yet," he later said. His biographer William Henry Channing does not specify the Hutcheson text, but tells us that it concerned "man's capacity for disinterested affection" and "virtue as the sacrifice of private interests and the bearing of private evils for the public good." [15] It is safe to assume that Hutcheson's *An Inquiry Concerning the Originals of Our Ideas of Virtue and Moral Good* (1725) was the vehicle of Channing's inspiration. Hutcheson was a popular thinker in those days, but not known ordinarily to produce such effects, so it is evident that the young Channing was fertile ground for his speculations. The nature of those speculations centered on Hutcheson's concept of the "moral sense," an innate power for discriminating between right and wrong that he posed against prevalent theories of virtue as self-interest. This concept was the core of Hutcheson's writings, and closely related to it was a concept of "disinterested affection,"[16] a capacity for acting wholly apart from, or even in opposition to, one's personal advantage, in deference to a worthier goal. Such an emotion established in Hutcheson's view "a *universal determination* to *benevolence* in mankind." Although he recognized the possibility of the degeneration of the moral sense, like any other sense, he also argued for its universal availability to humanity, and commented that its presence in human nature "is one of the strongest evidences of goodness in the Author of nature." [17]

To understand why such a theory would grip Channing with such force, one must place it in the context of the dominant theological system of the time, Calvinism. Since the middle eighteenth century, many New England theologians with liberal inclinations had chafed against the cold and vengeful God toward which Calvinism seemed to point, and they had felt similarly dissatisfied with the dogma of innate depravity, which seemed to rob human nature of the capacity for doing right. These liberal reactions in some ways exaggerated Calvinist dogma, but they did point to important distinguishing features of that system. It did stress God's justice over his benevolence, and it did find human moral effort, though perhaps a sign of election, certainly inadequate to effect salvation.

Hutcheson's positing of a moral sense, and his explicit linking of that sense to a human capacity for disinterested good, could be seen as challenge to the doctrine of innate depravity. Moreover, Hutcheson's assertion that the moral sense was strong evidence "of goodness in the Author of nature" emphasized the God of benevolence over the God of justice. And the fact that the evidence of the character of God could be found within human nature itself would be a theme of growing importance with Channing.

But Channing's spiritual development was not an even line of progress as this incident might at first suggest. The next incident of particular significance came after his study at Harvard, when Channing had taken a position as tutor with the family of David Meade Randolph of Richmond, Virginia. This interlude in Channing's life (1798–1800), his first venture out of New England, was a significant occasion for his growth, though that growth was achieved at some cost. "The Randolphs were Old Dominion aristocrats," as Jack Mendelsohn describes them: "cordial, elegant, sophisticated, and philosophical."[18] Although the Randolphs were Federalist in politics, like the New Englanders whom Channing had left, he was still introduced there to the currents of Jeffersonianism that were a challenge to his political outlook. Moreover, he confronted a social life far richer in both its temptations and its challenges than he had yet encountered. His reaction was at first to be charmed by the Southern manners and hospitality he found, seeing there a freer and more satisfying mode of social interaction than he had known before. But his ultimate reaction was to withdraw into ascetic isolation. He studied long hours in a poorly lighted and ill-heated building. He refused to buy clothing necessary for comfort or to carry on a social life. And in an intense inner struggle which seemed to consume him both spiritually and physically, he permanently damaged his health. He had been vigorously healthy as a youth, even a skilled wrestler. He spent his adult life nursing a very frail body and husbanding his ebbing strength.

Channing's own memory of the experience, in a letter of 1842, is worth considering:

> There I toiled as I have never done since, for gradually my constitution sank under the unremitting exertion. With not a human being to whom I could communicate my deepest thoughts and feelings, and shrinking from common society, I passed through intellectual and moral conflicts, through excitements of heart and mind, so absorbing as often to banish sleep, and to destroy almost wholly the power of digestion. I was worn well-nigh to a skeleton. Yet I look back on those days and nights of loneliness and frequent gloom with thankfulness. If I ever struggled with my whole soul for purity, truth, and goodness, it was there. There, amidst sore trials, the great question, I trust, was settled within me, whether I would obey the higher or

lower principles of my nature,—whether I would be the
victim of passion, the world, or the free child and servant
of God.[19]

Clearly there is a component of adolescent wrestling with physical
and emotional maturity in this experience. But there was also a related intellectual question, for Channing had been reading William
Godwin and other political radicals, and weighing the doctrines
which advocated the communal ownership of property in his search
for the key to a just society. Finally, this was a spiritual crisis for
him, rooted in part in his groping toward a decision to enter the
Christian ministry. Channing's self-consecration was at least in part
a dedication to a religious vocation, and he began to prepare himself
for it upon his return to Newport in 1800. At the time, Channing
ranked this Virginia experience as the spiritual turning point of his
life: "I never experienced that *change of heart* which is necessary to
constitute a Christian till within a few months past." But later in
life, when asked by an orthodox acquaintance "whether he had not
at some time experienced conversion," Channing's reply was different: "I should say not, unless the whole of my life may be called,
as it truly has been, a *process* of conversion."[20] A longer view of his
spiritual experience had led Channing to see it in terms of gradual
growth rather than a single and dramatic change.

Channing's reconception of spirituality in these dynamic terms
had important implications for the practice of the religious life. It
was liberating, for he explained that the Unitarians did not "consider
the written Word as a statute-book, by the letter of which every step
in life must be governed." In his view, Christianity offered "broad
views of duty" rather than "minute regulation." It "enjoined a pure
and disinterested spirit" which had to follow "the promptings of the
divine monitor within us," and respond to "the claims and exigencies of the ever varying conditions in which we are placed."[21] While
such an approach to moral duty avoided shallow legalism, it also extracted a cost through its perennial burden of judgment. Much the
same could also be said of the idea of perpetual dynamic growth itself. Although it remained for later followers of Channing to realize
it, the demand for an unceasing growth could be exhausting as well
as exhilarating.[22]

II

Upon returning to Newport, Channing continued to tutor one of the Randolph children, and pursued his theological studies with renewed vigor. There he came to know Samuel Hopkins, the greatest Calvinist thinker of the day. He was not attracted to him because of the famous Hopkinsian system of "consistent Calvinism," but rather for one element of that system which tallied with Channing's developing theological outlook. Hopkins insisted on a principle of "disinterestedness" in the religious affections, and one of his basic tenets was "that holiness consists in disinterested benevolence, which is in the nature of it, and in all its exercises, wholly contrary and opposed to self love." Hopkins is less famous for this principle than for a corollary which he wrung from it with a remorseless logic: that one should be willing to be damned eternally for the greater glory of God. Now it was not this corollary, but the principle of disinterestedness which attracted Channing, because it added confirmation to Hutcheson's definition of the working of the moral sense.[23]

Channing's studies led him back to Harvard, where he served as a regent, or proctor, and in that position he gained the leisure for further theological studies and for candidate preaching in the Boston area. In February, 1803, he accepted a call to the Federal Street Church in Boston, and was ordained there on June 1, 1803. He held this pastorate until his death. Although we cannot track with precision the progress of Channing's thinking in the early years of his pastorate, it is clear that he became part of the liberal party in Boston, which was beginning to emerge as a distinct movement in the first two decades of the nineteenth century. Though he would eventually become the leader of the movement, he was at first overshadowed by the brilliant young Joseph Stevens Buckminster, who led the liberals by virtue of his eloquent preaching, advanced Biblical scholarship, and literary expertise. Buckminster's early death by epilepsy in 1812 left a vacuum in the liberal movement's leadership. Channing, whose intellectual growth was slower but unwaveringly steady, eventually filled that vacuum.[24]

What called him to prominence was the building acrimony of the split between Calvinists and liberals. In 1805, Henry Ware, a liberal, was elected Hollis Professor of Divinity at Harvard. This disappointed many of the Calvinists, and outraged Jedidiah Morse, a talented but hot-headed defender of Calvinism, who was much given to a paranoia about plotting by the liberals, and carried a personal sense of persecution by them. He was a leader in the move to form Andover Seminary in 1808 as a conservative rival to Harvard, but that did not content him. In 1815, Morse found a book on English Unitarianism, Thomas Belsham's *Life of Theophilus Lindsey*, which included letters from Bostonian James Freeman concerning the growth of liberal ideas in New England. What Morse felt he had discovered in the book was proof that the liberals had conspired to drop Calvinism silently from their preaching, thus abandoning the essentials of the Christian faith. He published the evidence, and arranged for Jeremiah Evarts to review it in the orthodox periodical, the *Panoplist*.[25] It was this review which stung Channing into replying for the liberals. With it, the Unitarian controversy had begun and Channing emerged as the chief liberal spokesman.

It would be hard to improve upon John White Chadwick's concise description of Evarts' review:

> It had a threefold purpose: first, to identify American liberals with English Unitarians; second, to convict the former of dishonesty in covertly teaching or hypocritically concealing their Unitarian opinions; third, to demand the denial to all Unitarians of the Christian name and their exclusion from all Christian courtesy and fellowship.[26]

The liberals could quite easily refute the first of these charges, because the fact was that with the exception of James Freeman, they differed from the Socinian Christology of English Unitarianism, and held Arian views. The English Socinians attributed to Jesus a fully human nature; the New England Arians viewed Christ as supernatural, but not one with and equal to the Father. Channing agreed that there was prevalent "opposition to Trinitarianism" among the Boston clergy, but that did not make them Unitarian in the English sense of the word. In fact Christology continued to be important in Unitarian theology well into the century. "Still, I have not been accustomed to preach Christ *as a mere man*," Channing wrote in 1822. "I have spoken of him as a peculiar being." For Channing, as for most of the liberals at this time, Christ "existed in a state of glory before his birth, . . . is now a glorified, powerful agent in human affairs, . . . and hereafter he will be our judge."[27]

Although the liberals did wish to dinstinguish themselves from English Unitarianism, the last two points of Evarts' attack touched more sensitive issues. His characterization of the liberal program was designed to make it seem cunning, deceitful, and ultimately damaging to the faith of the people:

> Knowing that the cold skepticism of Socinianism cannot satisfy the wants nor alleviate the woes of plain common sense people, its advocates in general have not dared to be open. They have clandestinely crept into orthodox churches, by forbearing to contradict their faith, and then have gradually moulded them, by their *negative* preaching, to the shape which they would wish.[28]

By refusing to preach orthodox doctrines explicitly, it was charged, the liberals were subverting their flocks, and by refusing to disavow those doctrines publicly and explicitly, they were adding hypocrisy to their sins. Certainly these accusations hurt. Channing's reply to them confirmed the theological war which could now be declared.

Rather than viewing the liberal neglect of orthodox dogma as "negative" preaching, Channing saw it as positive. "We preach precisely as if no such doctrine as the Trinity had ever been known. We do not attempt to refute it, any more than to refute the systems of the Sabellians, the Eutychians, or the Nestorians, or of the other sects who have debated these questions with such hot and unprofitable zeal."[29] This reply reduced what the Calvinists saw as essential dogma to the status of a curious theological oddity. As a result, it gave Channing ground for vehement protest against the call for exclusion by Evarts, making the Calvinist attempt to preserve the Christian faith by excluding the liberals into an unchristian gesture of bigotry over an abstract question of theology. Channing had taken the high ground, and would never surrender it in his theological career.

It must be said, however, that Morse's attempt to distinguish and isolate the liberals from the Calvinists was beginning to succeed. Channing's reply confirmed publicly that many Boston ministers doubted the doctrine of the Trinity, a significant departure from the New England theological tradition. The liberals were beginning to see that they had passed the point of no return in becoming a separate sect, and a mood of assertion rather than compromise was the result. It was in that mood that in 1819 Channing delivered his famous "Baltimore Sermon," entitled "Unitarian Christianity." It has been called the "party platform" of the Unitarian movement.[30] Channing's speech was deliberately calculated to express the basis of the liberal movement, and it did so clearly and forcefully by defending the use of reason as a tool for theological investigation and Biblical analysis. Channing stressed that the Unitarian party was committed to the Bible as its source of truth. "Whatever doctrines seem to us to be clearly taught in the Scriptures, we receive without reserve or exception." This flat assertion certainly seems to confirm Chadwick's view that "no feature of Channing's early mind was more prominent than a devout biblicism." But of course the complexities involved in his affirmation of the Bible arose from the phrase "seem to us to be clearly taught." The next sentence in the sermon emphasizes those complexities: "We do not, however, attach equal importance to all the books in this collection."[31] Reason had to be brought into play to sort out apparently conflicting passages, place books in a proper historical context, and draw the proper interpretation from the Bible's metaphoric language. Channing was not, like Buckminster, a pioneer in Biblical criticism, but his address is an able summation of the movement toward historical and contextual scripture interpretation among the liberals.

Channing's Baltimore sermon was one sign of a mood of assertiveness among the liberals, and he maintained the momentum which had been established with a direct attack on Calvinist theology in 1820, "The Moral Argument Against Calvinism." Although this essay founded no movement as, in a sense, "Unitarian Christianity" did, it is an important sign-post of the end of the reign of Calvinism in American intellectual history. Channing's strategy was to strip Calvinism of its presumptive status as normative for Christian theology, and to suggest instead that it was a corruption, and a dangerous one, of Christian truth. "Calvinism owes its perpetuity to the influence of fear in palsying the moral nature," he wrote. The terror of the system so subdues the mind that individuals "come to vindicate in God what would disgrace his creatures."[32] Channing both begins and ends his essay by commenting on the warped vision of God which Calvinism engenders, and the significance of this emphasis should not be missed. For Channing, and for his movement as a whole, it signals the systematic reevaluation of human nature that was the defining tenet of liberal religion. Calvinism erred because its God departed so shockingly from any acceptable standard of human nature. "If it consist with divine rectitude to consign to everlasting misery, beings who have come guilty and impotent from his hand, we beg to know what interest we have in this rectitude, what pledge of good it contains, or what evil can be imagined which may not be its natural result?"[33] What have I to do with such a God? he asks. To emphasize the human measure of the divine, or, more accurately, the moral measure of the divine, Channing offered an example with enormous emotional appeal: "were a human parent to form himself on the universal Father, as described by Calvinism, that is, were he to bring his children into life totally depraved, and then to pursue them with endless punishment, we should charge him with a cruelty not surpassed in the annals of the world."[34] The parental nature of God, and the child-like nature of the believer, are images with deep roots in Christian piety. Channing's analogy was aimed, therefore, at one of Calvinism's tenderest spots.

Implicit in this analogy is the assumption that human nature and divine nature cohere. Channing made that assumption explicit in the essay, in language that calls to mind the moral sense philosophy of his early source of inspiration, Hutcheson. We cannot give praise to a God undeserving of it, he argued, because "in giving us a conscience," God "implanted a principle within us" that reveres only the good. Our deference to the authority of God, therefore, arises from "the perfect coincidence of his will and government with those great and fundamental principles of morality *written on our souls*" (emphasis added).[35] This firm conviction of the presence of God's attributes in human nature became for Channing the first principle of theological truth. Near the end of his life, as he wrote the preface for his collected works, he summarized his life's work simply: "The following writings will be found to be distinguished by nothing more, than by the high estimate which they express of human nature."[36] His whole spiritual pursuit can be thought of as an attempt to make plain those divine principles "written on our souls."

The spiritual import of the assumption was great. In Channing's view, it gave to acts of worship an air of filial devotion, and to moral relations a basis of love. It thereby eliminated the less disinterested motive of fear from the spiritual life. This purification of motive also meant a deeper commitment to moral actions which one undertook, because they were the natural or organic outgrowth of our nature. That part of human nature did need to be cultivated, as Channing readily agreed. As his anti-slavery writings show, he understood the deep capacity for evil in human nature. But the key to his view of evil, as his view of good, was that he saw it as potential, not as inevitable. He could therefore view human error as the failure to live up to the process of self-culture, and human achievement as the successful result of such culture.

This side of Channing's thinking, which based religious certitude in the human soul, appealed most strongly to later generations, especially the Transcendentalists. But it should be remembered that this tendency emerged most clearly in Channing's attack on the Calvinist doctrine of innate depravity. It did not signal a departure from more traditional ideas of Christian supernaturalism. While "Unitarian Christianity" is important as the Unitarian "party platform" and "The Moral Argument Against Calvinism" shows the breakup of the dominant New England theology, Channing's Dudleian Lecture of 1821 demonstrates the unquestionable fact that Channing and the liberal party still operated within the framework of a revealed and supernatural Christian truth. Paul Dudley's endowment of the lecture series in the mid-eighteenth century specified that the lectures should rotate through four set topics: a defense of natural and then of revealed religion, an attack on Papal infallibility, and a defense of congregational ordination.[37] Channing's task was to defend revealed religion, and to do so he focused on what he saw as "the great objection to Christianity." That objection, "oftener felt than expressed," was the belief "that miracles are incredible, and that the supernatural character of an alleged fact is proof enough of its falsehood."[38]

The root of Channing's problem in the defense can be traced to David Hume, whose skepticism about the miracles stood as both a threat and a stimulus to the theology of the era. Channing termed Hume's argument "specious," and in answering it he went directly to the heart of his disagreement. Hume had argued that a violation of the laws of nature was so contradictory to human experience that it outweighed the assent he might otherwise accord to human testimony. Thus Channing had to establish some standard of credibility strong enough to override that experience and provide a basis for belief in miracles. He did this by arguing that the order of nature is not the only standard of truth; by arguing, in effect, against experience as the sole criterion for assent. Assertions which seem to violate that order can be believed "if they agree with the known properties and attributes" of God, "a Being higher than nature."[39] The real problem, as Channing saw it, was not whether God could cause a miracle, but why he would do so. God had, after all, ordained the order of nature. But the establishment of that order was "a means, and not an end," its purpose being "to form and advance the mind." When, therefore, mind could be further advanced by departing from that order, we could expect God to do so. The miracles of the Bible were the instances where this had happened.[40]

What Channing expounded then was the harmonious blending of rational theology and a faith in the supernatural. This "supernatural rationalism," the dominant perspective in the 18th- and 19th-century Protestantism, embraced the natural theology of the Age of Reason, but preserved a place for revealed religion as well—to supplement and complete what reason could do only partially. Channing mentioned specifically that unaided nature could not establish the doctrine of "one God and Father" and "Immortality," so that the special revelation of the Bible was necessary to make religion complete.[41] It should also be noted that his explanation of the discernible purpose of the miracles, the formation and advancement of mind, accorded well with the developing focus of human moral ability that had been prominent in "The Moral Argument Against Calvinism." The supernatural context of the Dudleian Lecture, even though it argued for limitations on unaided human reason, provided Channing another avenue to show that the sum of religious progress was the cultivation of the spiritual capacities of the individual.

III

The decade of the 1820's, which began with the works we have been considering, was crucial in Channing's development. Channing was now being thrust into public prominence, but there was a price to pay for his pace of activity. In 1822, failing health forced him to take a leave from his ministerial duties and travel to Europe. The trip proved intellectually expansive for him, though it did not restore his health. Moreover, the death of his infant son George while he was away marred the trip emotionally. Still, Channing returned in 1823 somewhat changed, and whether the springs of that change were in the trip itself or before it, it does mark the place at which Channing's intellectual concerns start to become less exclusively theological. Although "he did not think of himself as a literary man," as Robert E. Spiller aptly put it, "he thought clearly of the nature of literature."[42] The same could be said about his writings on politics. He launched his career as a literary and social critic in the middle 1820's after returning from Europe, and the publication of his *Discourses, Reviews, and Miscellanies* in 1830 was the culmination of his move into cultural analysis. Emerson later remembered his essays on Milton and Napoleon as the first American examples of "that large criticism" characteristic of the influential English journal, the *Edinburgh Review*. The wide circulation and emulation of Channing's essays "lifted the style of Journalism" in America.[43] Those two essays, with his "Remarks on National Literature," constitute the major statements which first secured his reputation as a man of letters.

In the essays on both Milton and Napoleon, Channing confronted a figure of power, and attempted to take measure of that power. To do so, Channing began to expand the vision of the moral life which he developed in the Unitarian controversy, making the idea of the growth of inner capacity an idea that had literary and political consequences, as well as theological applications. In comparing Milton with another English genius, Samuel Johnson, Channing argued for Milton's higher place because of his greater sense of human potential. Johnson dwelt "on man's actual condition, on the realities of life," and "seems hardly to have dreamed of a higher state of the human mind that was then exhibited." While for modern readers this realism is the basis of Johnson's genius, Channing found it inferior to Milton's capacity for aspiration. Milton "thought, not so much of what man is, as of what he might become."[44] This emphasis on potential, expressed here in terms of the human race, was also the key to Milton himself. For Channing, Milton stood for the "culture of intellect" which took form in his expansive force of

mind. "Never was there a more unconfined mind," and that unbounded quality proved Milton's genius. The object of mind "is the
universe, which is strictly one, or bound together by infinite connexions and correspondences." This cosmological unity thus invites the
mind to perpetual expansion from one field of thought to another.
The "thirst for constantly enlarging knowledge," characteristic of
the mind, thus became a version of the kind of spiritual growth
which was central to Channing's religious vision.[45] It had emerged
in the debate against Calvinism, and expanded into a positive theological principle. It provided not only a theological touchstone, but
a standard of intellectual judgment also.

It had not escaped Channing's attention, of course, that Milton
dissented from the doctrine of the Trinity. Channing's cogent description of Milton's Christology in the newly published *Treatise on
Christian Doctrine* was in fact generally descriptive of the Arian
views of most of the Boston liberals.

> Milton teaches, that the Son of God is a distinct being
> from God, and inferior to him, that he existed before the
> world was made, that he is the first of the creation of God,
> and that afterwards all other things were made by him, as
> the instrument or minister of his Father.

Clearly then, Channing saw Milton as ammunition for the continuing war with the orthodox, and classed him with Locke and Newton
as one of "the three greatest and noblest minds of modern times."
All of them, in dissenting from Trinitarianism, helped to resurrect
"the long-obscured doctrine of the Divine Unity."[46]

Channing's interest in Milton suggests the widening of his concerns, but his essay on Napoleon took him even further into cultural
commentary. The appeal of Milton as an exemplary thinker was
clear. As he put it, "an enlightened and exalted mind is a brighter
manifestation of God than the outward universe."[47] Milton's biography stood as a kind of proof-text for natural theology. But what of
Napoleon, whose mind was neither enlightened nor exalted, but
whose path to empire "lay over wounded and slaughtered millions,
over putrefying heaps of his fellow-creatures"? The attraction of
Napoleon was that of sheer power, and Channing realized that
"great powers, even in their perversion, attest a glorious nature."

Napoleon's key fault was not difficult to recognize: an "egotistical, self-relying, self-exaggerating principle . . . was the most striking feature of his mind." It was this which made him "incapable . . . of understanding the character and answering the demands of his age," and led to his downfall.[48] Still, there is more to Channing's essay than simple condemnation, as Andrew Delbanco has aptly noted. Channing's fear of Napoleon was "truly an existential terror for the very reason that he is so attractive, so seductive."[49] In preaching the potential greatness of human nature, Channing had to see in Napoleon the cautionary reminder of individual human power gone awry. Thus he saw the tragedy of Napoleon's career: "We can conceive few subjects more worthy of Shakespeare than the mind of Napoleon, at the moment, when his fate was sealed."[50] Tragedy can ennoble, of course, and for Channing Napoleon's fate opened the difficult question of the relation of moral freedom to political fact. Napoleon's bondage to power had a moral cost, and he is the extreme example of the corrupting power of politics.

The essay moves toward the enunciation of a familiar theme, the central importance of the growth of the soul. Power did not make Napoleon free. "No man is wholly and immutably free but he who has broken every outward yoke, that he may obey his own deliberate conscience." Therefore, the outer social pursuits exemplified in politics were, for Channing, secondary. "To improve man's outward condition is a secondary agency, and is chiefly important as it gives the means of inward growth." It was this doctrine that Channing later would articulate fully as self-culture, and it became both an influential and controversial doctrine for him. In an age of rapid social transformation, he argued that progress was an individual thing. "The great hope of society is individual character."[51] This character was the product of the fuller expansion of that internal moral principle which had been the early object of Channing's faith.

It was in America that Channing felt this expansion of character would be most generally felt. He lamented Napoleon's despotism, for instance, not only as a weakness in the character of a potentially great man, but as the sign of a general moral malaise in European culture. "In the absolute governments of Europe, the very instruments of forming an enlightened and generous love of freedom are bent into the service of tyranny."[52] In his "Remarks on National Literature," Channing expanded this theme of America's unique position, and unique responsibilities. His essay is generally accorded prominence in the development of an American cultural identity in the early nineteenth century. For America, political independence preceded cultural independence by more than a half-century, and Channing's essay is one sign that the nation's intellectual conscience was beginning to awaken to this fact.

The heart of Channing's analysis was the connection between a national literature and the development of the individual. National literature was "the expression of a nation's mind in writing," of large importance because it attested to the existence of superior individuals as the flower of that culture. "The great distinction of a country, then, is, that it produces superior men," not great institutions. While social and political institutions are by no means worthless, they "have value only by the impulse which they give to the mind." With this premise, Channing established the basis for what becomes, as the essay unfolds, a long lament of the failures of American culture.

> There is among us much superficial knowledge, but little severe, persevering research; little of that consuming passion for new truth, which makes outward things worthless; little resolute devotion to a high intellectual culture. There is nowhere a literary atmosphere, or such an accumulation of literary influence, as determines the whole strength of the mind to its own enlargement, and to the manifestation of itself in enduring forms.[53]

Given Channing's commitment to American democracy as one vehicle of the expansion of human capacity, this was a failure of the greatest severity. What America offered, he felt, was a unique opportunity for human self-knowledge. The "consciousness of our own nature . . . contains, as a germ, all nobler thoughts." American writers could more easily than others expound that nature because "Man is not hidden from us by so many disguises as in the old world."[54] What seemed to be lacking was a commitment in America to that project, because of the general bondage to the immediately pragmatic. In a sense, America presented on a cultural level a tragedy akin to Napoleon's. Its enormous energy and power, its undeniable potential, was directed to unworthy and ultimately self-

defeating causes. The promotion of a national literature was the
means of breaking this cycle. The energy made available through
American freedom could be rechannelled into the activities which
advanced the development of the individual. "To literature we then
look, as the chief means of forming a better race of human
beings."[55]

IV

At the end of the 1820's, the decade of Channing's great intellectual expansion, he preached two of his most enduring sermons,
"Likeness to God" (1828) and "Spiritual Freedom" (1830). These
are not only remarkable texts in themselves, but points of both summation and departure in his growth. Their relation to his earlier development is clear, and they also forcefully articulate premises
which were the basis of some of his controversial work in the
1830's, when Channing became embroiled in the politics of anti-
slavery.

"Likeness to God" was, like "Unitarian Christianity," an ordination sermon. While Channing had felt it necessary to lay out the
premises of the liberal party on the earlier occasion, in "Likeness to
God" he took up a subject which was growing in importance to him,
the process of education. Since "a new teacher is to be given to the
church,"[56] the nature of religious instruction should be of primary
concern. In fact, religious learning, broadly conceived as moral and
spiritual growth, was the essence of religion itself for Channing. His
discourse suggests why education and religion have merged in the
liberal tradition. "True religion," he argued, "consists in proposing, as our great end, a growing likeness to the Supreme Being."
"Growing" should be emphasized here. As the "higher or spiritual
nature" is "unfolded," God's image within "is extended and
brightened." This is, in other words, a continuing process, not a
static condition which, when achieved, is an end in itself. Each step
of the process of spiritual growth or self-culture opens the possibility
of further steps, and the advancing spiritual growth continues infinitely.[57]

Channing's elusive spirituality can perhaps be felt by the reader
more strongly in "Likeness to God" than in any other work. Perry

Miller noted the sermon's assertion of "the supremacy of the intuitive assurance over all inductive reasoning," making it thus his "most 'Transcendental' " statement.[58] It is clear that his appeal to religious experience, to an intimacy with God, had great appeal to the younger Transcendentalists, who found the rationalism of some varieties of Unitarian theology cold.

> God becomes a real being to us, in proportion as his own nature is unfolded within us. To a man who is growing in the likeness of God, faith begins even here to change into vision. He carries within himself a proof of a Deity, which can only be understood by experience. He more than believes, he feels the Divine presence; and gradually rises to an intercourse with his Maker, to which it is not irreverent to apply the name of friendship and intimacy.[59]

Yet Channing feared the accusation of mysticism in these views. It should be noted that he based his experience of God on the presence of the divine attributes in the human soul, rather than the indwelling being of God. In other words, we follow a Divine pattern in our process of growth.

> To hold intellectual and moral affinity with the Supreme Being, to partake his spirit, to be his children *by derivations of kindred excellence,* to bear a growing conformity to the perfection which we adore, this is a felicity which obscures and annihilates all other good [emphasis added].[60]

Even so, Channing's elevation of the self, his complete reevaluation of human nature, was an impressive break from the Puritan past.

> Whence do we derive our knowledge of the attributes and perfections which constitute the Supreme Being? I answer, we derive them from our own souls. The divine attributes are first developed in ourselves, and thence transferred to our Creator. The idea of God, sublime and awful as it is, is the idea of our own spiritual nature, purified and enlarged to infinity.[61]

It was this emphasis of the spiritual capacity of the soul which appealed to Emerson and the Transcendentalists. The passage as it stands not only locates the assurance of God's nature within the soul, it moves toward a more completely human-centered religion. But Channing was careful to maintain the necessary connection of the individual and God. "The danger to which we are most exposed," he warned, "is that of severing the Creator from his creatures." Two years later in "Spiritual Freedom," he explicitly asserted the dependence of the human soul on God. "I am accustomed to speak of the greatness of human nature; but it is great only through its parentage; great, because descended from God, because connected with a goodness and power from which it is to be enriched forever."[62] But his emphasis in "Likeness to God" on the power of deriving Divine attributes from within was meant to add force to the argument for the continuing cultivation of the soul. For Channing, the great motivation toward spiritual education was the sense that inner discovery and cosmological truth parallel each other. It was no long step for Emerson later to assert, "Blessed is the day when the youth discovers that Within and Above are synonyms."[63]

This doctrine of the spiritual capacities of the soul and the resulting responsibility for inner growth had implications far beyond those of the private devotional life. When he was called upon to deliver the Massachusetts Annual Election Sermon in 1830, Channing felt it incumbent upon him to outline those implications. The occasion and tradition of that sermon required a look outward, a measuring of the inner God against the social and political environment. The sources of the election sermon were in the New England Puritan theocracy. It was the occasion to remind those in public office of their religious duties, and one of the traditional themes had been the interplay of religion and the conduct of political affairs. Channing saw this connection through the category of "freedom," a term not only dear to America's political self-conception, but an important part of Channing's spiritual vision as well. "Inward, spiritual liberty . . . is the supreme good of men, and civil and political liberty has but little worth, but as it springs from and invigorates this."[64]

Channing's "Spiritual Freedom" is thus a prolonged argument for the primacy of spiritual freedom over civil freedom, for the primacy of the moral over the political life. As the slavery issue grew, the convergence of moral and political questions became clearer to Channing, but his stance on slavery is best understood in the context of the priorities he established in "Spiritual Freedom." According to those priorities, social relations are a means of personal development, and not an end in themselves. "I know no wisdom but that which reveals man to himself, and which teaches him to regard all social institutions, and his whole life, as the means of unfolding and exalting the spirit within him."[65] The great danger of social institutions is their tendency to consume the individual, to overstep their proper role as aids to personal development and become ends in themselves. "Civilization, so far from being able of itself to give moral strength and elevation, includes causes of degradation, which nothing but the religious principle can withstand." Chief among those "causes of degradation" for Channing was the multiplication of "the comforts and enjoyments of life," and aid to "the sensual element in human nature . . . which allies, and too often enslaves us, to the earth." In contrast to material social progress, Channing suggested a truer ideal of society:

> To me, the progress of society consists in nothing more, than in bringing out the individual, in giving him a consciousness of his own being, and in quickening him to strengthen and elevate his own mind.[66]

In Channing's vision therefore, social freedom was but one element of an ultimate freedom which he termed spiritual in nature. "Our great error as a people is, that we put an idolatrous trust in our free institutions; as if these, by some magic power, must secure our rights, however we enslave ourselves to evil passions." "Spiritual Freedom" continues the worried denunciation of American materialism that was a prominent theme in "Remarks on National Literature." Material progress represented for Channing the greatest threat to American freedom. "We need to learn that the forms of liberty are not its essence," he noted.[67] Political abuse is possible even under a representative and constitutional government, and there is no political guarantee against it. One task of religion, therefore, was to augment the protection of the liberty of the people.

V

Channing's growing faith in human nature confronted one intractable fact in nineteenth century America—slavery. Channing had known slavery in the Newport of his youth, where his father had been a slave-holder, and again in Virginia. He experienced it freshly in a trip to the West Indies in 1830, and returned to Boston with plans to speak against it. But in the meantime anti-slavery sentiment was beginning to grow in Boston, and in the early 1830's, William Lloyd Garrison made abolitionism a hotly controversial movement. Channing was attracted to the cause of anti-slavery as a moral crusade, but at first repelled by the abolitionist movement. Thus in Chadwick's words, "Channing found himself between two fires, never pleasing the conservative part of the community and of his own society; seldom satisfying the abolitionists with the extent of his adhesion to their side." In these last twelve years of life, Channing's relations with his Federal Street church were reduced to chilly formality because of his public stance against slavery, but he was regarded by the radical abolitionists with suspicion and disdain because he refused to be counted among them.[68]

Slavery (1835) was Channing's major anti-slavery work. He had planned a statement as early as 1830, after his West Indies trip, but hesitated, evidently out of reluctance to become embroiled in abolitionist politics. Others began to speak out before him, notably Lydia Maria Child, who in 1833 published *An Appeal in Favor of That Class of Americans Called Africans*. Child emphasized the moral degradation to which both the slave and the slaveholder were subjected, and deplored this treatment "of beings, who, like ourselves, are heirs of immortality!" The argument drove itself home to Channing, who had staked so much of his vision on the moral potential of human nature. Thus, in *Slavery*, he charged that to enslave a person "is to offer an insult to his Maker."[69]

While *Slavery* is ostensibly a political book, it is at heart the application of a theological system to a particular social problem. We might expect to find the following sentence, for instance, in a theological work rather than a political one, even though it is the basis of Channing's whole argument: "Every human being has in him the germ of the greatest idea in the universe, the idea of God; and to unfold this is the end of his existence." It is clear that the developing idea of human spiritual resources has made itself felt forcefully here. The repression of this divine potential in humanity is to Channing's eye the great evil of slavery, and the depth of his faith in that divinity gives power to his moral condemnation, and fuels righteous indignation of this blistering intensity:

> Should we not deem it a wrong which no punishment could expiate, were one of our children seized as property, and driven by the whip to toil? And shall God's child, dearer to him than an only son to a human parent, be thus degraded? Every thing else may be owned in the universe; but a moral, rational being cannot be property. Suns and stars may be owned, but not the lowest spirit. Touch any thing but this. Lay not your hand on God's rational offspring. The whole spiritual world cries out, Forbear! The highest intelligences recognise their own nature, their own rights, in the humblest human being. By that priceless, immortal spirit which dwells in him, by that likeness of God which he wears, tread him not in the dust, confound him not with the brute.[70]

The phrase "likeness of God" of course leaps out from this passage to confirm the direct relation of Channing's important sermon to his entry into the ranks of the anti-slavery writers. While the Channing of the 1830's has in some respects a different emphasis from the Channing of "Likeness to God," the development toward *Slavery* is an organic one, and not a radical break from the past.

But if slavery should be opposed principally because it destroyed the moral and spiritual freedom of the slave, it also was a corrupting influence on the slaveholder. If the potential divinity of the slave was thwarted by external force, that of the slaveowner was similarly thwarted by the appeal of slavery to the base instincts of power. "I ask no documents to prove the abuses of this power, nor do I care what is said to disprove them. Millions may rise up and tell me that the slave suffers little from cruelty. I know too much of human nature, human history, human passion, to believe them." Now it may seem contradictory to argue against slavery on the basis of the divine potential of human nature, and then to speak of the inevitable abuses which will arise from human nature and human passion. But for Channing, that divine potential, though real, was incipient. The process of culture brought it more fully into being, but that growth was not inevitable. He realized that "absolute power always corrupts human nature more or less,"[71] and that nowhere was that power so nakedly absolute as in the relation of the master and slave.

Channing's indictment of slavery was one of the most damning attacks on the institution produced in America. But it did not win him ready acceptance among the abolitionists for three reasons. First, Channing did not advocate immediate abolition, and argued that "it would be cruelty, not kindness, . . . to give [the slave] a freedom, which he is unprepared to understand or enjoy." He advocated instead gradual change through moral persuasion, and asserted that "our proper and only means of action is to spread the truth on the subject of slavery." This he felt would eventually have its effect. In addition to this gradualism, Channing also refused to condemn slaveholders, even though he argued that slaveholding inevitably injured both slave and master. For him, the "motive" of an act determined the character of the actor, and injury could be done to another out of ignorance or misguided motive. Closely related to this argument was Channing's criticism of the abolitionists, the third point which alienated them from him. "They have fallen into the common error of enthusiasts, that of taking too narrow views, of feeling as if no evil existed but that which they opposed, and as if no guilt could be compared with that of countenancing or upholding it."[72] As to ends, Channing was an abolitionist; as to means, he was not. And for the more radical abolitionists, the question of means was the more pressing. Beneath this political question, Andrew Delbanco has rightly discerned a deeper moral question. Channing refused himself the luxury of identifying evil as "other," or alien to the self. In condemning slavery, he never allowed himself to be pulled into self-righteousness, always insisting "that a man must combat evil while never ceasing to combat himself."[73]

Channing continued an active spokesman in the anti-slavery crusade, and while his aversion to the abolitionists lessened somewhat, he remained independent. He accepted the responsibility to speak out that his public prominence thrust upon him, but never became an activist in the mold of Garrison and his followers. What he might have done had he lived into the 1850's is a very interesting subject of speculation. His last public speech in 1842 was a commemoration of the act of emancipation in the British West Indies, and a masterful condensation of his position on slavery and emancipation. His career ended, then, with that concern much on his mind. It would certainly have grown had he lived through the rising tensions of the 1840's and 1850's in America.

VI

Slavery was certainly the great issue in American politics before the Civil War, but the anti-slavery movement was only the most prominent feature of a series of agitations against the social structure. Various plans of reform in economics and property distribution, the movement for women's rights, and the crusade for temperance also challenged the accepted social and political norms of the day. Channing's most significant later works, "Self-Culture" and "On the Elevation of the Laboring Classes," addressed these issues through the concept of self-culture, which had grown for him now into a category which encompassed theology and politics. "Self-Culture," in particular, became one of his most influential essays, both a gainer of adherents and a provoker of important dissenters to its doctrine.

Channing's subject in both discourses was the working class, and the relation of the individual worker to the society in which he worked. Again, Channing insisted that this question had to be viewed not from the point of view of society, but of the individual. His interest in the working class was based "not on their usefulness to the community, so much as on what they are in themselves." In that view, work became secondary to self-culture in the life of the worker, and though Channing felt that work was a central means of that culture, it should not dominate life to the exclusion of other necessary activities.

I do not look on a human being as a machine, made to be kept in action by a foreign force, to accomplish an unvarying succession of motions, to do a fixed amount of work, and then to fall to pieces at death, but as a being of free

> spiritual powers; and I place little value on any culture, but
> that which aims to bring out these and to give them per-
> petual impulse and expansion.[74]

These views may not seem startling now, but they needed to be
heard at that historical moment, one much closer to feudalism than
our own. Early nineteenth-century America was still a society in
which brutally long hours, poor and unsafe working conditions, and
child labor were tolerated. Channing was no radical; he did not challenge the systems of property distribution that existed. But he did
relegate work to merely a supportive status in the development of an
individual's "free spiritual powers."

Channing argued that American democracy was succeeding in
distributing wealth equally, a fact which protected the property arrangements that existed. And he also noted that "property is in more
danger from those who are aspiring after wealth," that is, the entre-
preneurial speculators, investors, and business elite, "than from
those who live by the sweat of their brow."[75] Channing's plea is not
one which threatened the American social order with drastic change.
It rather appealed to the workers to keep their place in the social order in a proper moral perspective. There is an element of complacency in his confidence in the social order, but there is certainly a
fervor in the way he attacks the more disturbing complacency about
self-development. Admitting that "there are obstructions in the way
of improvement," he went on to argue that they were not definitive.
"But in this country, the chief obstructions lie, not in our lot, but in
ourselves, not in outward hardships, but in our worldy and sensual
propensities." Again, materialism was the great enemy to be
fought, and those whose financial resources were greater had no easier battle: "a true self-culture is as little thought of on exchange as in
the workshop, as little among the prosperous as among those of narrower conditions."[76] Channing did not intend to deny that outer circumstances could not inhibit self-culture. His argument against
slavery shows that. But he did feel that inner obstacles were much
the more prevalent deterrent to human development. For that reason
he put much faith in moral persuasion as a force for social change.

By the time Channing published *Self-Culture* (1838), the Transcendentalist movement in New England was at full boil. Emerson's
Divinity School Address, the focal point of the Transcendentalist

controversy, was delivered in 1838 and much significant discourse followed which not only changed New England theology, but spilled into politics and literature as well. Channing's relationship to that movement is complex, and has been much discussed, but two facts seem clear enough. The Transcendentalists shared with Channing, and in fact inherited from him and his tradition, an intractable faith in the potential divinity of the individual. Their spiritual quest to cultivate that divinity was his also. Moreover, the Transcendentalists, with many other religious groups as well, shared with Channing a conviction that materialism was the greatest threat to both the Americans as individuals, and to the American democracy. The opening of Thoreau's *Walden* is perhaps the most eloquent testimony to this, but the attack on material values as opposed to spiritual values permeated Transcendentalist writing. But Channing, however influential he was, was not one of the Transcendentalists. He remained an adherent of Lockean and Scottish common-sense epistemology, even though some of his statements on the "God within" gave support to Emerson's doctrine of intuition as the source of religious truth. And he clung much more firmly to a Christ-centered religion, never going as far as Emerson did in labelling Jesus' claim to divinity a poetic effusion. For Channing, that claim was real. Thus on July 6, 1841, he expressed to Elizabeth Palmer Peabody his reservations about Theodore Parker's *Discourse on the Transient and Permanent in Christianity,* a key document in the history of Transcendentalism. "I grieved that he did not give some clear, direct expression of his belief in the Christian miracles. His silence under such circumstances makes me fear that he does not believe them. I see not how the rejection of these can be separated from the rejection of Jesus Christ."[77] This strong affirmation seems to contradict the report of his son, that a year before his death (presumably the fall of 1841), Channing felt "more and more disposed to believe in [the] simple humanity" of Jesus.[78] But even if some liberalization of Channing's views on Christology was taking place in his last years, it was a private wrestling, too late and too personal to have had any public utterance. Indeed, we find in the closing portion of his last public address the following passage: "Come, Friend and Saviour of the race, who didst shed thy blood on the cross to reconcile man to man, and Earth to Heaven!"[79] Even if we make some allowance for the elements of traditional religious language which might permeate the peroration of the address, this seems a strongly Christological statement. Channing remained to the Transcendentalists a friend, and an inspiration, but not a brother-in-arms.

That Channing's last public statement concerned slavery indicates that his later thinking was pragmatic in nature rather than abstractly theological. He left unfinished a philosophical "Treatise on Man," a project which was the victim of both his failing health and his growing sense of responsibility to speak on public issues. His son reported that his commitment to human perfectibility remained strong to the very end of his life, and certainly it was this faith that fuelled much of his fervor for social reform.[80] The worth of human nature gave importance to the struggle to promote the causes which would improve it.

While Channing's impact on American intellectual and religious life was great, its largest impact was of course upon the denomination which he helped to found, Unitarianism. In many ways, the Unitarians led the way in the general American movement toward theological modernism, remaining a denomination of relatively small numbers and large influence. The Transcendentalist movement was the first of several waves of radicalism in Unitarian history, including the Free Religion movement of the 1860's and 1870's, and the Humanist movement of the 1920's and 1930's. And in the continuing debate over the nature of liberal religion which these movements have created, Channing's name has been prominent. In the middle and late nineteenth century, the more moderate Unitarians claimed the name "Channing Unitarians," associating themselves with the Christian and supernatural positions which Channing had espoused. Others argued that since Channing's theology continued to develop, it falsified his legacy to associate him with a particular creed frozen in time. "What would Channing think, . . . how would he deal with the living questions of today?" asked Minot J. Savage at the centenary of Channing's birth. For him, these were the more important questions, ones which might align Channing more closely with the radical wing of the denomination.[81] But whether viewed as a support to adherents of a more traditional and Christian form of Unitarianism, or as the forefather of the radicals, Channing's name has continued to carry great weight among Unitarians. The recent celebration of the Channing Bicentennial by the Unitarian Universalist Association is evidence of his continuing influence as a religious teacher. Recent scholarly interest in him suggests his historical stature.

The changes in Channing's career are real enough, but there is also a tenacious continuity in his thinking which is perhaps a more valuable way to assess it. From his early encounter with Hutcheson, through his polemical war with Calvinism, to his stature as an anti-slavery reformer and forerunner of Transcendentalism, Channing articulated an ever-deepening faith in the individual's spiritual resources. His principal message was the urgent insistence that these be developed. More than anything else, his faith and message lent him the air of "spirituality" which set him apart. It was as if his ultimate act of faith was to live out his own sense of expanding potential. He thus climbed to a height in his own spiritual experience from which his words entered the souls of his hearers with all the "searching force" which Hedge noted. Those words have not lost their force.

Notes

1. "Address of Rev. Frederic H. Hedge," in *Services in Memory of Rev. William E. Channing, D.D., at the Arlington-Street Church, Boston, on Sunday Evening, October 6, 1867* (Boston: John Wilson and Son, 1867), 27.

2. Theodore Parker, *An Humble Tribute to the Memory of William Ellery Channing, D. D.* (Boston: Charles C. Little and James Brown, 1842), 6.

3. *The Complete Works of Ralph Waldo Emerson,* ed. Edward Waldo Emerson, 12 vols. (Boston and New York: Houghton Mifflin, 1903–04), 10:339.

4. Parker, 7.

5. Ralph Waldo Emerson, "Literary Intelligence," *Dial* 3 (1843): 387.

6. Hedge, 27.

7. Sydney E. Ahlstrom, "The Interpretation of Channing," *New England Quarterly* 30 (1957): 99–105.

8. John White Chadwick, *William Ellery Channing: Minister of Religion* (Boston and New York: Houghton, Mifflin, 1903), 14.

9. *The Journals and Miscellaneous Notebooks of Ralph Waldo Emerson, (JMN),* ed. William H. Gilman et al, 16 vols. (Cambridge: Har-

vard University Press and the Belknap Press of Harvard University Press, 1960–82), 8:470.

10. This is a familiar anecdote to students of Channing. See William Henry Channing, *The Life of William Ellery Channing, D.D.* (Boston: American Unitarian Association, 1887), 16–17; Elizabeth Palmer Peabody, *Reminiscences of Rev. Wm. Ellery Channing, D.D.* (Boston: Roberts Brothers, 1880), 62–63; Chadwick, 23–24; and Jack Mendelsohn, *Channing: The Reluctant Radical* (Boston: Little, Brown, 1971), 22–24.

11. Peabody, 63.

12. On Unitarian origins, see Conrad Wright, *The Beginnings of Unitarianism in America* (Boston: Starr King, 1955).

13. Conrad Wright, *The Liberal Christians: Essays on American Unitarian History* (Boston: Beacon, 1970), 33.

14. Ibid., 29–33. Wright argues against Hopkins as a major influence on Channing.

15. William Henry Channing, pp. 32–33.

16. Francis Hutcheson, *An Inquiry Concerning the Originals of Our Idea of Virtue and Moral Good* (1725), reprinted in part in *British Moralists, 1650–1800,* ed. D. D. Raphael, 2 vols. (Oxford: Clarendon Press, 1969), 1:259–321. The quotation is from page 278. This discussion of Hutcheson is reprinted from my earlier essay "The Legacy of Channing: Culture as a Religious Category in New England Thought," *Harvard Theological Review* 74 (1981): 221–39, with permission of *Harvard Theological Review,* copyright 1981 by the President and Fellows of Harvard College.

17. Hutcheson, 289, 299.

18. Mendelsohn, 37.

19. William Henry Channing, 75–76.

20. Ibid., 74–75.

21. *The Works of William E. Channing, D.D.,* 6 vols. (Boston: James Munroe, 1841–43), 3:164.

22. See Robert Leet Patterson, *The Philosophy of William Ellery Channing* (New York: Bookman, 1952); and Robinson, "The Legacy of Channing."

23. Samuel Hopkins, *The System of Doctrines, Contained in Divine Revelation, Explained and Defended,* 2 vols. (Boston: Thomas and Andrews, 1793), 1:545. This discussion of Hopkins is also based on my previous essay, "The Legacy of Channing." See also Conrad Wright, *The Liberal Christians,* 23–33.

24. On Buckminster, see Lawrence Buell, "Joseph Stevens Buckminster: The Making of a New England Saint," *The Canadian Review of*

American Studies 10 (1979), 1–29. For details on the Boston milieu of Channing's early career see Chadwick, 55–114, and Mendelsohn, 56–81.

25. See William Wallace Fenn, "The Revolt Against the Standing Order," in *The Religious History of New England: King's Chapel Lectures* (Cambridge: Harvard University Press, 1917), 77–133, and Conrad Wright, "The Controversial Career of Jedidiah Morse," *Harvard Library Bulletin* 31 (1983), 64–87.

26. Chadwick, 130.

27. William Henry Channing, 198, 311.

28. Jeremiah Evarts, "Review of American Unitarianism," *Panoplist and Missionary Magazine* 11 (1815), as reprinted in *Tracts on the Unitarian Controversy* (Boston: Wells and Lilly, 1816), 20.

29. *A Letter to the Rev. Samuel C. Thacher, on the Aspersions Contained in a late Number of the Panoplist, on the Ministers of Boston and the Vicinity*, 3rd ed. (Boston: Wells and Lilly, 1815), p. 13.

30. Conrad Wright, *Three Prophets of Religious Liberalism: Channing-Emerson-Parker* (Boston: Beacon, 1961), 6.

31. Channing, *Works*, 3:60; Chadwick, 123.

32. Channing, *Works*, 1:218–19.

33. Channing, *Works*, 1:236–37.

34. Channing, *Works*, 1:238.

35. Channing, *Works*, 1:232–33.

36. Channing, *Works*, 1:vi.

37. See Perry Miller, "The Insecurity of Nature," *Nature's Nation* (Cambridge: The Belknap Press of Harvard University Press, 1967), 121–133; and Conrad Wright, *The Liberal Christians*, 1–21.

38. Channing, *Works*, 3:106.

39. Channing, *Works*, 3:115–16.

40. Channing, *Works*, 3:112–13.

41. See Wright's discussion of Supernatural Rationalism in *The Liberal Christians*, 1–21.

42. On the impact of Channing's trip, see Chadwick, 184–89; Van Wyck Brooks, *The Flowering of New England* (New York: Dutton, 1936), 104–10; and Robert E. Spiller, "A Case for W.E. Channing," *New England Quarterly* 3 (January 1930), 55–81. Quotation is from Spiller, 71.

43. Emerson, *Complete Works*, 10:339. Channing's "Remarks on National Literature" has been chosen here as the representative piece from his literary essays of this period.

44. Channing, *Works*, 1:37.

45. Channing, *Works*, 1:6, 64.

46. Channing, *Works*, 1:45, 46.

47. Channing, *Works,* 1:68.

48. Channing, *Works,* 1:95, 74, 100, 95–96.

49. Andrew Delbanco, *William Ellery Channing: An Essay on the Liberal Spirit in America* (Cambridge: Harvard University Press, 1981), 46.

50. Channing, *Works,* 1:105.

51. Channing, *Works,* 1:134, 140, 163.

52. Channing, *Works,* 1:132.

53. Channing, *Works,* 1:243, 245, 254.

54. Channing, *Works,* 1:268.

55. Channing, *Works,* 1:250.

56. Channing, *Works,* 3:227.

57. Channing, *Works,* 3:228. For further discussion of this issue see Patterson, and Robinson, ''The Legacy of Channing.''

58. Perry Miller, *The Transcendentalists: An Anthology* (Cambridge: Harvard University Press, 1950), 228.

59. Channing, *Works,* 3:229–30.

60. Channing, *Works,* 3:229.

61. Channing, *Works,* 3:233.

62. Channing, *Works,* 3:238 and 4:80.

63. Emerson, *JMN,* 4:365.

64. Channing, *Works,* 4:68. On the election sermon see A.W. Plumstead, *The Wall and the Garden: Selected Massachusetts Election Sermons, 1670–1775* (Minneapolis: University of Minnesota Press, 1968), 3–37.

65. Channing, *Works,* 4:69.

66. Channing, *Works,* 4:82, 78.

67. Channing, *Works,* 4:95.

68. Chadwick, 63. On Channing and the Unitarian anti-slavery movement, see Wright, *The Liberal Christians,* 62–80, and Douglas C. Stange, *Patterns of Antislavery Among American Unitarians, 1831–1860* (Rutherford, N.J.: Fairleigh Dickinson University Press, 1977).

69. Lydia Maria Child, *An Appeal in Favor of That Class of Americans Called Africans* (2nd ed., 1836; rpt. New York: Arno, 1968), 16. Channing, *Works,* 2:26.

70. Channing, *Works,* 2:27, 29.

71. Channing, *Works,* 2:75.

72. Channing, *Works,* 2:109, 117, 51, 126.

73. Delbanco, 150.

74. Channing, *Works,* 2:350, 368.

75. Channing, *Works,* 2:392.

76. Channing, *Works,* 2:408.

77. On Channing's adherence to Lockean epistemology, see Wright,

The Liberal Christians, 34–38. Quotation from Channing in William Henry Channing, 449.

78. Thomas Wentworth Higginson, "Two New England Heretics: Channing and Parker," *Independent* 54 (22 May 1902), 1235.

79. William Ellery Channing, *An Address Delivered at Lenox, on the First of August, 1842, the Anniversary of Emancipation in the British West Indies* (Lenox, Mass.: J.G. Stanly, 1842), 38.

80. On his unfinished work, see Morton deCorcey Nachlas, "A Study and Transcription of William Ellery Channing's Unfinished Treatise on Man" (B.D. diss., Meadville Theological School, 1942). On his later thoughts, see Higginson (note 78).

81. Minot J. Savage, "Channing Unitarianism," *The Channing Centenary in America, Great Britain, and Ireland* (Boston: George H. Ellis, 1881), 117.

A LETTER TO THE
REV. SAMUEL C. THACHER (1815)*

*The original text that follows this introduction is *A Letter to the Rev. Samuel C. Thacher, on the Aspersions Contained in a Late Number of the Panoplist, on the Ministers of Boston and the Vicinity*, 3rd ed. (Boston: Wells and Lilly, 1815). The marginal quotation marks used in early printing practice have been silently deleted here.

The Unitarian controversy, which had been simmering in New England for several decades around the turn of the nineteenth century, exploded into the open in 1815. Channing's Letter to the Rev. Samuel C. Thacher *is the document which finally established that there could be no reconciliation between the orthodox Calvinists and the emerging sect of liberal Christians, those who would soon openly accept the name "Unitarian." There is no text which better suggests the uncomfortable mixture of reluctance and rage with which Channing entered the arena of controversy and debate. If a tone of general exasperation prevails in this piece, it is a testament to Channing's self-control, because the sense of almost dumbfounded anger plays beneath its surface and boils up at key moments. The provocation of this letter, as noted in the introduction to this volume, was the general accusation of dishonesty which Jedediah Morse and Jeremiah Evarts had levelled at the Boston liberals, and the further suggestion that they be denied Christian fellowship. For Channing, this was a declaration of theological war which could not be ignored or taken lightly.*

Channing's use of the "private" letter written for public consumption as the vehicle of his defense is revealing. It suggests the fundamental reluctance with which he brought theological controversy into the public sphere. The letter is intended to convey the impression that issues better left for private discussion and debate have been forced into the public media. Similarly, his choice of Samuel Cooper Thacher (1785–1818) as the letter's nominal recipient is also notable. Thacher was, as Jack Mendelsohn aptly put it, "the Harry Percy of the young liberals." He was not only one of the most intellectually and socially promising of the young Boston ministers, but perhaps the most aggressive of them in defending the liberal cause.

Moreover, as Channing noted after Thacher's untimely death by consumption, "never was a man more universally beloved." [1] *He and Channing had enjoyed a close friendship. The possessor of social grace, intelligence, deep piety, and a strong devotion to the liberal cause, Thacher was an ideal representative of the sort of man whom the orthodox were unjustly attacking and attempting to exclude from the Christian community.*

This letter is full of the details of Evarts's charges against the liberals, and Channing's defenses and counterattacks. Measured against many of his other works then, this piece lacks the range of reference and application that is one mark of Channing's excellence and continuing relevance. But the compensations of the letter are its plain emotion, and the particularity with which it allows the reader to enter into one era's great intellectual conflict. For Channing, and indeed for liberal religion in America, this was a significant beginning.

LETTER TO THE

REV. SAMUEL C. THACHER,

ON THE ASPERSIONS CONTAINED IN A

LATE NUMBER OF THE PANOPLIST,

ON THE MINISTERS OF BOSTON AND THE VICINITY

My Friend and Brother,

I have recollected with much satisfaction the conversation, which we held the other morning, on the subject of the late *Review* in the *Panoplist* for *June*, of a pamphlet, called "American Unitarianism." [1] I was not surprised, but I was highly gratified, by the spirit with which you spoke of that injurious publication. Grief rather than indignation marked your countenance, and you mourned, that men, who bear the sacred and pacifick name of Christian, could prove so insensible to the obligations of their profession. Our conversation

---

1. Jack Mendelsohn, *Channing: The Reluctant Radical* (Boston: Little, Brown, 1971), 90. For biographical information on Thacher, see the sketches collected in William B. Sprague, *Annals of the American Unitarian Pulpit* (New York: Robert Carter and Brothers, 1865), 435–45. For Channing's eulogy of Thacher, see "Notice of the Rev. S.C. Thacher," in *The Works of William E. Channing, D.D.*, 6 vols. (Boston: James Munroe, 1841–43), 5:439.

turned, as you recollect, on the *falsehood* of that Review; on its *motives*; and on the *duties* which are imposed on those ministers, whose good name and whose influence it was designed to destroy.

After leaving you, my thoughts still dwelt on the subject; and, painful as is the task, I have thought it my duty to exhibit to the publick the topicks which we discussed, as well as to add some reflections suggested by private meditation.

I bring to the subject a feeling, which I cannot well express in words, but which you can easily understand. It is a feeling, as if I were degrading myself by noticing the false and injurious charges contained in this review. I feel as if I were admitting, that we need vindication, that our reputations want support, that our characters and lives do not speak for themselves. My self respect too is wounded, by coming into contact with assailants, who not only deny us the name of Christians, but withhold from us the treatment of gentlemen. These feelings, united with my love of peace, would induce me to pass over the Review in silence, if it were limited to the sphere within which we are personally known. In this sphere, I trust, its bitterness, coarseness, and misrepresentations will work their own cure; and that no other defence is required, but the tenour of our ministry and lives. But the work, in which this article is published, is industriously spread through the country, and through all classes of society. The aspersions which it contains are also diffused, as widely as possible, by conversation and even by newspapers. We owe then to ourselves, and what is more important to the cause of christian truth and charity, some remarks on the representations and spirit of the Review. You can easily conceive, how difficult it is to read again and again such a publication without catching some portion of an unchristian spirit. I do indeed feel myself breathing an atmosphere to which I am not accustomed. But my earnest desire is to remember whose disciple I am, and to temper displeasure with meekness and forgiveness.

The Panoplist Review, though extended over so many pages, may be compressed into a very narrow space. It asserts, 1. That the ministers of this town and its vicinity, and the great body of liberal christians are Unitarians in Mr. Belsham's[2] sense of the word: that is, they believe that Jesus Christ is a mere man, who when on earth was liable to errour and sin; to whom we owe no gratitude for benefits which we are now receiving; and for whose future interposition we have no reason to hope.

2. The Review asserts, that these ministers and liberal christians are guilty of hypocritical concealment of their sentiments, and behave in a base, cowardly and hypocritical manner.

3. Christians are called to come out and separate themselves from these ministers and the liberal body of christians, and to withhold from them christian communion.

I will consider these three heads in their order, and may then notice some other topicks introduced into the Review.

The *first* assertion to be considered is, that the ministers of this town and vicinity, and the great body of liberal christians are Unitarians, in Mr. Belsham's sense of that word; and I wish every reader to look back and distinctly impress this sense on his memory. I am sensible that almost every liberal christian,* who reads these pages, will regard this charge with a mixture of surprise and indignation, and will almost doubt the correctness of my statement of the Review. I therefore add the following extracts from the last number of the Panoplist, in which the Review is contained. (P. 267.) ''We feel entirely warranted to say that the *predominant religion* of the liberal party is decidedly Unitarian, in Mr. Belsham's sense of the word.'' P. 254, ''We shall feel ourselves warranted hereafter, to speak of the fact as certain, that Unitarianism,'' meaning Mr. Belsham's, ''is the predominant religion among the ministers and churches of Boston.'' P. 271, ''The liberal party mutilate the New Testament, reject nearly all the fundamental doctrines of the gospel, and degrade the Saviour to the condition of a fallible, peccable, and ignorant man.'' It is unnecessary to multiply extracts to show, that not only Boston, but its vicinity, is involved in the charge. In fact, the liberal party, in general, as you see, is ranged under the standard of Mr. Belsham. Now we both of us know this statement to be false. This misrepresentation is founded chiefly on some letters written by the Rev. Dr. Freeman, and Mr. William Wells, of Boston, to the Rev. Mr. Lindsey and the Rev. Mr. Belsham, of London,[3] which letters state, that many of the ministers and laymen of this quarter are Unitarian. You informed me in our late conversation, that Mr. Wells has assured you, that in his letter to Mr. Belsham, he used the word *Unitarian* in its proper and

---

*See Note A.

usual sense, as *opposed* to *Trinitarian*, as denoting a man who believes that God is *one* person, and not *three* persons. That Dr. Freeman attached the same meaning to the word, I cannot doubt, because I have once and again heard him give this very definition. If you will consult Miss Adams' View of Religions,[4] the only authority which I have at hand, you will see, that this term belongs to persons, who differ widely in their views of Jesus Christ. She particularly quotes Mosheim,[5] as saying, that Unitarians are Anti-Trinitarians. "The Socinians," Mosheim adds, "are also so called. The term is comprehensive, and is applicable to a great variety of persons, who, notwithstanding, agree in this common principle, that there is no *distinction in the Divine nature.*" The word Unitarian, taken in this its true sense, as including all who believe that there is no distinction of persons in God, is indeed, as Mosheim observes, of great extent. Dr. Watts, in the latter part of his life, was decidedly an Unitarian. So was Dr. Samuel Clarke; so was the late Dr. Eckley,* of this town;[6] so, I am told by respectable authorities, are several Hopkinsian clergymen in New-England. The word *Unitarianism*, as denoting this opposition to Trinitarianism, undoubtedly expresses the character of a considerable part of the ministers of this town and its vicinity, and the commonwealth. But we both of us know, that their Unitarianism is of a very different kind from that of Mr. Belsham.[7] We both agreed in our late conference, that a majority of our brethren believe, that Jesus Christ is more than man, that he existed before the world, that he literally came from heaven to save our race, that he sustains other offices than those of a teacher and witness to the truth, and that he still acts for our benefit, and is our intercessor with the Father. This we agreed to be the prevalent sentiment of our brethren. There is another class of liberal christians, who, whilst they reject the distinction of three persons in God, are yet unable to pass a definitive judgment on the various systems, which prevail, as to the nature and rank of Jesus Christ. They are met by difficulties on every side, and generally rest in the conclusion, that *He*, whom God has appointed to be our Saviour, must be precisely adapted to his work, and that acceptable faith consists in regarding and following him as our Lord, Teacher, and Saviour; without deciding on his nature or rank in the universe. There is another class, who believe the

---

*See Note B.

simple humanity of Jesus Christ; but these form a small proportion of the great body of Unitarians in this part of our country; and I very much doubt, whether of these, one individual can be found, who could conscientiously subscribe to Mr. Belsham's creed as given in the Review. The conduct of the Reviewer, in collecting all the opinions of that gentleman, not only on the Trinity, but on every other theological subject, in giving to the *whole* collection the name of *Unitarianism*, and in exhibiting this to the world as the creed of liberal christians in this region, is perhaps as criminal an instance of unfairness, as is to be found in the records of theological controversy. The fact is, that the great body of liberal christians would shrink from some of these opinions with as much aversion as from some of the gloomy doctrines of Calvin. You, my friend, well know, that Mr. Belsham is not acknowledged as a leader by any Unitarians in our country. I have heard from those, who are thought to approach him most nearly in opinion, complaints of the extravagance of some of his positions, as unjust and prejudicial to the cause which he has undertaken to defend.

I trust, that the statement which has now been made, will not be considered as casting the least reproach on those amongst us, who believe in the simple humanity of Jesus Christ. Whilst I differ from them in opinion, I have certainly no disposition to deny them the name and privileges of christians. There are gentlemen of this class, whom I have the happiness to know, in whom I discover the evidences of a scrupulous uprightness, and a genuine piety; and there are others, whose characters, as portrayed by their biographers, appear to me striking examples of the best influences of christianity.

After considering the letters of Mr. Wells and Dr. Freeman, it is not necessary to enlarge on the other evidences of our adopting Mr. Belsham's creed, which have been adduced by the Reviewer. The Monthly Anthology is summoned as a proof. I have read as little of that work as of most periodical publications; but you, who know more of it, have expressed to me your confident persuasion, that, from beginning to end, the doctrine of the simple humanity of Christ is not once asserted. As to the General Repository,[8] which is brought forward as another proof, I never for a moment imagined, that its editor was constituted or acknowledged as the organ of his brethren; and while its high literary merit has been allowed, I have heard some of its sentiments disapproved by the majority of those with whom I have conversed. With respect to the "Improved Version of the New Testament,"[9] I can speak with greater confidence. It is false, that this work was patronized and circulated by the ministers of Boston and the vicinity. It is impossible that such a fact could have escaped my notice, and I can scarcely remember an individual, who, in speaking of this version, has not expressed an unfavourable opinion at least of some of its notes.

I repeat it, these remarks are not offered for the purpose of throwing any reproach on any class of Christians, but simply to repel a statement which is untrue, and which is intended to rank us under a denomination, which the people of this country have been industriously taught to abhor. It is this intention of rendering us odious, which constitutes the criminality of the charge, and which exposes its author to severe indignation. A man, who is governed by christian principles, will slowly and reluctantly become "the accuser of his brethren."[10] He will inquire long and impartially before he attempts to fasten a bad name, (the most injurious method of assailing reputation) on an individual, and especially on a large class of the community. What severity of reproof then is merited by the author of this Review, who has laboured to attach, not only to professors, but to ministers of religion, a name and character which he hoped would awaken popular alarm, and endanger their influence, although a large majority of the accused have no participation in the pretended crime. That he intended to deceive, I am unwilling to assert; but the most charitable construction which his conduct will admit is, that his passions and party spirit have criminally blinded him, and hurried him into an act, which could have been authorized only by the strongest evidence, and the most impartial inquiry. The time may come, when he will view this transaction with other eyes; when the rage of party will have subsided; when the obligation of a fair and equitable temper will appear at least as solemn as the obligation of building up a sect; when misrepresentation, intended to injure, and originating, if not in malignity, yet in precipitancy and passion, will be felt to be a crime of no common aggravation. That this time may soon come, and may bring with it not only remorse, but sincere repentance, I know to be your wish, and I trust it is my own.

II. I now come to the *second* charge of the Review: That the ministers of Boston and the vicinity, and the most considerable

members of the liberal party "operate in secret; entrust only the in-
itiated with their measures; are guilty of hypocritical concealment of
their sentiments; behave in a base and hypocritical manner, compared with which Mr. Belsham's conduct, rotten as he is in doctrine
to the very core, is purity itself."* Such is the *decent* language scattered through this Review. This charge is infinitely more serious
than the first. To believe with Mr. Belsham is no crime. But artifice,
plotting, hypocrisy, *are* crimes; and if we practise them, we deserve
to be driven not only from the ministry, not only from the church,
but from the society of the decent and respectable. Our own hearts,
I trust, tell us at once how gross are these aspersions; and our acquaintance with our brethren authorizes us to speak in their vindication with the same confidence as in our own.

It is not to be wondered at, that those, who have charged us
with holding sentiments which we reject, should proceed to charge
us with hypocritically concealing our sentiments. Most of us have
often contradicted Mr. Belsham's opinions: and they who insist that
these opinions are ours, will be forced to maintain that we practise
deceit. They start with a falsehood, and their conclusion cannot
therefore be true.

I am not, however, disposed to dismiss this charge of artifice
and hypocrisy so lightly. The proofs on which it rests are perhaps the
most extraordinary which were ever adduced on so serious an occasion. The first evidence of our baseness is a letter from Dr. Freeman.
It is unnecessary to enter into any examination of this letter. It is sufficient to observe, that it was written, according to the Review, in
the year 1796 or 1797, that is, it was written when all the present

---

*We are accused of "the systematick practice of artifice," p. 242; of "hyp-
ocritical concealment," 251; of "cowardice in the concealment of our opinions,"
260; of "cunning and dishonesty," 260; of "acting in a base, hypocritical manner," a manner "at which common honesty revolts," 260; a manner "incompatible
with fidelity or integrity," 261. "The conduct of Mr. Belsham," we are told, "rotten as he is to the very core in point of doctrine, is purity itself, compared with the
conduct of these men," 262. "In pretence all is politeness and liberality; in practice
we find a rancour bitter as death, and cruel as the grave," 264. Let it be remembered that this is not to be considered as the invective and exaggeration, which we
are unhappily accustomed to permit in a political pamphlet. It is found in a grave
theological publication, and uttered by a man who declares that he "never took his
pen in hand with greater caution, nor with a more imperious sense of duty," 259.

congregational ministers in Boston, with the single exception of the venerated Dr. Lathrop, [11] were receiving their education either at school or in college, and had not probably directed their thoughts towards the sacred office; and before a considerable part of our brethren, now in the vicinity, were settled in the ministry. It is a melancholy thought, that accusations which would place us among the profligate part of society, are bitterly and furiously urged on such foundation as this!

But the next proof of our base concealment is still more remarkable. It is the letter of Mr. Wells to Mr. Belsham. In this letter Mr. Wells says, "Most of our Boston clergy and respectable laymen, among whom we have many enlightened theologians, are Unitarian. Nor do they think it at all necessary to conceal their sentiments, but express them without reserve when they judge it proper. I may safely say, the general habit of thinking and speaking upon this question is Unitarian." Can a more explicit passage be conceived? The method in which it is distorted by the Reviewer can hardly be recollected without expressions of indignation. Towards the close of his Review, p. 269, in speaking of the persons on whom Mr. Wells "lavishes commendation," he represents him as mentioning "most of the Boston clergy and respectable laymen, many of whom are enlightened theologians, who do not conceal their sentiments, but express them *when they judge it proper.*" This passage, as it stands in the Review, has the marks of quotation, as if taken from Mr. Wells' letter. Let me ask you to look back, and compare it carefully with the second sentence, which I have extracted from that letter. You perceive, that by mutilating that sentence, and by printing the last words in Italicks, the reviewer has entirely done away the meaning of Mr. Wells, and contrived to give to the common reader a directly opposite impression to what that gentleman intended to convey. An unperverted mind turns with sorrow and disgust from such uncharitable and disingenuous dealing; and why all this labour to distort what is so plain? The object is, to fix the character of knaves and hypocrites on a large class of christians and christian ministers. I might here be permitted to dip my pen in gall; but I do not write for those, whose moral feeling is so dull, as to need indignant comment on practices like these.

With respect to yourself, my friend, I presume no one will charge you with hypocritical concealment. Your situation offers you no temptation; and no one who has heard you preach, can ever have suspected you of a leaning towards Trinitarianism. As to myself, I have ever been inclined to cherish the most exalted views of Jesus Christ, which are consistent with the supremacy of the Father; and I have felt it my duty to depart from Mr. Belsham, in perhaps every sentiment which is peculiar to him on this subject. I have always been pleased with some of the sentiments of Dr. Watts on the intimate and peculiar union between the Father and the Son. But I have always abstained most scrupulously from every expression which could be construed into an acknowledgement of the Trinity. My worship and sentiments have been Unitarian in the proper sense of that word. In conversation with my people, who have requested my opinion upon the subject, especially with those who consider themselves Trinitarians, I have spoken with directness and simplicity. Some of those who differ from me most widely, have received from me the most explicit assurances of my disbelief of the doctrine of the Trinity, and of my views in relation to the Saviour. As to my brethren in general, never have I imagined for a moment, from their preaching or conversation, that they had the least desire to be considered as Trinitarians; nor have I ever heard from them any views of God or of Jesus Christ, but Unitarian in the proper meaning of that word.

It is indeed true, as Mr. Wells says, that we seldom or never introduce the Trinitarian controversy into our pulpits. We are accustomed to speak of the Father as the only living and true God, and of Jesus Christ as his son, as a distinct being from him, as dependent on him, subordinate to him, and deriving all from him. This phraseology pervades all our prayers, and all our preaching. We seldom or never, however, refer to any different sentiments, embraced by other christians, on the nature of God or of Jesus Christ. We preach precisely as if no such doctrine as the Trinity had ever been known. We do not attempt to refute it, any more than to refute the systems of the Sabellians, the Eutychians, or the Nestorians,[12] or of the other sects who have debated these questions with such hot and unprofitable zeal. But, in following this course, we are not conscious of having contracted, in the least degree, the guilt of insincerity. We have aimed at making no false impression. We have only followed a general system, which we are persuaded to be best for our people and for the cause of christianity; the system of excluding controversy as much as possible from our pulpits. In compliance with this system, I have never assailed Trinitariansim; nor have I ever said one word against Methodism, Quakerism, Episcopalianism, or the denomination of Baptists; and I may add Popery, if I except a few occasional remarks on the intolerance of that system. The name of these sects, with that single exception, has never passed my lips in preaching, through my whole ministry, which has continued above twelve years. We all of us think it best to preach the truth, or what we esteem to be the truth, and to say very little about errour, unless it be errour of a strictly practical nature. A striking proof of our sentiments and habits on this subject may be derived from the manner in which you and myself have treated Calvinism. We consider the errours which relate to Christ's person as of little or no importance compared with the errour of those who teach, that God brings us into life wholly depraved and wholly helpless, that he leaves multitudes without that aid which is indispensably necessary to their repentance, and then plunges them into everlasting burnings and unspeakable torture, for not repenting. This we consider as one of the most injurious errours which ever darkened the christian world; and none will pretend that we have anything to fear from exposing this errour to our people. On the contrary, we could hardly select a more popular topick;—and yet our hearers will bear witness how seldom we introduce this topick into our preaching. The name of Calvinist has never, I presume, been uttered by us in the pulpit. Our method is, to state what we conceive to be more honourable, and ennobling, and encouraging views of God's character and government, and to leave these to have their effect, without holding up other christians to censure or contempt. We could, if we were to make strenuous efforts, render the name of Calvinist as much a word of reproach in our societies, as that of Unitarian is in some parts of our country. But we esteem it a solemn duty to disarm instead of exciting the bad passions of our people. We wish to promote among them a spirit of universal charity. We wish to make them condemn their own bad practices, rather than the erroneous speculations of their neighbour. We love them too sincerely to imbue them with the spirit of controversy.

In thus avoiding controversy, we have thought that we deserved, not reproach, but some degree of praise for our self denial. Every preacher knows how much easier it is to write a controversial than a practical discourse; how much easier it is to interest an audience by attacking an opposite party, than by stating to them the duties and motives of the gospel. We often feel, that our mode of preaching exposes us to the danger of being trite and dull; and I presume we have often been tempted to gratify the love of disputation which lurks in every society. But so deeply are we convinced, that the great end of preaching is to promote a spirit of love, a sober, righteous and godly life, and that every doctrine is to be urged simply and exclusively for this end, that we have sacrificed our ease, and have chosen to be less striking preachers, rather than to enter the lists of controversy.

We have seldom or never assailed the scheme of the Trinity, not only from our dislike to controversy in general, but from a persuasion that this discussion would, above all others, perplex and needlessly perplex a common congregation, consisting of persons of all ages, capacities, degrees of improvement and conditions in society. This doctrine we all regard as the most unintelligible about which christians have ever disputed. If it do not mean that there are Three Gods, (a construction which its advocates indignantly repel,) we know not what it means; and we have not thought that we should edify common hearers by attacking a doctrine, altogether inconceivable and wholly beyond the grasp of our faculties.—We have recollected too the mischiefs of the Trinitarian controversy in past ages, that it has been a firebrand lighting the flames of persecution, and kindling infernal passions in the breasts of christians; and we have felt no disposition to interest the feelings of our congregation in a dispute, which has so disgraced the professed disciples of the meek and lowly Jesus.—Many of us have been disinclined, not only to assail systems which we do not believe, but even to enforce the views which we have given of the rank and character of Jesus Christ; because we have known, how divided the best men have been on these topicks, and how largely we ourselves partake of the fallibility of our nature; because we have wished, that our hearers should derive their impressions on these points as much as possible from the scriptures; and because we have all been persuaded, that precision of views upon these subjects is in no degree essential to the faith or practice of a christian.—We have considered the introduction of the Trinitarian controversy into the pulpit, as the less necessary, because we have generally found that common christians admit that distinction between God and his Son, and that subordination of the Son, which we believe to be the truth; and as to that very small part of our hearers, who are strongly attached to the doctrine of the Trinity, while we have not wished to conceal from them our difference of opinion, we have been fully satisfied, that the most effectual method of promoting their holiness and salvation was to urge on them perpetually those great truths and precepts, about which there is little contention, and which have an immediate bearing on the temper and the life.— To conclude, we have never entered into discussions of the doctrine of the Trinity, because we are not governed by a proselyting temper. I will venture to assert, that there is not on earth a body of men who possess less of the spirit of proselytism, than the ministers of this town and vicinity. Accustomed as we are to see genuine piety in all classes of christians, in Trinitarians and Unitarians, in Calvinists and Arminians, in Episcopalians, Methodists, Baptists, and Congregationalists, and delighting in this character wherever it appears, we are little anxious to bring men over to our peculiar opinions. I could smile at the idea of a *Unitarian plot,* were not this fiction intended to answer so unworthy an end. There cannot be a doubt, that had we seriously united for the purpose of spreading Unitarianism by any and every means, by secret insinuations against those who differ from us, by *uncharitable denunciations,* and by the other usual arts of sects, we might have produced in this part of the country an Unitarian heat and bitterness not inferior to that with which Trinitarianism is too often advocated. But not the slightest whisper of any concert for this end has ever reached me; and as to these arts, our people can best say how far we have practised them. Our people will testify, how little we have sought to influence them on the topicks of dispute among christians, how little we have laboured to make them partisans, how constantly we have besought them to look with candour on other denominations, and to delight in all the marks which others exhibit of piety, and goodness. Our great and constant object has been to promote the spirit of Christ, and we have been persuaded, that in this way we should most effectually promote the interests of christian truth.

These remarks will shew, how entirely unfounded are the charges, which are adduced against us, of insincerity and base hypocrisy. And are we not authorized, my brother, to repel these charges with some degree of warmth? Are we not called to speak in the language of indignant and insulted virtue, as well as of pity and sorrow, in relation to the man, who is propagating these unmerited reproaches? We are christians by profession, and ministers of the Gospel, governed, as we humbly hope, by the principles of Jesus Christ. We honour his name; we remember his dying love with gratitude; and I hope we are ready to meet the loss of all things in his service; and yet we are represented to our people as unprincipled men, wearing a mask, and practising the basest arts. And we are thus loaded with invective and abuse, that we may be robbed of that influence, which, if we know ourselves, we wish to exert for the honour of God, and the salvation of mankind; that we may be robbed of the confidence and affection of our societies, and may be forsaken by them as unworthy the christian name. Need I ask, whether this be a light injury or an ordinary crime?

On the present occasion, when our moral character is impeached, we are justified, I think, in an appeal to our respective societies; and I trust, my friend, that we and our accused brethren can say with confidence to those to whom we minister, "Brethren, you know us, for we live among you; we visit you in your families, we speak to you from the pulpit; we repair to you in your sorrows, and we sit too at the table of your festivity. You know something of our conduct in our families, and in the common relations of life. We are, indeed sensible, that in all these situations, we have exhibited to you much of human imperfection, and our frequent prayer to God is, that he will forgive our deficiencies. But, brethren, we ask you to recollect our general deportment and ministrations. Have we seemed to you men of artifice and deceit, men without reverence for truth, and without the fear of God, men of sordid and selfish views, seeking your wealth or applause, and careless of your souls? Have we ever seemed to you to be labouring to build up a cause, or to establish a party, which we were ashamed to acknowledge? Have we ever directed you to any foundation of hope or guide of life, but the Gospel of Christ? Have we not continually exhorted you, as a father doth his children, that you would walk worthy of this religion from heaven? In your affliction have we not administered to you the consolations which it offers? and in the more dangerous seasons of enjoyment, have we not discovered the purity and moderation which it inculcates? To what work of christian usefulness have you found us reluctant? In what relation of life have you found us unfaithful? On what occasion have we discovered, that our christian profession is a cloak of hypocrisy? It is not our design, by these questions, to advance our own glory; God forbid it: But we wish to impress you deeply with the criminality of those aspersions, which are cast habitually on your teachers; and with the urgent necessity of discouraging that unrelenting party spirit, which has no respect for innocence or virtue, and which threatens to overwhelm our churches with discord and contention.''

III. I now come to the third head of the Review, which I propose to consider. The Reviewer, having charged us with holding the opinions of Mr. Belsham, and hypocritically concealing them, solemnly calls on christians who differ from us in sentiment, " to come out and be separate from us, and to withhold communion with us;" and a paragraph of the bitterest contempt and insult is directed against those ministers who, whilst they disagree on the controverted points of theology, are yet disposed to love and treat us as brethren. This language does not astonish me, when I recollect the cry of heresy which has been so loudly raised against this part of the country. But I believe that this is the first instance, in which christians have been deliberately called to deny us the christian name and privileges. As such let it be remembered; and let the consequences of it lie on its authors.

Why is it that our brethren are thus instigated to cut us off, as far as they have power, from the body and church of Christ? Let every christian weigh well the answer. It is not because we refuse to acknowledge Jesus Christ as our Lord and Master; it is not because we neglect to study his word; it is not, because our lives are wanting in the spirit and virtues of his gospel. It is, because after serious investigation, we cannot find in the Scriptures, and cannot adopt as instructions of our Master, certain doctrines, which have divided the church for ages, which have perplexed the best and wisest men, and which are very differently conceived even by those who profess to receive them. It is, in particular, because we cannot adopt the language of our brethren, in relation to a doctrine, which we cannot understand, and which is expressed in words not only unauthorized by the Scripture, but as we believe, in words employed without meaning, (unless they mean that there are three Gods,) by those who insist upon them. This is our crime, that we cannot think and speak with our brethren on subjects the most difficult and perplexing, on which the human mind was ever engaged. For this we are pursued with the cry of heresy, and are to have no rest until virtually excommunicated by our brethren.

Were the christian world more enlightened on the nature of heresy, they would not be so much alarmed when they hear it attached to their brethren. Most earnestly do I wish that the Dissertation of Dr. Campbell on Heresy, in his "Translation of the Four Gospels,"[13] were more generally read and considered. He has proved, I think, very satisfactorily, that *heresy,* as the word is used in the Scriptures, does not consist in the adoption or profession of wrong opinions, but in a *spirit of division, of dissension, of party,* in a *factious and turbulent temper;* and that the heretick is not a man who entertains erroneous or even injurious sentiments, but *one who loves to be called Rabbi and master;* who has a *disposition to separate christians, to create or to extend sects and parties.* The conclusion of the Dissertation of this most judicious writer on Heresy, deserves to be imprinted on every mind in these days of discussion. "No person, who, in the spirit of candour and charity, adheres to that which to the best of his judgment is right, though in this opinion he should be mistaken, is in the *scriptural* sense either *schismatick* or *heretick*; and *he,* on the contrary, whatever sect he belongs to, is more entitled to these odious appellations, *who is most apt to throw the imputation upon others.* Both terms, (for they denote only different degrees of the same bad quality,) *always indicate a disposition and practice unfriendly to peace and harmony and love."** If these views be correct, there is no difficulty in deciding, to what persons among us the name of heretick most justly belongs; and we shall be forced to conclude, that of all publications which have issued from our press, no one is more tinctured with the spirit of heresy, than the Review, which it is my painful office to examine.

Most earnestly do I hope that christians will weigh well the nature and guilt of schism, the consequences of separation, and the spirit of their religion, before they adopt the measure recommended in this Review. For myself, the universe would not tempt me to bear a part in this work of dividing Christ's church, and of denouncing his followers. If there be an act which, above all others, is a transgres-

---

*Campbell's Gospels, Vol. II, p. 141, Boston edition.

sion of the christian law, it is this. What is the language of our Master? "A *new* commandment I give unto you, that ye *love one another. By this shall all men know, that ye are my disciples,* if ye have *love one to another."* "Bear ye one another's burdens," says St. Paul, "and so fulfil *the law of Christ."*[14] But what says this Review? "Cast out your brethren, and treat them as heathens." I know it will be said, that christians are not called upon to reject real christians, but hereticks and false pretenders to the name. But heresy, we have seen, is not a false opinion, but a sectarian spirit; and as to false pretences, we desire those who know us, to put their hands on their hearts, and to say, whether they can for a moment believe that we hypocritically profess to follow the instructions of Jesus Christ? Does charity discover nothing in our language and lives to justify the hope that we are united to Jesus Christ by love for his character, and by participation of his spirit? Most earnestly would I advise those persons who are inclined to follow the instigations of this Review, to think seriously before they act; to remember, that Jesus Christ has solemnly forbidden uncharitable judgment, that he regards the injuries which are done to his followers, through a censorious spirit, as done to himself, and that christians cannot more surely forsake their Lord, the Prince of peace, than by following an inciter to denunciation and division.

I wish that my motives for these earnest remonstrances against division may be understood. I feel as little personal interest in the subject as any individual in the community. Were the proposed separation to take place, I should still enjoy the ordinances of the gospel in the society of those whom I best love. The excommunication which is threatened gives me no alarm. I hear this angry thunder murmur at a distance, with as little concern as if it were the thunder of the pope, from whom it seems indeed to be borrowed. But whilst I fear nothing for myself, I do fear and feel for that body of which Christ is the head, which has been bleeding for ages under the contests of christians, and which is now threatened with a new wound. I feel for the cause of our common christianity, which I am set to defend, and which has suffered inconceivably more from the bad passions and divisions of its friends, than from all the arts and violence of its foes. I cannot but look forward with pain to the irritations, hatreds, bitter recriminations, censoriousness, spiritual pride, and schismatical spirit which will grow up under this system of denunciation and exclusion, and which may not only convulse many churches at the present moment, but will probably end in most unhappy divisions among the very christians who denounce us; who seem indeed to be united, now that a common enemy is to be trodden under foot, but who have sufficient diversities of opinion, to awaken against each other all the fury of intolerance, when this shall have become the temper and habit of their minds. I repeat it, I have no interest in this point, but as a christian; and as such, I look with a degree of horrour on this attempt to inflame and distract our churches. Errour of opinion is an evil too trifling to be named in comparison with this practical departure from the Gospel, with this proud, censorious, overbearing temper, which says to a large body of christians, "stand off, we are holier than you."

Before I leave this question of separation, let me just observe, that by this Review, not only we and our brethren are cut off from the body of Christ; but the most venerable men who have left us, and who, when living, were esteemed ornaments of the church, such men as the late President Willard, Dr. Howard, Dr. Eckley, Dr. Eliot, and Dr. Barnard,[15] are declared unworthy of the communion of the church on earth, and of course unfit for the fellowship of saints in heaven. It would be easy to show, that the same dreadful sentence is past on some of the most exemplary men in civil life, to whom this commonwealth is indebted for the stability of its civil and religious institutions.* These all having lived, as they thought, in the faith of Christ, and having died with a hope in his precious promises, are now cut off from his church, and denied his name. What christian does not shudder at this awful temerity in a frail and erring fellow-being, who thus presumes to sit in judgment on men, who in purity and sincerity and devotion to God, were certainly not inferiour to himself? I stop here, for I wish not to indulge in language of severity; and this subject, if any, may be left to speak for itself to the heart of the christian.

---

*Were it an object to enumerate all who are involved in this sweeping sentence of condemnation, I might mention Locke, Newton, Grotius, Dr. Samuel Clarke, Lardner, Price, Paley,[16] and other names most conspicuous among the friends of science and religion. All these were decided Unitarians; and can any imagine that christianity is to be promoted by driving these men from the christian church?

Having thus considered the three principal heads in the Review, I now proceed, as I proposed, to offer a few words of friendly admonition, as to the temper and conduct which become our brethren and ourselves, under the injuries which we receive. The first suggestion you have undoubtedly anticipated. It is, that we remember the great duty which belongs to us as christians, of regarding our enemies with good will, if possible with a degree of approbation, at least with displeasure tempered with compassion. We profess to accord with that apostle, who has taught us that charity is greater than faith and hope, more excellent than the tongue of angels and the understanding of all mysteries. Let us prove our sincerity by our deeds. Let us cheerfully avail ourselves of every circumstance, which will justify the belief, that the cruel and bitter remarks of our adversaries proceed not from a wanton and unblushing contempt of truth, but from deep rooted prejudices, false views of religion, unsuspected biasses to censoriousness, and disordered imagination; and whilst we lament that they do not partake more largely of the best influences of the gospel, let us be induced to hope that their profession of the gospel is sincere, and that their departure from its spirit is unknown to themselves. As to the great mass of those christians, who view us with so much jealousy, we must remember, that they know us only by report, that they believe as they are taught by men to whom they ascribe an eminent sanctity, and that they are liable to be carried away on this, as on every other subject, by loud assertion, and by addresses to their fears. Accustomed as they are to hear us branded with names and epithets, to which they have attached no definite ideas, but which seem to them to express every thing depraved, can we wonder that they shrink from us with a kind of terrour? Towards this great class of our opposers, we certainly owe nothing but kindness; and we should esteem it an unspeakable happiness, that we can look with so much pleasure and hope on those by whom we are dreaded and shunned; that we are not obliged by our system to regard *our* adversaries as the enemies of God, and the objects of his wrath. On this point, above all others, I would be urgent. Our danger is, that reproach will hurry us into language or conduct unbecoming the spirit of our master. Let us remember that our opposers cannot ultimately injure us, unless we permit them to awaken bad passions, and to impair our virtues. Let us remember what is due from us to our religion. The more that our age is uncharitable, the more that the glory of the gospel is obscured by its being exhibited as a source of censoriousness and contention, the more we owe it to our Lord to wipe off this reproach from his truth, to shew the loveliness of his religion, to show its power in changing the heart into the image of divine forbearance and forgiveness. Is the gospel at this moment receiving deep wounds in the house of its friends? Let us guard with new jealousy its interests and honour.

The second suggestion I would offer, is this. Whilst we disapprove and lament the unchristian spirit of some of our opposers, and the efforts which are used to make us odious, let us yet acknowledge that there is kindness in that Providence, which permits this trial to befall us. We esteem it indeed a hardship to be numbered by our brethren among the enemies of that Saviour whom we love. But let us remember, that we as well as others need affliction: and it is my persuasion and hope that God intends by this dispensation to purify our characters and extend our usefulness. The singular prosperity which we have enjoyed, has undoubtedly exposed us to peculiar temptations. Perhaps in no part of the world is the condition of ministers more favoured than ours. Whilst we receive nothing of a superstitious homage or a blind submission, we find ourselves respected by all classes of society, and, may I not say, distinguished by the eminent, the enlightened and the good? We are received with a kind of domestick affection into the families of our parishioners. Our sufferings call forth their sympathy, and in sickness we enjoy every aid which tenderness and liberality can bestow. Our ministrations are attended with a seriousness, which, however due to the truth which we deliver, we often feel to be poorly deserved, by the imperfect manner in which it is dispensed. In our societies there are no divisions, no jealousies, no parties to disturb us. Whilst for these singular blessings, we should give thanks to the Author of all good, we should remember, that human virtue is often unable to sustain uninterrupted prosperity; that a condition so favoured tends to awaken pride and self-indulgence; and that God, who knows us better than we know ourselves, may see that we need reproach and opposition to make us better men and better ministers. I can certainly say for myself, that the spirit of denunciation in our country, has led me to a more serious and habitual study of the scriptures, and to a deeper feeling of my responsibility, than I should have attained in a more peaceful condition. Let us then resign ourselves to God, who in infinite wisdom sees fit to expose us to the scourge of evil tongues. Let this trial awaken us to new watchfulness, devotion, and fidelity; and we may trust that it will be overruled to the extension of our usefulness, and to the promotion of pure and undefiled religion.

A third, and a very important suggestion is this: Let us hold fast our uprightness. I have said, that the opposition to which we are exposed has its advantages; but whilst it preserves us from the temptation of prosperity, it brings some temptation of its own, which we cannot too steadfastly resist. It will try our integrity. That our churches are to be generally shaken by the assault which is made upon them, I am far from believing. But some may suffer. It is not impossible, that the efforts which are now employed to direct against us the uncharitableness and mistaken zeal of the country, and to spread disaffection through the most uninstructed and the most easily excited classes of society, may produce some effect. We know the fluctuations of the human mind. We know that the sincerest christians are often unduly influenced by timidity, and may be brought to suspect a minister, when he is decried as a heretick, who is leading souls to hell. It requires more strength of nerves and more independence of mind than all good people possess, to withstand this incessant clamour. A storm then may be gathering over some of us, and the sufferers may be tempted to bend to it. But God forbid, my friend, that any of us should give support to the aspersions cast on our uprightness, by ever suppressing our convictions, or speaking a language foreign to our hearts. Through good report and through evil report, let us with simplicity and sincerity declare what we believe to be the will of God and the way to Heaven, and thus secure to ourselves that peace of conscience which is infinitely better than the smiles of the world. Let us never forget, that the most honoured condition on earth is that of being sufferers for the sake of righteousness, for adherence to what we deem the cause of God and holiness, and let us welcome suffering, if it shall be appointed us, as bringing us nearer to our persecuted Lord, and his injured apostles. My brother, we profess to count man's judgment as a light thing, to esteem this world and all which it offers to be vanity. We profess to look up to a heavenly inheritance, and to hope that we shall one day mingle with angels and just men made perfect. And with these sub-

lime hopes, shall we tremble before frail and fallible fellow creatures, be depressed by difficulties, or shrink from the expression of
what we deem important and useful truth? God forbid.

I have time to add but one more suggestion. Let us beware lest
opposition and reproach lead any of us into a sectarian attachment to
our peculiar opinions. This is a danger to which persons of ardent
and irritable temper are peculiarly exposed. Too many of us are apt
to cling to a system in proportion as it is assailed, to consider ourselves pledged to doctrines which we have openly espoused, to rally
round them as if our own honour and interest were at stake, and to
assert them with more and more positiveness, as if we were incapable of errour. This is the infirmity of our frail nature; and whilst we
condemn it in others, let us not allow it in ourselves. Let us be what
we profess to be, patient inquirers after truth, open to conviction,
willing to listen to objections, willing to renounce errour, willing to
believe that we as well as others may have been warped in our opinions, by education and situation, and that others may have acquired
important truths which, through weakness or prejudice, we may
have overlooked. Were we a party, anxious to make proselytes, we
should do well to be positive and overbearing. But we profess to be
anxious that our fellow christians should inquire for themselves into
the difficulties of religion, instead of implicitly receiving what we
have embraced. We profess to believe, that candid and impartial research will guide mankind to a purer system of christianity, than is
now to be found in any church or country under Heaven. Most earnestly do I hope that we shall not be betrayed by any violence of assault into a sectarian heat and obstinacy, which will discredit our
profession, and obstruct this glorious reformation of the church of
God.

I have thus, my brother, considered the charges, by which we
and our brethren have been assailed, and have endeavoured to recommend the temper with which we should meet reproach and insult.
I intended to offer a few remarks on some other topicks introduced
into the Review: but this letter is already extended far beyond the
limits which I originally prescribed. I cannot, however, pass over in
silence the charges against Harvard University, that venerable institution, which so many excellent men in this commonwealth are accustomed to regard with filial affection and honour, and to which we
are all so much indebted for the light of knowledge, and for what-

ever capacities of usefulness to society we may possess. The statement of the Reviewer, that the propagation of Unitarianism in that University is the object of regular and well concerted exertion, is altogether false, I am persuaded that such a plan never entered the thoughts of those to whom the department of theological instruction is entrusted. The books in which the classes are taught, were selected for the very purpose of avoiding, as far as possible, the controversies of theologians, and the communication of any peculiarities of opinion to the students. They are, "Grotius on the Truth of the Christian Religion," "Paley's Evidences," "Butler's Analogy," and "Griesbach's New Testament."[17] The charge of the Reviewer, that the students, instructed as they are in these works, by a professor of exemplary purity and uprightness, are yet *taught to deny Jesus Christ*, will, I trust, excite the indignation and abhorrence of every unperverted mind.*

Had I time, I should feel it my duty to offer some remarks on the general *style* of the publication which I am called to examine. It not only abounds in misrepresentation, and breathes an unchristian spirit, but it is written in a style which tends to deprave the taste and manners of the community. It is suited to give a coarse and vulgar character to the conversation and deportment of those christians whom it may influence. It abounds in sneer and insult, and bears the marks of a writer better fitted to fill the pages of an inflammatory newspaper, than to be the guide of the mild and benevolent disciples of Jesus Christ. I trust, however, that its style and spirit will do much to counteract its pernicious tendency. I have too much respect for this people to believe that wanton assaults on the moral character of ministers and private christians will be encouraged and approved. I even hope that good will in many cases result from this publication. I trust, that those christians who have been partially misled by the denouncing spirit of the times, will now pause and consider; that all christians, of whatever name, who have any delicacy and tenderness of feeling, will learn the true character of that unhallowed zeal which is seeking to divide our churches; and that in this way, some important aid will be given to the cause of peace and charity. May God, whose glory it is to bring good from evil, thus cause "the wrath of man to praise him."[18]

---

*See Note C.

I think it proper, in conclusion, to observe that I shall not feel myself bound to notice any replies which may be made to this letter, especially if they appear in the Panoplist. I consider that work as having forfeited all claim on the confidence of candid, upright, and honourable men. If any remarks on this letter shall appear, written with the spirit of a christian, or in the style of a gentleman, I shall read them with care, and I hope with impartiality; and I shall readily retract any of my opinions or statements which I shall see to be erroneous, if they shall be thought sufficiently important to demand publick acknowledgment.

I now commit this humble effort to promote the peace and union of the church, and the cause of truth and free inquiry, to the blessing of Almighty God. That in writing it, I have escaped every unchristian feeling, I dare not hope; and for every departure from the spirit of his gospel, I implore his forgiveness. If I have fallen into errour, I beseech him to discover it to my own mind, and to prevent its influence on the minds of others. It is an unspeakable consolation that we and our labours are in his hand, and that the cause of the gospel is his peculiar care. That he may honour us as the instruments of extending the knowledge and the spirit of the gospel, is the earnest prayer of your friend and brother in Christ,

W. E. Channing.
Boston, June 20, 1815.

CHANNING'S
NOTES

Note A

I have used the phrase or denomination *Liberal Christians* because it is employed by the Reviewer to distinguish those whom he assails. I have never been inclined to claim this appellation for myself or my friends, because as the word *liberality* expresses the noblest qualities of the human mind, freedom from local prejudices and narrow feelings, the enlargement of the views and affections,—I have thought that the assumption of it would savour of that spirit, which has attempted to limit the words *orthodox* and *evangelical* to a particular body of christians. As the appellation, however, cannot well be avoided, I will state, the meaning which I attach to it.

By a liberal christian I understand one, who is disposed to receive as his brethren in Christ, all who in the judgment of charity, sincerely profess to receive Jesus Christ as their Lord and Master. He rejects all tests or standards of christian faith and of christian character, but the word of Jesus Christ and of his inspired apostles. He thinks it an act of disloyalty to his Master to introduce into the church creeds of fallible men as bonds of union, or terms of christian fellowship. He calls himself by no name derived from human leaders, disclaims all exclusive connexion with any sect or party, professes himself a member of the church universal on earth and in heaven, and cheerfully extends the hand of brotherhood to every man of every name who discovers the spirit of Jesus Christ.

According to this view of liberal christians, they cannot be called a party. They are distinguished only by refusing to separate themselves in any form or degree from the great body of Christ. They are scattered too through all classes of Christians. I have known Trinitarians and Calvinists, who justly deserve the name of liberal, who regard with affection all who appear to follow Jesus Christ in temper and life, however they may differ on the common points of theological controversy. To this class of christians, which is scattered over the earth, and which I trust has never been extinct in any age, I profess and desire to belong. God send them prosperity.—In this part of the country, liberal christians, as they have been above described, are generally, though by no means universally, Unitarians in the proper sense of that word. It is of this part of them that I chiefly speak in this letter.

I cannot forbear enforcing the sentiments of this note and of the letter by a passage from the venerable Baxter, as I find it quoted by Grove from the preface to the second part of "Saints' Everlasting Rest."[19]

"Two things have set the church on fire, and been the plagues of it above one thousand years;—1st. Enlarging our creed, and making more fundamentals than ever God made. 2d. Composing, and so *imposing*, our creeds and confessions in our own words and phrases.

When men have learned more manners and humility than to accuse God's language as too general and obscure, as if they could mend it—and have more dread of God and compassion on themselves, than to make those to be fundamentals or certainties which God never made so; and when they reduce their confessions, 1st. to their due extent, and 2d. to *scripture phrases*, that dissenters may not scruple subscribing—then, and I think never till then, shall the church have peace about doctrinals. It seems to me no heinous *Socinian* notion which Chillingworth is blamed for, viz. *Let all men believe the Scripture, and that only, and endeavour to believe it in the true sense, and promise this, and require no more of others, and they shall find this not only a better, but the only means to suppress heresy and restore unity."*

Note B

I have mentioned the name of Dr. Eckley, because his opinions on this subject were again and again expressed before me with perfect frankness, and are stated with great distinctness in his letter to the Rev. Thomas Worcester of Salisbury,[20] from which I subjoin an extract.

"My plan, when I saw you, as I think I intimated, respecting the Son of God, was very similar to what your brother* has now adopted. The common plan of three self-existent persons forming one *Essence* or infinite *Being*, and one of these persons being *united to a man*, but not in the least humbling himself or suffering, completely leads to and ends in Socinianism; and though it claims the form of *orthodoxy*, it is a *shadow* without the *substance*; it eludes inspection; and I sometimes say to those who are strenuous for this doctrine, that they take away my Lord, and I know not where they place him."—"The *orthodoxy*, so called, of *Waterland*, is as repugnant to my reason and views of religion, as the *heterodoxy of Lardner*; and I am at a loss to see that any solid satisfaction, for a person who wishes to find salvation through the death of the SON OF GOD, can be found in either."—"I seek for a plan which exalts the personal character and attributes of the SON OF GOD in the *highest pos-*

---

*Rev. Noah Worcester.

sible degree. The plan which your brother hath chosen does this— The scheme he has adopted affords light and comfort to the christian. I have long thought so; and I continue to think I have not been mistaken.''

Additional Remarks

Note C

I have been surprised and grieved at hearing, since the publication of this letter, that some readers have thought, that the charges in the Review against the President of Harvard University ought to have received from me a degree of attention. The important station, which that gentleman fills with so much usefulness and honour, seemed to me to render the introduction of his name into a controversy like the present improper and perhaps indecorous. I thought too, that it would be an imputation on the understanding of the plainest reader, to attempt the refutation of that singular argument in support of a Unitarian plot at the University, which the Reviewer has derived from the *omissions* of certain topicks in the President's *prayer* on the Commencement in the year 1813. I did suppose, that this argument might be safely left without a word of comment, and that the importance given to it in the Review would be regarded as one of the strongest possible proofs of a desperate cause. An assailant when he is driven to the use of such a weapon, ceases to be formidable. What christian on earth will escape denunciation, if his character is to be decided by *omissions* in a *prayer*? I very much fear, that the holy men, whose prayers are recorded in scripture, will, if tried by this standard of *omission*, be often found wanting in some essential articles of faith; and what is more, I fear, that the Author of the Lord's prayer will, according to this rule, be driven as a heretick from the very church which he has purchased with his own blood. In that well known prayer I can discover no reference to the ''inspiration of the holy scriptures, to the supreme divinity of the Son and Holy Ghost, to the atonement and intercession of Jesus Christ, to the native and total depravity of the unregenerate, and to the reality and necessity of special divine grace to renew and sanctify the souls of men;'' and these, let it be remembered, are *five* out of the *six* articles which are given by the Reviewer as fundamental articles of a christian's faith, p. 249. These omissions, it is to be observed, are not found in a prayer used on a special occasion by our Lord; but in a prayer given by him to his disciples as a *form* or *model,* and which he designed should be *published through the whole earth,* and transmitted for the *use and imitation of all future ages.* I cannot adopt the style of the Reviewer, and exhort christian parents to beware of placing their children under the guidance of our Lord as a teacher, because such a prayer, which omits so many essentials, proceeded from his lips.

I neglected to notice this argument in my letter, because *as an argument* it seemed unworthy of notice. There is, however, another view of it, in which it deserves attention. I refer to the spirit which it indicates in *some* of our opponents. The story which the Reviewer tells, of a number of men assembling on the evening of Commencement, and putting together their observations on the President's prayer, sounds badly. One has reason to fear, that these men listened to the prayer, with something of the temper of certain persons in the time of our Saviour, who assembled to heaɪ him, that they might "catch something out of his mouth, that they might accuse him."[21] We learn too, that it is not impossible, that we are surrounded by spies, when we suspect no evil; that our words may be treasured up, and may be published after months, and even years, have passed away, and have blotted every recollection of them from our minds; and that we may be summoned to answer, at that distant period, not only for what we said, but for what we omitted to say. I think that we discover something of this system of *espionage* in the story told by the Reviewer, of the complaint of a Boston minister on visiting New-York, where he was not invited to preach. The peace of society and of the church, and the freedom and confidence of social intercourse demand, that this very degrading practice of publishing what people *say,* should be exposed with great plainness and strong disapprobation.

There is another charge against the President of Harvard University, which no one certainly will expect me to notice; it is the charge of having written an article in the Anthology above four years ago. I am not in the habit of asking gentlemen, whether they are the authors of pieces which appear without a name; nor do I conceive that the President of Harvard University is bound to answer to the publick, whenever an anonymous publication shall be laid to his charge.

Notes

1. For details on this review, see the introduction to this volume and also Conrad Wright, "The Controversial Career of Jedidiah Morse," *Harvard Library Bulletin* 31 (Winter 1983): 64–87.

2. Thomas Belsham (1750–1829) wrote *Memoir of the Late Reverend Theophilus Lindsey* (London: 1812), part of which was reprinted as *American Unitarianism* by Jedidiah Morse in 1815. Jeremiah Evarts's review of that pamphlet provoked Channing's response.

3. James Freeman (1759–1835) was minister at King's Chapel, Boston, and the first avowed Unitarian minister in New England. Unlike most of the other New England liberals, he held a Socinian Christology, which stressed the humanity of Jesus. Theophilus Lindsey (1723–1808) was a presbyter of the Church of England who held anti-trinitarian views. See Wright, "The Controversial Career of Jedidiah Morse." William Wells, Jr. (1773–1860) was a publisher and later school proprietor in Boston, and a friend of James Freeman.

4. Hannah Adams (1755–1831) was the author of *A View of Religions* (Boston: 1711).

5. Johann Lorenz von Mosheim (c.1694–1755) was author of *An Ecclesiastical History, Ancient and Modern*, translated by Archibald Maclaine (London: 1765, and many other editions).

6. Isaac Watts (1674–1748) was a noted hymnist; Samuel Clarke (1675–1729) was an English theologian of much influence on the New England Liberals; Joseph Eckley (1750–1811) was minister of the Old South Church in Boston.

7. Channing's distinction between the Boston liberals and Belsham is important. The Boston liberals were largely Arian in their Christology—they held that Jesus was divine, but subordinate to God the Father. The English Unitarians, influenced by Joseph Priestley, were Socinian in their Christology.

8. *The Monthly Anthology and Boston Review*, published in Boston from 1803 to 1811, was an important early American religious and literary magazine, and an organ for liberal opinion. It was superseded by *The General Repository and Review*. For more information on *The Monthly Anthol-*

ogy, see Lewis P. Simpson, *The Federalist Literary Mind* (Baton Rouge, La.: 1972).

9. The reference is probably to *The New Testament, in an Improved Version, Upon the Basis of Archbishop Newcome's New Translation: With a Corrected Text, and Notes Critical and Explanatory*, edited by Thomas Belsham (London: 1808).

10. Revelation 12:10—". . . for the accuser of our brethren is cast down, which accused them before our God day and night."

11. John Lathrop (1740–1816) was pastor of the Second Church in Boston.

12. The Sabellians were followers of Sabellius, a third-century theologian who taught the radical unity of the Godhead and was excommunicated as a heretic. The Eutychians were the followers of Eutyches of Constantinople (ca.380–ca.456) who taught that Christ had a divine nature only. He was excommunicated as a heretic. The Nestorians were followers of Nestorius of Constantinople (ca.381–451) who believed that two separate natures adhered in Christ, divine and human. He claimed that the title "Mother of God" could not be used for Mary, since she was mother only of the human nature of Jesus. This doctrine was pronounced heretical in 431. Channing's choice of these sects is meant not only to make Calvinism seem an obscure and unessential doctrine, but to suggest the vexed history of the doctrine of the relation of God the Father to Jesus.

13. George Campbell, *The Four Gospels, Translated from the Greek, With Preliminary Dissertations and Notes Critical and Explanatory . . . With the Author's Last Corrections* (Boston: 1811).

14. The verses quoted are John 13:34–35 and Galatians 6:2.

15. Joseph Willard (1738–1804) was president of Harvard College from 1781–1804; Simeon Howard (1733–1804) was pastor of Boston's West Church; Joseph Eckley (1750–1811) was pastor of Boston's Old South Church; John Eliot (1754-1813) was pastor of Boston's New North Church; Thomas Barnard, Jr. (1748–1814) was pastor of Salem's North Church.

16. John Locke (1632–1704), philosopher; Isaac Newton (1642–1727), philosopher and scientist; Hugo Grotius (1583–1645), theologian; Samuel Clarke (1675–1729), theologian; Nathaniel Lardner (1684–1768), theologian; Richard Price (1723–1791), moral philosopher; William Paley (1743–1805), theologian.

17. Hugo Grotius, *The Truth of the Christian Religion, . . .* translated by Symon Patrick (London: 1680); William Paley, *A View of the Evidences of Christianity* (London: 1794); Joseph Butler, *The Analogy of Religion, Natural and Revealed, to the Constitution and Course of Nature*

(London: 1736); *Novum Testamentum Graece* . . . edited by Johann Jakob Griesbach (Halae: 1775–77).

18. Psalms 76:10—''Surely the wrath of man shall praise thee: the remainder of wrath shalt thou restrain.''

19. Channing refers to Richard Baxter's classic devotional work *The Saints' Everlasting Rest* (London: 1649, and many other editions).

20. Thomas Worcester (1768–1831) was pastor at Salisbury, New Hampshire.

21. Luke 11:54—''Laying wait for him, and seeking to catch something out of his mouth, that they might accuse him.''

UNITARIAN CHRISTIANITY (1819)*

*The original text that follows this introduction is from *The Works of William E. Channing, D. D.* (Boston: James Munroe, 1841–43), 3: 59–103.

Channing's *"Unitarian Christianity"* was an address composed with an acute awareness of its potential historical significance. That it lived up to that potential, to be the single most important sermon in Unitarian history, seems to have been confirmed by historical consensus. John White Chadwick, writing in 1903, noted that the sermon *"is agreed to have been the strongest ever preached by Channing on distinctly Unitarian lines, his most important contribution to the Unitarian controversy, and to the definite integration of the Unitarian body."*[1] It was this integrating effect, this function of the sermon as an organizational call-to-arms, that more than anything has secured its historical place. It was not only a theological statement, but a basis upon which to act. In Conrad Wright's apt phrase, it was a *"party proclamation."*[2]

Both the time of the sermon, and the occasion which prompted it, gave it significance. In 1819 the theological battle between the Calvinists and the liberals had reached its greatest intensity, and the liberals were beginning to assert their independence, and to accept, however reluctantly, the label *"Unitarian."* Channing's sermon was the signal that the name had not only been accepted, but seized and affirmed. Moreover, Channing's preaching the sermon at a new liberal church outside Boston signalled the intention of the Unitarians to make theirs a national movement. Six years later, in 1825, the American Unitarian Association would be founded.

1. John White Chadwick, *William Ellery Channing: Minister of Religion* (Boston and New York: Houghton Mifflin, 1903), 144.

2. Conrad Wright, *Three Prophets of Religious Liberalism: Channing-Emerson-Parker* (Boston: Beacon, 1961), 6.

UNITARIAN CHRISTIANITY
DISCOURSE AT THE ORDINATION OF
THE REV. JARED SPARKS. BALTIMORE, 1819.

I Thes. v. 21: "Prove all things; hold fast that which
is good."

The peculiar circumstances of this occasion not only justify,
but seem to demand a departure from the course generally followed
by preachers at the introduction of a brother into the sacred office. It
is usual to speak of the nature, design, duties, and advantages of the
Christian ministry; and on these topics I should now be happy to insist, did I not remember that a minister is to be given this day to a
religious society, whose peculiarities of opinion have drawn upon
them much remark, and may I not add, much reproach.[1] Many good
minds, many sincere Christians, I am aware, are apprehensive that
the solemnities of this day are to give a degree of influence to principles which they deem false and injurious. The fears and anxieties
of such men I respect; and, believing that they are grounded in part
on mistake, I have thought it my duty to lay before you, as clearly as
I can, some of the distinguishing opinions of that class of Christians
in our country, who are known to sympathize with this religious society. I must ask your patience, for such a subject is not to be despatched in a narrow compass. I must also ask you to remember, that
it is impossible to exhibit, in a single discourse, our views of every
doctrine of Revelation, much less the differences of opinion which
are known to subsist among ourselves. I shall confine myself to topics, on which our sentiments have been misrepresented, or which
distinguish us most widely from others. May I not hope to be heard
with candor? God deliver us all from prejudice and unkindness, and
fill us with the love of truth and virtue.

There are two natural divisions under which my thoughts will
be arranged. I shall endeavour to unfold, 1st, The principles which
we adopt in interpreting the Scriptures. And 2dly, Some of the doctrines, which the Scriptures, so interpreted, seem to us clearly to express.

I. We regard the Scriptures as the records of God's successive
revelations to mankind, and particularly of the last and most perfect

revelation of his will by Jesus Christ. Whatever doctrines seem to us to be clearly taught in the Scriptures, we receive without reserve or exception. We do not, however, attach equal importance to all the books in this collection.[2] Our religion, we believe, lies chiefly in the New Testament. The dispensation of Moses, compared with that of Jesus, we consider as adapted to the childhood of the human race, a preparation for a nobler system, and chiefly useful now as serving to confirm and illustrate the Christian Scriptures. Jesus Christ is the only master of Christians, and whatever he taught, either during his personal ministry, or by his inspired Apostles, we regard as of divine authority, and profess to make the rule of our lives.

This authority, which we give to the Scriptures, is a reason, we conceive, for studying them with peculiar care, and for inquiring anxiously into the principles of interpretation, by which their true meaning may be ascertained. The principles adopted by the class of Christians in whose name I speak, need to be explained, because they are often misunderstood. We are particularly accused of making an unwarrantable use of reason in the interpretation of Scripture. We are said to exalt reason above revelation, to prefer our own wisdom to God's. Loose and undefined charges of this kind are circulated so freely, that we think it due to ourselves, and to the cause of truth, to express our views with some particularity.

Our leading principle in interpreting Scripture is this, that the Bible is a book written for men, in the language of men, and that its meaning is to be sought in the same manner as that of other books. We believe that God, when he speaks to the human race, conforms, if we may so say, to the established rules of speaking and writing. How else would the Scriptures avail us more, than if communicated in an unknown tongue?

Now all books, and all conversation, require in the reader or hearer the constant exercise of reason; or their true import is only to be obtained by continual comparison and inference. Human language, you well know, admits various interpretations; and every word and every sentence must be modified and explained according to the subject which is discussed, according to the purposes, feelings, circumstances, and principles of the writer, and according to the genius and idioms of the language which he uses. These are acknowledged principles in the interpretation of human writings; and a man, whose words we should explain without reference to these principles, would reproach us justly with a criminal want of candor, and an intention of obscuring or distorting his meaning.

Were the Bible written in a language and style of its own, did it consist of words, which admit but a single sense, and of sentences wholly detached from each other, there would be no place for the principles now laid down. We could not reason about it, as about other writings. But such a book would be of little worth; and perhaps, of all books, the Scriptures correspond least to this description. The Word of God bears the stamp of the same hand, which we see in his works. It has infinite connexions and dependences. Every proposition is linked with others, and is to be compared with others; that its full and precise import may be understood. Nothing stands alone. The New Testament is built on the Old. The Christian dispensation is a continuation of the Jewish, the completion of a vast scheme of providence, requiring great extent of view in the reader. Still more, the Bible treats of subjects on which we receive ideas from other sources besides itself; such subjects as the nature, passions, relations, and duties of man; and it expects us to restrain and modify its language by the known truths, which observation and experience furnish on these topics.

We profess not to know a book, which demands a more frequent exercise of reason than the Bible. In addition to the remarks now made on its infinite connexions, we may observe, that its style nowhere affects the precision of science, or the accuracy of definition. Its language is singularly glowing, bold, and figurative, demanding more frequent departures from the literal sense, than that of our own age and country, and consequently demanding more continual exercise of judgment.— We find, too, that the different portions of this book, instead of being confined to general truths, refer perpetually to the times when they were written, to states of society, to modes of thinking, to controversies in the church, to feelings and usages which have passed away, and without the knowledge of which we are constantly in danger of extending to all times, and places, what was of temporary and local application. — We find, too, that some of these books are strongly marked by the genius and character of their respective writers, that the Holy Spirit did not so guide the Apostles as to suspend the peculiarities of their minds, and that a knowledge of their feelings, and of the influences under which they were placed, is one of the preparations for understanding their writings. With these views of the Bible, we feel it our bounden duty to exercise our reason upon it perpetually, to compare, to infer, to look beyond the letter to the spirit, to seek in the nature of the subject, and the aim of the writer, his true meaning; and, in general, to make use of what is known, for explaining what is difficult, and for discovering new truths.

Need I descend to particulars, to prove that the Scriptures demand the exercise of reason? Take, for example, the style in which they generally speak of God, and observe how habitually they apply to him human passions and organs. Recollect the declarations of Christ, that he came not to send peace, but a sword; that unless we eat his flesh, and drink his blood, we have no life in us; that we must hate father and mother, and pluck out the right eye; and a vast number of passages equally bold and unlimited. Recollect the unqualified manner in which it is said of Christians, that they possess all things, know all things, and can do all things. Recollect the verbal contradiction between Paul and James, and the apparent clashing of some parts of Paul's writings with the general doctrines and end of Christianity. I might extend the enumeration indefinitely; and who does not see, that we must limit all these passages by the known attributes of God, of Jesus Christ, and of human nature, and by the circumstances under which they were written, so as to give the language a quite different import from what it would require, had it been applied to different beings, or used in different connexions.

Enough has been said to show, in what sense we make use of reason in interpreting Scripture. From a variety of possible interpretations, we select that which accords with the nature of the subject and the state of the writer, with the connexion of the passage, with the general strain of Scripture, with the known character and will of God, and with the obvious and acknowledged laws of nature. In other words, we believe that God never contradicts, in one part of Scripture, what he teaches in another; and never contradicts, in revelation, what he teaches in his works and providence. And we therefore distrust every interpretation, which, after deliberate attention, seems repugnant to any established truth. We reason about the Bible precisely as civilians do about the constitution under which we live; who, you know, are accustomed to limit one provision of that venerable instrument by others, and to fix the precise import of its parts, by inquiring into its general spirit, into the intentions of its authors, and into the prevalent feelings, impressions, and circumstances of the time when it was framed. Without these principles of interpretation, we frankly acknowledge, that we cannot defend the divine authority of the Scriptures. Deny us this latitude, and we must abandon this book to its enemies.

We do not announce these principles as original, or peculiar to ourselves. All Christians occasionally adopt them, not excepting those who most vehemently decry them, when they happen to menace some favorite article of their creed. All Christians are compelled to use them in their controversies with infidels. All sects employ them in their warfare with one another. All willingly avail themselves of reason, when it can be pressed into the service of their own party, and only complain of it, when its weapons wound themselves. None reason more frequently than those from whom we differ. It is astonishing what a fabric they rear from a few slight hints about the fall of our first parents; and how ingeniously they extract, from detached passages, mysterious doctrines about the divine nature. We do not blame them for reasoning so abundantly, but for violating the fundamental rules of reasoning, for sacrificing the plain to the obscure, and the general strain of Scripture to a scanty number of insulated texts.

We object strongly to the contemptuous manner in which human reason is often spoken of by our adversaries, because it leads, we believe, to universal skepticism. If reason be so dreadfully darkened by the fall, that its most decisive judgments on religion are unworthy of trust, then Christianity, and even natural theology, must be abandoned; for the existence and veracity of God, and the divine original of Christianity, are conclusions of reason, and must stand or fall with it. If revelation be at war with this faculty, it subverts itself, for the great question of its truth is left by God to be decided at the bar of reason. It is worthy of remark, how nearly the bigot and the skeptic approach. Both would annihilate our confidence in our faculties, and both throw doubt and confusion over every truth. We honor revelation too highly to make it the antagonist of reason, or to believe that it calls us to renounce our highest powers.

We indeed grant, that the use of reason in religion is accompanied with danger. But we ask any honest man to look back on the history of the church, and say, whether the renunciation of it be not still more dangerous. Besides, it is a plain fact, that men reason as erroneously on all subjects, as on religion. Who does not know the wild and groundless theories, which have been framed in physical and political science? But who ever supposed, that we must cease to exercise reason on nature and society, because men have erred for ages in explaining them? We grant, that the passions continually, and sometimes fatally, disturb the rational faculty in its inquiries into revelation. The ambitious contrive to find doctrines in the Bible, which favor their love of dominion. The timid and dejected discover there a gloomy system, and the mystical and fanatical, a visionary theology. The vicious can find examples or assertions on which to build the hope of a late repentance, or of acceptance on easy terms. The falsely refined contrive to light on doctrines which have not been soiled by vulgar handling. But the passions do not distract the reason in religious, any more than in other inquiries, which excite strong and general interest; and this faculty, of consequence, is not to be renounced in religion, unless we are prepared to discard it universally. The true inference from the almost endless errors, which have darkened theology, is, not that we are to neglect and disparage our powers, but to exert them more patiently, circumspectly, uprightly. The worst errors, after all, having sprung up in that church, which proscribes reason, and demands from its members implicit faith. The most pernicious doctrines have been the growth of the darkest times, when the general credulity encouraged bad men and enthusiasts to broach their dreams and inventions, and to stifle the faint remonstrances of reason, by the menaces of everlasting perdition. Say what we may, God has given us a rational nature, and will call us to account for it. We may let it sleep, but we do so at our peril. Revelation is addressed to us as rational beings. We may wish, in our sloth, that God had given us a system, demanding no labor of comparing, limiting, and inferring. But such a system would be at variance with the whole character of our present existence; and it is the part of wisdom to take revelation as it is given to us, and to interpret it by the help of the faculties, which it everywhere supposes, and on which it is founded.

To the views now given, an objection is commonly urged from the character of God. We are told, that God being infinitely wiser than men, his discoveries will surpass human reason. In a revelation from such a teacher, we ought to expect propositions, which we cannot reconcile with one another, and which may seem to contradict established truths; and it becomes us not to question or explain them away, but to believe, and adore, and to submit our weak and carnal reason to the Divine Word. To this objection, we have two short answers. We say, first, that it is impossible that a teacher of infinite wisdom should expose those, whom he would teach, to infinite error. But if once we admit, that propositions, which in their literal sense appear plainly repugnant to one another, or to any known truth, are still to be literally understood and received, what possible limit can we set to the belief of contradictions? What shelter have we from the wildest fanaticism, which can always quote passages, that, in their literal and obvious sense, give support to its extravagances? How can the Protestant escape from transubstantiation, a doctrine most clearly taught us, if the submission of reason, now contended for, be a duty? How can we even hold fast the truth of revelation, for if one apparent contradiction may be true, so may another, and the proposition, that Christianity is false, though involving inconsistency, may still be a verity?

We answer again, that, if God be infinitely wise, he cannot sport with the understandings of his creatures. A wise teacher discovers his wisdom in adapting himself to the capacities of his pupils, not in perplexing them with what is unintelligible, not in distressing them with apparent contradictions, not in filling them with a skeptical distrust of their own powers. An infinitely wise teacher, who knows the precise extent of our minds, and the best method of enlightening them, will surpass all other instructors in bringing down truth to our apprehension, and in showing its loveliness and harmony. We ought, indeed, to expect occasional obscurity in such a book as the Bible, which was written for past and future ages, as well as for the present. But God's wisdom is a pledge, that whatever is necessary for *us*, and necessary for salvation, is revealed too plainly to be mistaken, and too consistently to be questioned, by a sound and upright mind. It is not the mark of wisdom, to use an unintelligible phraseology, to communicate what is above our capacities, to confuse and unsettle the intellect by appearances of contradiction. We honor our Heavenly Teacher too much to ascribe to him such a revelation. A revelation is a gift of light. It cannot thicken our darkness, and multiply our perplexities.

II. Having thus stated the principles according to which we interpret Scripture, I now proceed to the second great head of this discourse, which is, to state some of the views which we derive from that sacred book, particularly those which distinguish us from other Christians.

1. In the first place, we believe in the doctrine of God's UNITY, or that there is one God, and one only. To this truth we give infinite importance, and we feel ourselves bound to take heed, lest any man spoil us of it by vain philosophy. The proposition, that there is one God, seems to us exceedingly plain. We understand by it, that there is one being, one mind, one person, one intelligent agent, and one only, to whom underived and infinite perfection and dominion belong. We conceive, that these words could have conveyed no other meaning to the simple and uncultivated people, who were set apart to be the depositaries of this great truth, and who were utterly incapable of understanding those hair-breadth distinctions between being and person, which the sagacity of later ages has discovered. We find no intimation, that this language was to be taken in an unusual sense, or that God's unity was a quite different thing from the oneness of other intelligent beings.

We object to the doctrine of the Trinity, that, whilst acknowledging in words, it subverts in effect, the unity of God.[3] According to this doctrine, there are three infinite and equal persons, possessing supreme divinity, called the Father, Son, and Holy Ghost. Each of these persons, as described by theologians, has his own particular consciousness, will, and perceptions. They love each other, converse with each other, and delight in each other's society. They perform different parts in man's redemption, each having his appropriate office, and neither doing the work of the other. The Son is mediator and not the Father. The Father sends the Son, and is not himself sent; nor is he conscious, like the Son, of taking flesh. Here, then, we have three intelligent agents, possessed of different consciousnesses, different wills, and different perceptions, performing different acts, and sustaining different relations; and if these things do not imply and constitute three minds or beings, we are utterly at a loss to know how three minds or beings are to be formed. It is difference of properties, and acts, and consciousness, which leads us to the belief of different intelligent beings, and, if this mark fails us, our whole knowledge falls; we have no proof, that all the agents and persons in the universe are not one and the same mind. When we attempt to conceive of three Gods, we can do nothing more than represent to ourselves three agents, distinguished from each other by similar marks and peculiarities to those which separate the persons of the Trinity; and when common Christians hear these persons spoken of as conversing with each other, loving each other, and performing different acts, how can they help regarding them as different beings, different minds?

We do, then, with all earnestness, though without reproaching our brethren, protest against the irrational and unscriptural doctrine of the Trinity. "To us," as to the Apostle and the primitive Christians, "there is one God, even the Father." With Jesus, we worship the Father; as the only living and true God. We are astonished, that any man can read the New Testament, and avoid the conviction, that the Father alone is God. We hear our Saviour continually appropriating this character to the Father. We find the Father continually distinguished from Jesus by this title. "God sent his Son." "God anointed Jesus." Now, how singular and inexplicable is this phraseology, which fills the New Testament, if this title belong equally to Jesus, and if a principal object of this book is to reveal him as God, as partaking equally with the Father in supreme divinity! We challenge our opponents to adduce one passage in the New Testament, where the word God means three persons, where it is not limited to one person, and where, unless turned from its usual sense by the connexion, it does not mean the Father. Can stronger proof be given, that the doctrine of three persons in the Godhead is not a fundamental doctrine of Christianity?

This doctrine, were it true, must, from its difficulty, singularity, and importance, have been laid down with great clearness, guarded with great care, and stated with all possible precision. But where does this statement appear? From the many passages which treat of God, we ask for one, one only, in which we are told, that he is a threefold being, or that he is three persons, or that he is Father, Son, and Holy Ghost. On the contrary, in the New Testament, where, at least, we might expect many express assertions of this nature, God is declared to be one, without the least attempt to prevent the acceptation of the words in their common sense; and he is always spoken of and addressed in the singular number, that is, in language which was universally understood to intend a single person, and to which no other idea could have been attached, without an express admonition. So entirely do the Scriptures abstain from stating the Trinity, that when our opponents would insert it into their creeds and doxologies, they are compelled to leave the Bible, and to invent forms of words altogether unsanctioned by Scriptural phraseology. That a doctrine so strange, so liable to misapprehension, so fundamental as this is said to be, and requiring such careful exposition, should be left so undefined and unprotected, to be made out by inference, and to be hunted through distant and detached parts of Scripture, this is a difficulty, which, we think, no ingenuity can explain.

We have another difficulty. Christianity, it must be remembered, was planted and grew up amidst sharp-sighted enemies, who overlooked no objectionable part of the system, and who must have fastened with great earnestness on a doctrine involving such apparent contradictions as the Trinity. We cannot conceive an opinion, against which the Jews, who prided themselves on an adherence to God's unity, would have raised an equal clamor. Now, how happens it, that in the apostolic writings, which relate so much to objections against Christianity, and to the controversies which grew out of this religion, not one word is said, implying that objections were brought against the Gospel from the doctrine of the Trinity, not one word is uttered in its defence and explanation, not a word to rescue it from reproach and mistake? This argument has almost the force of demonstration. We are persuaded, that had three divine persons been announced by the first preachers of Christianity, all equal, and all infinite, one of whom was the very Jesus who had lately died on a cross, this peculiarity of Christianity would have almost absorbed every other, and the great labor of the Apostles would have been to repel the continual assaults, which it would have awakened. But the fact is, that not a whisper of objection to Christianity, on that account, reaches our ears from the apostolic age. In the Epistles we see not a trace of controversy called forth by the Trinity.

We have further objections to this doctrine, drawn from its practical influence. We regard it as unfavorable to devotion, by dividing and distracting the mind in its communion with God. It is a great excellence of the doctrine of God's unity, that it offers to us ONE OBJECT of supreme homage, adoration, and love, One Infinite Father, one Being of beings, one original and fountain, to whom we may refer all good, in whom all our powers and affections may be concentrated, and whose lovely and venerable nature may pervade all our thoughts. True piety, when directed to an undivided Deity, has a chasteness, a singleness, most favorable to religious awe and love. Now, the Trinity sets before us three distinct objects of supreme adoration; three infinite persons, having equal claims on our hearts; three divine agents, performing different offices, and to be acknowledged and worshipped in different relations. And is it possible, we ask, that the weak and limited mind of man can attach itself to these with the same power and joy, as to One Infinite Father, the only First Cause, in whom all the blessings of nature and redemption meet as their centre and source? Must not devotion be distracted by the equal and rival claims of three equal persons, and must not the worship of the conscientious, consistent Christian, be disturbed by an apprehension, lest he withhold from one or another of these, his due proportion of homage?

We also think, that the doctrine of the Trinity injures devotion, not only by joining to the Father other objects of worship, but by taking from the Father the supreme affection, which is his due, and transferring it to the Son. This is a most important view. That Jesus Christ, if exalted into the infinite Divinity, should be more interesting than the Father, is precisely what might be expected from history, and from the principles of human nature. Men want an object of worship like themselves, and the great secret of idolatry lies in this propensity. A God, clothed in our form, and feeling our wants and sorrows, speaks to our weak nature more strongly, than a Father in heaven, a pure spirit, invisible and unapproachable, save by the reflecting and purified mind.— We think, too, that the peculiar offices ascribed to Jesus by the popular theology, make him the most attractive person in the Godhead. The Father is the depositary of the justice, the vindicator of the rights, the avenger of the laws of the Divinity. On the other hand, the Son, the brightness of the divine mercy, stands between the incensed Deity and guilty humanity, exposes his meek head to the storms, and his compassionate breast to the sword of the divine justice, bears our whole load of punishment, and purchases with his blood every blessing which descends from heaven. Need we state the effect of these representations, especially on common minds, for whom Christianity was chiefly designed, and whom it seeks to bring to the Father as the loveliest being? We do believe, that the worship of a bleeding, suffering God, tends strongly to absorb the mind, and to draw it from other objects, just as the human tenderness of the Virgin Mary has given her so conspicuous a place in the devotions of the Church of Rome. We believe, too, that this worship, though attractive, is not most fitted to spiritualize the mind, that it awakens human transport, rather than that deep veneration of the moral perfections of God, which is the essence of piety.

2. Having thus given our views of the unity of God, I proceed in the second place to observe, that we believe in the unity of Jesus Christ. We believe that Jesus is one mind, one soul, one being, as truly one as we are, and equally distinct from the one God. We complain of the doctrine of the Trinity, that, not satisfied with making God three beings, it makes Jesus Christ two beings, and thus introduces infinite confusion into our conceptions of his character. This corruption of Christianity, alike repugnant to common sense and to the general strain of Scripture, is a remarkable proof of the power of a false philosophy in disfiguring the simple truth of Jesus.

According to this doctrine, Jesus Christ, instead of being one mind, one conscious intelligent principle, whom we can understand, consists of two souls, two minds; the one divine, the other human; the one weak, the other almighty; the one ignorant, the other omniscient. Now we maintain, that this is to make Christ two beings. To denominate him one person, one being, and yet to suppose him made up of two minds, infinitely different from each other, is to abuse and confound language, and to throw darkness over all our conceptions of intelligent natures. According to the common doctrine, each of these two minds in Christ has its own consciousness, its own will, its own perceptions. They have, in fact, no common properties. The divine mind feels none of the wants and sorrows of the human, and the human is infinitely removed from the perfection and happiness of the divine. Can you conceive of two beings in the universe more distinct? We have always thought that one person was constituted and distinguished by one consciousness. The doctrine, that one and the same person should have two consciousnesses, two wills, two souls, infinitely different from each other, this we think an enormous tax on human credulity.

We say, that if a doctrine, so strange, so difficult, so remote from all the previous conceptions of men, be indeed a part and an essential part of revelation, it must be taught with great distinctness, and we ask our brethren to point to some plain, direct passage, where Christ is said to be composed of two minds infinitely different, yet constituting one person. We find none. Other Christians, indeed, tell us, that this doctrine is necessary to the harmony of the Scriptures, that some texts ascribe to Jesus Christ human, and others divine properties, and that to reconcile these, we must suppose two minds, to which these properties may be referred. In other words, for the purpose of reconciling certain difficult passages, which a just criticism can in a great degree, if not wholly, explain, we must invent an hypothesis vastly more difficult, and involving gross absurdity. We are to find our way out of a labyrinth, by a clue which conducts us into mazes infinitely more inextricable.

Surely, if Jesus Christ felt that he consisted of two minds, and that this was a leading feature of his religion, his phraseology respecting himself would have been colored by this peculiarity. The universal language of men is framed upon the idea, that one person is one person, is one mind, and one soul; and when the multitude heard this language from the lips of Jesus, they must have taken it in its usual sense, and must have referred to a single soul all which he spoke, unless expressly instructed to interpret it differently. But where do we find this instruction? Where do you meet, in the New Testament, the phraseology which abounds in Trinitarian books, and which necessarily grows from the doctrine of two natures in Jesus? Where does this divine teacher say, "This I speak as God, and this as man; this is true only of my human mind, this only of my divine"? Where do we find in the Epistles a trace of this strange phraseology? Nowhere. It was not needed in that day. It was demanded by the errors of a later age.

We believe, then, that Christ is one mind, one being, and, I add, a being distinct from the one God. That Christ is not the one God, not the same being with the Father, is a necessary inference from our former head, in which we saw that the doctrine of three persons in God is a fiction. But on so important a subject, I would add a few remarks. We wish, that those from whom we differ, would weigh one striking fact. Jesus, in his preaching, continually spoke of God. The word was always in his mouth. We ask, does he, by this word, ever mean himself? We say, never. On the contrary, he most plainly distinguishes between God and himself, and so do his disci-

ples. How this is to be reconciled with the idea, that the manifestation of Christ, as God, was a primary object of Christianity, our
adversaries must determine.

If we examine the passages in which Jesus is distinguished from
God, we shall see, that they not only speak of him as another being,
but seem to labor to express his inferiority. He is continually spoken
of as the Son of God, sent of God, receiving all his powers from
God, working miracles because God was with him, judging justly
because God taught him, having claims on our belief, because he
was anointed and sealed by God, and was able of himself to do nothing. The New Testament is filled with this language. Now we ask,
what impression this language was fitted and intended to make?
Could any, who heard it, have imagined that Jesus was the very God
to whom he was so industriously declared to be inferior; the very
Being by whom he was sent, and from whom he professed to have
received his message and power? Let it here be remembered, that the
human birth, and bodily form, and humble circumstances, and mortal sufferings of Jesus, must all have prepared men to interpret, in
the most unqualified manner, the language in which his inferiority to
God was declared. Why, then, was this language used so continually, and without limitation, if Jesus were the Supreme Deity, and
if this truth were an essential part of his religion? I repeat it, the human condition and sufferings of Christ tended strongly to exclude
from men's minds the idea of his proper Godhead; and, of course,
we should expect to find in the New Testament perpetual care and
effort to counteract this tendency, to hold him forth as the same
being with his Father, if this doctrine were, as is pretended, the soul
and centre of his religion. We should expect to find the phraseology
of Scripture cast into the mould of this doctrine, to hear familiarly of
God the Son, of our Lord God Jesus, and to be told, that to us there
is one God, even Jesus. But, instead of this, the inferiority of Christ
pervades the New Testament. It is not only implied in the general
phraseology, but repeatedly and decidedly expressed, and unaccom-
panied with any admonition to prevent its application to his whole
nature. Could it, then, have been the great design of the sacred writers to exhibit Jesus as the Supreme God?

I am aware that these remarks will be met by two or three texts,
in which Christ is called God, and by a class of passages, not very
numerous, in which divine properties are said to be ascribed to him.

To these we offer one plain answer. We say, that it is one of the most established and obvious principles of criticism, that language is to be explained according to the known properties of the subject to which it is applied. Every man knows, that the same words convey very different ideas, when used in relation to different beings. Thus, Solomon *built* the temple in a different manner from the architect whom he employed; and God *repents* differently from man. Now we maintain, that the known properties and circumstances of Christ, his birth, sufferings, and death, his constant habit of speaking of God as a distinct being from himself, his praying to God, his ascribing to God all his power and offices, these acknowledged properties of Christ, we say, oblige us to interpret the comparatively few passages which are thought to make him the Supreme God, in a manner consistent with his distinct and inferior nature. It is our duty to explain such texts by the rule which we apply to other texts, in which human beings are called gods, and are said to be partakers of the divine nature, to know and possess all things, and to be filled with all God's fulness. These latter passages we do not hesitate to modify, and restrain, and turn from the most obvious sense, because this sense is opposed to the known properties of the beings to whom they relate; and we maintain, that we adhere to the same principle, and use no greater latitude, in explaining, as we do, the passages which are thought to support the Godhead of Christ.

Trinitarians profess to derive some important advantages from their mode of viewing Christ. It furnishes them, they tell us, with an infinite atonement, for it shows them an infinite being suffering for their sins. The confidence with which this fallacy is repeated astonishes us. When pressed with the question, whether they really believe, that the infinite and unchangeable God suffered and died on the cross, they acknowledge that this is not true, but that Christ's human mind alone sustained the pains of death. How have we, then, an infinite sufferer? This language seems to us an imposition on common minds, and very derogatory to God's justice, as if this attribute could be satisfied by a sophism and a fiction.

We are also told, that Christ is a more interesting object, that his love and mercy are more felt, when he is viewed as the Supreme God, who left his glory to take humanity and to suffer for men. That Trinitarians are strongly moved by this representation, we do not mean to deny; but we think their emotions altogether founded on a misapprehension of their own doctrines. They talk of the second person of the Trinity's leaving his glory and his Father's bosom, to visit and save the world. But this second person, being the unchangeable and infinite God, was evidently incapable of parting with the least degree of his perfection and felicity. At the moment of his taking flesh, he was as intimately present with his Father as before, and equally with his Father filled heaven, and earth, and immensity. This Trinitarians acknowledge; and still they profess to be touched and overwhelmed by the amazing humiliation of this immutable being! But not only does their doctrine, when fully explained, reduce Christ's humiliation to a fiction, it almost wholly destroys the impressions with which his cross ought to be viewed. According to their doctrine, Christ was comparatively no sufferer at all. It is true, his human mind suffered; but this, they tell us, was an infinitely small part of Jesus, bearing no more proportion to his whole nature, than a single hair of our heads to the whole body, or than a drop to the ocean. The divine mind of Christ, that which was most properly himself, was infinitely happy, at the very moment of the suffering of his humanity. Whilst hanging on the cross, he was the happiest being in the universe, as happy as the infinite Father; so that his pains, compared with his felicity, were nothing. This Trinitarians do, and must, acknowledge. It follows necessarily from the immutableness of the divine nature, which they ascribe to Christ; so that their system, justly viewed, robs his death of interest, weakens our sympathy with his sufferings, and is, of all others, most unfavorable to a love of Christ, founded on a sense of his sacrifices for mankind. We esteem our own views to be vastly more affecting. It is our belief, that Christ's humiliation was real and entire, that the whole Saviour, and not a part of him, suffered, that his crucifixion was a scene of deep and unmixed agony. As we stand round his cross, our minds are not distracted, nor our sensibility weakened, by contemplating him as composed of incongruous and infinitely differing minds, and as having a balance of infinite felicity. We recognise in the dying Jesus but one mind. This, we think, renders his sufferings, and his patience and love in bearing them, incomparably more impressive and affecting than the system we oppose.

3. Having thus given our belief on two great points, namely, that there is one God, and that Jesus Christ is a being distinct from, and inferior to, God, I now proceed to another point, on which we

lay still greater stress. We believe in the *moral perfection of God.* We consider no part of theology so important as that which treats of God's moral character; and we value our views of Christianity chiefly as they assert his amiable and venerable attributes.

It may be said, that, in regard to this subject, all Christians agree, that all ascribe to the Supreme Being infinite justice, goodness, and holiness. We reply, that it is very possible to speak of God magnificently, and to think of him meanly; to apply to his person high-sounding epithets, and to his government, principles which make him odious. The Heathens called Jupiter the greatest and the best; but his history was black with cruelty and lust. We cannot judge of men's real ideas of God by their general language, for in all ages they have hoped to soothe the Deity by adulation. We must inquire into their particular views of his purposes, of the principles of his administration, and of his disposition towards his creatures.

We conceive that Christians have generally leaned towards a very injurious view of the Supreme Being. They have too often felt, as if he were raised, by his greatness and sovereignty, above the principles of morality, above those eternal laws of equity and rectitude, to which all other beings are subjected. We believe, that in no being is the sense of right so strong, so omnipotent, as in God. We believe that his almighty power is entirely submitted to his perceptions of rectitude; and, this is the ground of our piety. It is not because he is our Creator merely, but because he created us for good and holy purposes; it is not because his will is irresistible, but because his will is the perfection of virtue, that we pay him allegiance. We cannot bow before a being, however great and powerful, who governs tyrannically. We respect nothing but excellence, whether on earth or in heaven. We venerate not the loftiness of God's throne, but the equity and goodness in which it is established.

We believe that God is infinitely good, kind, benevolent, in the proper sense of these words; good in disposition, as well as in act; good, not to a few, but to all; good to every individual, as well as to the general system.

We believe, too, that God is just; but we never forget, that his justice is the justice of a good being, dwelling in the same mind, and acting in harmony, with perfect benevolence. By this attribute, we understand God's infinite regard to virtue or moral worth, expressed in a moral government; that is, in giving excellent and equitable laws, and in conferring such rewards, and inflicting such punishments, as are best fitted to secure their observance. God's justice has for its end the highest virture of the creation, and it punishes for this end alone, and thus it coincides with benevolence; for virtue and happiness, though not the same, are inseparably conjoined.

God's justice thus viewed, appears to us to be in perfect harmony with his mercy. According to the prevalent systems of theology, these attributes are so discordant and jarring, that to reconcile them is the hardest task, and the most wonderful achievement, of infinite wisdom. To us they seem to be intimate friends, always at peace, breathing the same spirit, and seeking the same end. By God's mercy, we understand not a blind instinctive compassion, which forgives without reflection, and without regard to the interests of virtue. This, we acknowledge, would be incompatible with justice, and also with enlightened benevolence. God's mercy, as we understand it, desires strongly the happiness of the guilty, but only through their penitence. It has a regard to character as truly as his justice. It defers punishment, and suffers long, that the sinner may return to his duty, but leaves the impenitent and unyielding, to the fearful retribution threatened in God's Word.

To give our views of God in one word, we believe in his Parental character. We ascribe to him, not only the name, but the dispositions and principles of a father. We believe that he has a father's concern for his creatures, a father's desire for their improvement, a father's equity in proportioning his commands to their powers, a father's joy in their progress, a father's readiness to receive the penitent, and a father's justice for the incorrigible. We look upon this world as a place of education, in which he is training men by prosperity and adversity, by aids and obstructions, by conflicts of reason and passion, by motives to duty and temptations to sin, by a various discipline suited to free and moral beings, for union with himself, and for a sublime and ever-growing virtue in heaven.[4]

Now, we object to the systems of religion, which prevail among us, that they are adverse, in a greater or less degree, to these purifying, comforting, and honorable views of God; that they take from us our Father in heaven, and substitute for him a being, whom we cannot love if we would, and whom we ought not to love if we could. We object, particularly on this ground, to that system, which arrogates to itself the name of Orthodoxy, and which is now industriously propagated through our country. This system indeed takes various shapes, but in all it casts dishonor on the Creator. According to its old and genuine form, it teaches, that God brings us into life wholly depraved, so that under the innocent features of our childhood is hidden a nature averse to all good and propense to all evil, a nature which exposes us to God's displeasure and wrath, even before we have acquired power to understand our duties, or to reflect upon our actions. According to a more modern exposition, it teaches, that we came from the hands of our Maker with such a constitution, and are placed under such influences and circumstances, as to render certain and infallible the total depravity of every human being, from the first moment of his moral agency; and it also teaches, that the offence of the child, who brings into life this ceaseless tendency to unmingled crime, exposes him to the sentence of everlasting damnation. Now, according to the plainest principles of morality, we maintain, that a natural constitution of the mind, unfailingly disposing it to evil and to evil alone, would absolve it from guilt; that to give existence under this condition would argue unspeakable cruelty; and that to punish the sin of this unhappily constituted child with endless ruin, would be a wrong unparalleled by the most merciless despotism.

This system also teaches, that God selects from this corrupt mass a number to be saved, and plucks them, by a special influence, from the common ruin; that the rest of mankind, though left without that special grace which their conversion requires, are commanded to repent, under penalty of aggravated woe; and that forgiveness is promised them, on terms which their very constitution infallibly disposes them to reject, and in rejecting which they awfully enhance the punishments of hell. These proffers of forgiveness and exhortations of amendment, to beings born under a blighting curse, fill our minds with a horror which we want words to express.[5]

That this religious system does not produce all the effects on character, which might be anticipated, we most joyfully admit. It is often, very often, counteracted by nature, conscience, common sense, by the general strain of Scripture, by the mild example and precepts of Christ, and by the many positive declarations of God's universal kindness and perfect equity. But still we think that we see its unhappy influence. It tends to discourage the timid, to give excuses to the bad, to feed the vanity of the fanatical, and to offer shelter to the bad feelings of the malignant. By shocking, as it does, the fundamental principles of morality, and by exhibiting a severe and partial Deity, it tends strongly to pervert the moral faculty, to form a gloomy, forbidding, and servile religion, and to lead men to substitute censoriousness, bitterness, and persecution, for a tender and impartial charity. We think, too, that this system, which begins with degrading human nature, may be expected to end in pride; for pride grows out of a consciousness of high distinctions, however obtained, and no distinction is so great as that which is made between the elected and abandoned of God.[5a]

The false and dishonorable views of God, which have now been stated, we feel ourselves bound to resist unceasingly. Other errors we can pass over with comparative indifference. But we ask our opponents to leave to us a GOD, worthy of our love and trust, in whom our moral sentiments may delight, in whom our weaknesses and sorrows may find refuge. We cling to the Divine perfections. We meet them everywhere in creation, we read them in the Scriptures, we see a lovely image of them in Jesus Christ; and gratitude, love, and veneration call on us to assert them. Reproached, as we often are, by men, it is our consolation and happiness, that one of our chief offences is the zeal with which we vindicate the dishonored goodness and rectitude of God.

4. Having thus spoken of the unity of God; of the unity of Jesus, and his inferiority to God; and of the perfections of the Divine character; I now proceed to give our views of the mediation of Christ, and of the purposes of his mission. With regard to the great object which Jesus came to accomplish, there seems to be no possibility of mistake. We believe, that he was sent by the Father to effect a moral, or spiritual deliverance of mankind; that is, to rescue men from sin and its consequences, and to bring them to a state of everlasting purity and happiness. We believe, too, that he accomplishes this sublime purpose by a variety of methods; by his instructions respecting God's unity, parental character, and moral government, which are admirably fitted to reclaim the world from idolatry and impiety, to the knowledge, love, and obedience of the Creator; by his promises of pardon to the penitent, and of divine assistance to those who labor for progress in moral excellence; by the light which he has thrown on the path of duty; by his own spotless example, in which the loveliness and sublimity of virtue shine forth to warm and

quicken, as well as guide us to perfection; by his threatenings against incorrigible guilt; by his glorious discoveries of immortality; by his sufferings and death; by that signal event, the resurrection, which powerfully bore witness to his divine mission, and brought down to men's senses a future life; by his continual intercession, which obtains for us spiritual aid and blessings; and by the power with which he is invested of raising the dead, judging the world, and conferring the everlasting rewards promised to the faithful.

We have no desire to conceal the fact, that a difference of opinion exists among us, in regard to an interesting part of Christ's mediation; I mean, in regard to the precise influence of his death on our forgiveness. Many suppose, that this event contributes to our pardon, as it was a principal means of confirming his religion, and of giving it a power over the mind; in other words, that it procures forgiveness by leading to that repentance and virtue, which is the great and only condition on which forgiveness is bestowed. Many of us are dissatisfied with this explanation, and think that the Scriptures ascribe the remission of sins to Christ's death, with an emphasis so peculiar, that we ought to consider this event as having a special influence in removing punishment, though the Scriptures may not reveal the way in which it contributes to this end.

Whilst, however, we differ in explaining the connexion between Christ's death and human forgiveness, a connexion which we all gratefully acknowledge, we agree in rejecting many sentiments which prevail in regard to his mediation. The idea, which is conveyed to common minds by the popular system, that Christ's death has an influence in making God placable, or merciful, in awakening his kindness towards men, we reject with strong disapprobation. We are happy to find, that this very dishonorable notion is disowned by intelligent Christians of that class from which we differ. We recollect, however, that, not long ago, it was common to hear of Christ, as having died to appease God's wrath, and to pay the debt of sinners to his inflexible justice; and we have a strong persuasion, that the language of popular religious books, and the common mode of stating the doctrine of Christ's mediation, still communicate very degrading views of God's character. They give to multitudes the impression, that the death of Jesus produces a change in the mind of God towards man, and that in this its efficacy chiefly consists. No error seems to us more pernicious. We can endure no shade over the pure goodness of God. We earnestly maintain, that Jesus, instead of calling forth, in any way or degree, the mercy of the Father, was sent by that mercy, to be our Saviour; that he is nothing to the human race, but what he is by God's appointment; that he communicates nothing but what God empowers him to bestow; that our Father in heaven is originally, essentially, and eternally placable, and disposed to forgive; and that his unborrowed, underived, and unchangeable love is the only fountain of what flows to us through his Son. We conceive, that Jesus is dishonored, not glorified, by ascribing to him an influence, which clouds the splendor of Divine benevolence.

We farther agree in rejecting, as unscriptural and absurd, the explanation given by the popular system, of the manner in which Christ's death procures forgiveness for men. This system used to teach as its fundamental principle, that man, having sinned against an infinite Being, has contracted infinite guilt, and is consequently exposed to an infinite penalty. We believe, however, that this reasoning, if reasoning it may be called, which overlooks the obvious maxim, that the guilt of a being must be proportioned to his nature and powers, has fallen into disuse. Still the system teaches, that sin, of whatever degree, exposes to endless punishment, and that the whole human race, being infallibly involved by their nature in sin, owe this awful penalty to the justice of their Creator. It teaches, that this penalty cannot be remitted, in consistency with the honor of the divine law, unless a substitute be found to endure it or to suffer an equivalent. It also teaches, that, from the nature of the case, no substitute is adequate to this work, save the infinite God himself; and accordingly, God, in his second person, took on him human nature, that he might pay to his own justice the debt of punishment incurred by men, and might thus reconcile forgiveness with the claims and threatenings of his law. Such is the prevalent system. Now, to us, this doctrine seems to carry on its front strong marks of absurdity; and we maintain that Christianity ought not to be encumbered with it, unless it be laid down in the New Testament fully and expressly. We ask our adversaries, then, to point to some plain passages where it is taught. We ask for one text, in which we are told, that God took human nature that he might make an infinite satisfaction to his own justice; for one text, which tells us, that human guilt requires an infinite substitute; that Christ's sufferings owe their efficacy to their being borne by an infinite being; or that his divine nature gives infinite value to the sufferings of the human. Not *one word* of this description can we find in the Scriptures; not a text, which even hints at these strange doctrines. They are altogether, we believe, the fictions of theologians. Christianity is in no degree responsible for them. We are astonished at their prevalence. What can be plainer, than that God cannot, in any sense, be a sufferer, or bear a penalty in the room of his creatures? How dishonorable to him is the supposition, that his justice is now so severe, as to exact infinite punishment for the sins of frail and feeble men, and now so easy and yielding, as to accept the limited pains of Christ's human soul, as a full equivalent for the endless woes due from the world? How plain is it also, according to this doctrine, that God, instead of being plenteous in forgiveness, never forgives; for it seems absurd to speak of men as forgiven, when their whole punishment, or an equivalent to it, is borne by a substitute? A scheme more fitted to obscure the brightness of Christianity and the mercy of God, or less suited to give comfort to a guilty and troubled mind, could not, we think, be easily framed.

We believe, too, that this system is unfavorable to the character. It naturally leads men to think, that Christ came to change God's mind rather than their own; that the highest object of his mission was to avert punishment, rather than to communicate holiness; and that a large part of religion consists in disparaging good works and human virtue, for the purpose of magnifying the value of Christ's vicarious sufferings. In this way, a sense of the infinite importance and indispensable necessity of personal improvement is weakened, and high-sounding praises of Christ's cross seem often to be substituted for obedience to his precepts. For ourselves, we have not so learned Jesus. Whilst we gratefully acknowledge, that he came to rescue us from punishment, we believe, that he was sent on a still nobler errand, namely, to deliver us from sin itself, and to form us to a sublime and heavenly virtue. We regard him as a Saviour, chiefly as he is the light, physician, and guide of the dark, diseased, and wandering mind. No influence in the universe seems to us so glorious, as that over the character; and no redemption so worthy of thankfulness, as the restoration of the soul to purity. Without this, pardon, were it possible, would be of little value. Why pluck the sinner from hell, if a hell be left to burn in his own breast? Why raise him to heaven, if he remain a stranger to its sanctity and love? With these impressions, we are accustomed to value the Gospel chiefly as it abounds in effectual aids, motives, excitements to a generous and divine virtue. In this virtue, as in a common centre, we see all its doctrines, precepts, promises meet; and we believe, that faith in this religion is of no worth, and contributes nothing to salvation, any farther than as it uses these doctrines, precepts, promises, and the whole life, character, sufferings, and triumphs of Jesus, as the means of purifying the mind, of changing it into the likeness of his celestial excellence.

5. Having thus stated our views of the highest object of Christ's mission, that it is the recovery of men to virtue, or holiness, I shall now, in the last place, give our views of the nature of Christian virtue, or true holiness. We believe that all virtue has its foundation in the moral nature of man, that is, in conscience, or his sense of duty, and in the power of forming his temper and life according to conscience. We believe that these moral faculties are the grounds of responsibility, and the highest distinctions of human nature, and that no act is praiseworthy, any farther than it springs from their exertion. We believe, that no dispositions infused into us without our own moral activity, are of the nature of virtue, and therefore, we reject the doctrine of irresistible divine influence on the human mind, moulding it into goodness, as marble is hewn into a statue. Such goodness, if this word may be used, would not be the object of moral approbation, any more than the instinctive affections of inferior animals, or the constitutional amiableness of human beings.

By these remarks, we do not mean to deny the importance of God's aid or Spirit; but by his Spirit, we mean a moral, illuminating, and persuasive influence, not physical, not compulsory, not involving a necessity of virtue. We object, strongly, to the idea of many Christians respecting man's impotence and God's irresistible agency on the heart, believing that they subvert our responsibility and the laws of our moral nature, that they make men machines, that they cast on God the blame of all evil deeds, that they discourage good minds, and inflate the fanatical with wild conceits of immediate and sensible inspiration.

Among the virtues, we give the first place to the love of God. We believe, that this principle is the true end and happiness of our being, that we were made for union with our Creator, that his infinite perfection is the only sufficient object and true resting-place for the insatiable desires and unlimited capacities of the human mind, and that, without him, our noblest sentiments, admiration, veneration, hope, and love, would wither and decay. We believe, too, that the love of God is not only essential to happiness, but to the strength and perfection of all the virtues; that conscience, without the sanction of God's authority and retributive justice, would be a weak director; that benevolence, unless nourished by communion with his good-ness, and encouraged by his smile, could not thrive amidst the self-ishness and thanklessness of the world; and that self-government, without a sense of the divine inspection, would hardly extend be-yond an outward and partial purity. God, as he is essentially good-ness, holiness, justice, and virtue, so he is the life, motive, and sustainer of virtue in the human soul.

But, whilst we earnestly inculcate the love of God, we believe that great care is necessary to distinguish it from counterfeits. We think that much which is called piety is worthless. Many have fallen into the error, that there can be no excess in feelings which have God for their object; and, distrusting as coldness that self-possession, without which virtue and devotion lose all their dignity, they have abandoned themselves to extravagances, which have brought con-tempt on piety. Most certainly, if the love of God be that which often bears its name, the less we have of it the better. If religion be the shipwreck of understanding, we cannot keep too far from it. On this subject, we always speak plainly. We cannot sacrifice our reason to the reputation of zeal. We owe it to truth and religion to maintain, that fanaticism, partial insanity, sudden impressions, and ungovern-able transports, are any thing rather than piety.[6]

We conceive, that the true love of God is a moral sentiment, founded on a clear perception, and consisting in a high esteem and veneration, of his moral perfections. Thus, it perfectly coincides, and is in fact the same thing, with the love of virtue, rectitude, and goodness. You will easily judge, then, what we esteem the surest and only decisive signs of piety. We lay no stress on strong excite-ments. We esteem him, and him only a pious man, who practically conforms to God's moral perfections and government; who shows his delight in God's benevolence, by loving and serving his neigh-bour; his delight in God's justice, by being resolutely upright; his sense of God's purity, by regulating his thoughts, imagination, and

desires; and whose conversation, business, and domestic life are
swayed by a regard to God's presence and authority. In all things
else men may deceive themselves. Disordered nerves may give them
strange sights, and sounds, and impressions. Texts of Scripture may
come to them as from Heaven. Their whole souls may be moved,
and their confidence in God's favor be undoubting. But in all this
there is no religion. The question is, Do they love God's commands,
in which his character is fully expressed, and give up to these their
habits and passions? Without this, ecstasy is a mockery. One surrender of desire to God's will, is worth a thousand transports. We do not
judge of the bent of men's minds by their raptures, any more than we
judge of the natural direction of a tree during a storm. We rather suspect loud profession, for we have observed, that deep feeling is generally noiseless, and least seeks display.

We would not, by these remarks, be understood as wishing to
exclude from religion warmth, and even transport. We honor, and
highly value, true religious sensibility. We believe, that Christianity
is intended to act powerfully on our whole nature, on the heart as
well as the understanding and the conscience. We conceive of
heaven as a state where the love of God will be exalted into an unbounded fervor and joy; and we desire, in our pilgrimage here, to
drink into the spirit of that better world. But we think, that religious
warmth is only to be valued, when it springs naturally from an improved character, when it comes unforced, when it is the recom-
pense of obedience, when it is the warmth of a mind which
understands God by being like him, and when, instead of disorder-
ing, it exalts the understanding, invigorates conscience, gives a
pleasure to common duties, and is seen to exist in connexion with
cheerfulness, judiciousness, and a reasonable frame of mind. When
we observe a fervor, called religious, in men whose general character expresses little refinement and elevation, and whose piety seems
at war with reason, we pay it little respect. We honor religion too
much to give its sacred name to a feverish, forced, fluctuating zeal,
which has little power over the life.

Another important branch of virtue, we believe to be love to
Christ. The greatness of the work of Jesus, the spirit with which he
executed it, and the sufferings which he bore for our salvation, we
feel to be strong claims on our gratitude and veneration. We see in
nature no beauty to be compared with the loveliness of his character,

nor do we find on earth a benefactor to whom we owe an equal debt. We read his history with delight, and learn from it the perfection of our nature. We are particularly touched by his death, which was endured for our redemption, and by that strength of charity which triumphed over his pains. His resurrection is the foundation of our hope of immortality. His intercession gives us boldness to draw nigh to the throne of grace, and we look up to heaven with new desire, when we think, that, if we follow him here, we shall there see his benignant countenance, and enjoy his friendship for ever.

I need not express to you our views on the subject of the benevolent virtues. We attach such importance to these, that we are sometimes reproached with exalting them above piety. We regard the spirit of love, charity, meekness, forgiveness, liberality, and beneficence, as the badge and distinction of Christians, as the brightest image we can bear of God, as the best proof of piety. On this subject, I need not, and cannot enlarge; but there is one branch of benevolence which I ought not to pass over in silence, because we think that we conceive of it more highly and justly than many of our brethren. I refer to the duty of candor, charitable judgment, especially towards those who differ in religious opinion. We think, that in nothing have Christians so widely departed from their religion, as in this particular. We read with astonishment and horror, the history of the church; and sometimes when we look back on the fires of persecution, and on the zeal of Christians, in building up walls of separation, and in giving up one another to perdition, we feel as if we were reading the records of an infernal, rather than a heavenly kingdom. An enemy to every religion, if asked to describe a Christian, would, with some show of reason, depict him as an idolator of his own distinguishing opinions, covered with badges of party, shutting his eyes on the virtues, and his ears on the arguments, of his opponents, arrogating all excellence to his own sect and all saving power to his own creed, sheltering under the name of pious zeal the love of domination, the conceit of infallibility, and the spirit of intolerance, and trampling on men's rights under the pretence of saving their souls.

We can hardly conceive of a plainer obligation on beings of our frail and fallible nature, who are instructed in the duty of candid judgment, than to abstain from condemning men of apparent conscientiousness and sincerity, who are chargeable with no crime but that of differing from us in the interpretation of the Scriptures, and differing, too, on topics of great and acknowledged obscurity.[7] We are astonished at the hardihood of those, who, with Christ's warnings sounding in their ears, take on them the responsibility of making creeds for his church, and cast out professors of virtuous lives for imagined errors, for the guilt of thinking for themselves. We know that zeal for truth is the cover for this usurpation of Christ's prerogative; but we think that zeal for truth, as it is called, is very suspicious, except in men, whose capacities and advantages, whose patient deliberation, and whose improvements in humility, mildness, and candor, give them a right to hope that their views are more just than those of their neighbours. Much of what passes for a zeal for truth, we look upon with little respect, for it often appears to thrive most luxuriantly where other virtues shoot up thinly and feebly; and we have no gratitude for those reformers, who would force upon us a doctrine which has not sweetened their own tempers, or made them better men than their neighbours.

We are accustomed to think much of the difficulties attending religious inquiries; difficulties springing from the slow development of our minds, from the power of early impressions, from the state of society, from human authority, from the general neglect of the reasoning powers, from the want of just principles of criticism and of important helps in interpreting Scripture, and from various other causes. We find, that on no subject have men, and even good men, ingrafted so many strange conceits, wild theories, and fictions of fancy, as on religion; and remembering, as we do, that we ourselves are sharers of the common frailty, we dare not assume infallibility in the treatment of our fellow-Christians, or encourage in common Christians, who have little time for investigation, the habit of denouncing and contemning other denominations, perhaps more enlightened and virtuous than their own. Charity, forbearance, a delight in the virtues of different sects, a backwardness to censure and condemn, these are virtues, which, however poorly practised by us, we admire and recommend; and we would rather join ourselves to the church in which they abound, than to any other communion, however elated with the belief of its own orthodoxy, however strict in guarding its creed, however burning with zeal against imagined error.

I have thus given the distinguishing views of those Christians in whose names I have spoken. We have embraced this system, not hastily or lightly, but after much deliberation; and we hold it fast, not merely because we believe it to be true, but because we regard it as purifying truth, as a doctrine according to godliness, as able to "work mightily" and to "bring forth fruit" in them who believe.[8] That we wish to spread it, we have no desire to conceal; but we think, that we wish its diffusion, because we regard it as more friendly to practical piety and pure morals than the opposite doctrines, because it gives clearer and nobler views of duty, and stronger motives to its performance, because it recommends religion at once to the understanding and the heart, because it asserts the lovely and venerable attributes of God, because it tends to restore the benevolent spirit of Jesus to his divided and afflicted church, and because it cuts off every hope of God's favor, except that which springs from practical conformity to the life and precepts of Christ. We see nothing in our views to give offence, save their purity, and it is their purity, which makes us seek and hope their extension through the world.

My friend and brother;—You are this day to take upon you important duties; to be clothed with an office, which the Son of God did not disdain; to devote yourself to that religion, which the most hallowed lips have preached, and the most precious blood sealed. We trust that you will bring to this work a willing mind, a firm purpose, a martyr's spirit, a readiness to toil and suffer for the truth, a devotion of your best powers to the interests of piety and virtue. I have spoken of the doctrines which you will probably preach; but I do not mean, that you are to give yourself to controversy. You will remember, that good practice is the end of preaching, and will labor to make your people holy livers, rather than skilful disputants. Be careful, lest the desire of defending what you deem truth, and of repelling reproach and misrepresentation, turn you aside from your great business, which is to fix in men's minds a living conviction of the obligation, sublimity, and happiness of Christian virtue. The best way to vindicate your sentiments, is to show, in your preaching and life, their intimate connexion with Christian morals, with a high and delicate sense of duty, with candor towards your opposers, with inflexible integrity, and with an habitual reverence for God. If any light can pierce and scatter the clouds of prejudice, it is that of a pure example. My brother, may your life preach more loudly than your lips. Be to this people a pattern of all good works, and may your instructions derive authority from a well-grounded belief in your hearers, that you speak from the heart, that you preach from experience, that the truth which you dispense has wrought powerfully in your own heart, that God, and Jesus, and heaven, are not merely words on your lips, but most affecting realities to your mind, and springs of hope and consolation, and strength, in all your trials. Thus laboring, may you reap abundantly, and have a testimony of your faithfulness, not only in your own conscience, but in the esteem, love, virtues, and improvements of your people.

To all who hear me, I would say, with the Apostle, Prove all things, hold fast that which is good. Do not, brethren, shrink from the duty of searching God's Word for yourselves, through fear of human censure and denunciation. Do not think, that you may innocently follow the opinions which prevail around you, without investigation, on the ground, that Christianity is now so purified from errors, as to need no laborious research. There is much reason to believe, that Christianity is at this moment dishonored by gross and cherished corruptions. If you remember the darkness which hung over the Gospel for ages; if you consider the impure union, which still subsists in almost every Christian country, between the church and state, and which enlists men's selfishness and ambition on the side of established error; if you recollect in what degree the spirit of intolerance has checked free inquiry, not only before, but since the Reformation; you will see that Christianity cannot have freed itself from all the human inventions, which disfigured it under the Papal tyranny. No. Much stubble is yet to be burned; much rubbish to be removed; many gaudy decorations, which a false taste has hung around Christianity, must be swept away; and the earth-born fogs, which have long shrouded it, must be scattered, before this divine fabric will rise before us in its native and awful majesty, in its harmonious proportions, in its mild and celestial splendors. This glorious reformation in the church, we hope, under God's blessing, from the progress of the human intellect, from the moral progress of society, from the consequent decline of prejudice and bigotry, and, though last not least, from the subversion of human authority in matters of religion, from the fall of those hierarchies, and other human institutions, by which the minds of individuals are oppressed under the weight of numbers, and a Papal dominion is perpetuated in the Protestant church. Our earnest prayer to God is, that he will over-turn, and overturn, and overturn the strong-holds of spiritual usur-pation, until HE shall come, whose right it is to rule the minds of men; that the conspiracy of ages against the liberty of Christians may be brought to an end; that the servile assent, so long yielded to hu-man creeds, may give place to honest and devout inquiry into the Scriptures; and that Christianity, thus purified from error, may put forth its almighty energy, and prove itself, by its ennobling influence on the mind, to be indeed ''the power of God unto salvation.''[9]

Notes

1. Channing here refers to the founding of the Unitarian society in Baltimore and the installation of Jared Sparks as its minister. Sparks's de-cision to take the Baltimore church rather than a more secure Boston pulpit, or a professorship, was one sign of the Unitarian determination to make their movement national. Sparks was from 1819–1823 not only the minister in Baltimore, but an important Unitarian representative to the South. He went on to a prominent career as editor of the *North American Review,* and historian of the American Revolutionary period. It is the edition of *The Writings of George Washington* (1834–37) which secured his prominence as a historical editor, and he later became a professor of history, and then president, of Harvard. For details, see Samuel Eliot Morison, ''Jared Sparks,'' in *Dictionary of American Biography* (New York: Scribner's 1928–37), vol. 16, 430–34, and Conrad Wright, *Three Prophets of Reli-gious Liberalism: Channing-Emerson-Parker* (Boston: Beacon, 1961).

2. In resisting the tendency to read the Bible as a unified whole, and in insisting on reading it in its historical context, Channing is articulating one of the major premises of the higher criticism of the Bible which the lib-erals had embraced. For details, see Jerry Wayne Brown, *The Rise of Bib-lical Criticism in America, 1800–1870* (Middletown: Wesleyan University Press, 1969).

3. In attacking the doctrine of the Trinity, Channing was in effect ac-cepting the designation ''Unitarian,'' which as Wright notes (*Three Proph-ets of Religious Liberalism*) had been given to the liberals as a pejorative name.

4. The conception of life as a process of spiritual education and growth which Channing introduces here would be a dominant part of his re-ligious teaching throughout his career.

5. The Calvinist doctrine of election to grace, which Channing attacks here, was seen by the liberals as one of the most repulsive aspects of Orthodox Calvinist belief.

5a. *Textual emendation:* "be" has been substituted for "by" in the original text.

6. Channing's attack here on the emotional excesses of evangelical revivalism is much in line with a whole tradition in New England liberalism of opposition to revivalism. That opposition can be traced to Charles Chauncy's attacks on the Great Awakening in the 1740's. See Edward M. Griffin, *Old Brick: Charles Chauncy of Boston, 1705–1787* (Minneapolis: University of Minnesota Press, 1980).

7. This passage is in part a veiled reference to Channing's dispute with Jedidiah Morse and Jeremiah Evarts, in which those defenders of Calvinism had proposed to exclude the liberals from fellowship. See, for details, the introduction to this volume, and also John White Chadwick, *William Ellery Channing: Minister of Religion* (Boston and New York: Houghton Mifflin, 1903); and Jack Mendelsohn, *Channing: The Reluctant Radical* (Boston: Little, Brown, 1971).

8. See Colossians 1:29—"Whereunto I also labour, striving according to his working, which worketh in me mightily;" and John 15:16—"Ye have not chosen me, but I have chosen you, and ordained you, that ye should go and bring forth fruit, and *that* your fruit should remain: that whatsoever ye shall ask of the Father in my name, he may give it to you."

9. See Romans 1:16—"For I am not ashamed of the Gospel of Christ: for it is the power of God unto salvation to every one that believeth; to the Jew first, and also to the Greek."

THE MORAL ARGUMENT
AGAINST CALVINISM (1820)*

*The original text that follows this introduction is from *The Works of William E. Channing, D.D.*, 6 vols. (Boston: James Munroe, 1841-43, 1:217-41.

The enormous intellectual energy which we sense in the early phase of the liberal movement can be traced in part to the growing boldness with which its members attacked the prevailing theology of New England, Calvinism. The price of that boldness can be best understood when we remember that in attacking Calvinism, the liberals were also attacking their ancestral religion, the very faith by which their culture had been founded and their churches built. It is fair to say that Channing did not at first seek theological confrontation with Calvinism. Even so, he did come to see that the divisiveness of sectarian controversy had already erupted, and that principles were at stake which had to be protected. Thus in 1815 he became America's most powerful critic of Calvinism, and in 1820 he wrote his polemical masterpiece, "The Moral Argument Against Calvinism." The essay is a superb complement to "Unitarian Christianity" because it brings out explicitly the system against which the early Unitarians were defining themselves. Of necessity, therefore, the early liberals spent much time attacking and refuting Calvinist doctrine, and defending themselves from similar attacks. Ralph Waldo Emerson later sarcastically referred to "the pale negations of Boston Unitarianism," as he tried to distance himself from these embroilments of theological debate.[1] But as Channing's essay here will demonstrate, some of those negations were anything but pale. Channing's "No!" to Calvinism was said in thunder.

---

1. *The Complete Works of Ralph Waldo Emerson*, ed. Edward Waldo Emerson, 12 vols. (Boston and New York: Houghton Mifflin, 1903–04), 10:552.

THE MORAL ARGUMENT
AGAINST CALVINISM

Illustrated in a Review of a Work entitled "A General View of the Doctrines of Christianity, designed more especially for the Edification and Instruction of Families. Boston. 1809."

The work, of which we have prefixed the title to this article, was published several years ago, and has been read by many among us with pleasure and profit.[1] But it is not known as widely as it should be, and we wish to call to it the notice which it merits. It is not an original work, but was compiled chiefly from the writings of the Rev. Robert Fellowes, whose name is probably known to most of our readers. The title we think not altogether happy, because it raises an expectation which the book does not answer. We should expect from it a regular statement of the great truths of our religion; but we find, what at present is perhaps as useful, a vindication of Christianity from the gross errors, which Calvinism has labored to identify with this divine system. This may easily be supposed from the table of contents. The book professes to treat of the following subjects:—The nature of religion and the mistakes that occur on that subject; the free-agency and accountableness of man; the fall of Adam, and original sin; the doctrine of faith in general, and of religious faith in particular; the doctrine of works; the doctrine of regeneration; the doctrine of repentance; the doctrine of grace; the doctrine of election and reprobation; the doctrine of perseverance; the visiting of the iniquities of the fathers upon the children; and the sin against the Holy Ghost.—By those, who are acquainted with the five thorny points of Calvinism,[2] the design of this compilation will be sufficiently understood from the enumeration of topics now given; and few designs are more praiseworthy, than to free Christianity from the reproach brought upon it by that system.

The work under review is professedly popular in its style and mode of discussion. It has little refined and elaborate reasoning, but appeals to the great moral principles of human nature, and to the general strain of the Scriptures. It expresses strongly and without circumlocution the abhorrence with which every mind, uncorrupted by false theology, must look on Calvinism; and although some of its delineations may be overcharged, yet they are substantially correct, and their strength is their excellence. The truth is, that nothing is so necessary on this subject as to awaken moral feeling in men's breasts. Calvinism owes its perpetuity to the influence of fear in palsying the moral nature. Men's minds and consciences are subdued by terror, so that they dare not confess, even to themselves, the shrinking, which they feel, from the unworthy views which this system gives of God; and, by thus smothering their just abhorrence, they gradually extinguish it, and even come to vindicate in God what would disgrace his creatures. A voice of power and solemn warning is needed to rouse them from this lethargy, to give them a new and a juster dread, the dread of incurring God's displeasure, by making him odious, and exposing religion to insult and aversion.—In the present article, we intend to treat this subject with great freedom. But we beg that it may be understood that by Calvinism we intend only the peculiarities or distinguishing features of that system. We would also have it remembered, that these peculiarities form a small part of the religious faith of a Calvinist. He joins with them the general, fundamental, and most important truths of Christianity, by which they are always neutralized in a greater or less degree, and in some cases nullified. Accordingly it has been our happiness to see in the numerous body by which they are professed, some of the brightest examples of Christian virtue. Our hostility to the doctrine does not extend to its advocates. In bearing our strongest testimony against error, we do not the less honor the moral and religious worth, with which it is often connected.

The book under review will probably be objected to by theologians, because it takes no notice of a distinction, invented by Calvinistic metaphysicians, for rescuing their doctrines from the charge of aspersing God's equity and goodness. We refer to the distinction between *natural* and *moral inability*, a subtilty which may be thought to deserve some attention, because it makes such a show in some of the principal books of this sect. But, with due deference to its defenders, it seems to us groundless and idle, a distinction without a difference. An inability to do our duty, which is *born* with us, is to all intents and according to the established meaning of the word, *natural*. Call it moral, or what you please, it is still a part of the nature which our Creator gave us, and to suppose that he punishes us for it, because it is an inability seated in the will, is just as absurd, as to suppose him to punish us for a weakness of sight or of a limb. Common people cannot understand this distinction, cannot split this hair; and it is no small objection to Calvinism, that, according to its ablest defenders, it can only be reconciled to God's perfections, by a metaphysical subtilty, which the mass of people cannot comprehend.

If we were to speak as critics of the style of this book, we should say, that, whilst generally clear, and sometimes striking, it has the faults of the style which was very current not many years ago in this country, and which, we rejoice to say, is giving place to a better. The style to which we refer, and which threatened to supplant good writing in this country, intended to be elegant, but fell into jejuneness and insipidity. It delighted in words and arrangements of words, which were little soiled by common use, and mistook a spruce neatness for grace. We had a Procrustes' bed for sentences, and there seemed to be a settled war between the style of writing and the free style of conversation. Times we think have changed. Men have learned more to write as they speak, and are ashamed to dress up familiar thoughts, as if they were just arrived from a far country, and could not appear in public without a foreign and studied attire. They have learned that common words are common, precisely because most fitted to express real feeling and strong conception, and that the circuitous, measured phraseology, which was called elegance, was but the parade of weakness. They have learned that words are the signs of thought, and worthless counterfeits without it, and that style is good, when, instead of being anxiously cast into a mould, it seems a free and natural expression of thought, and gives to us with power the workings of the author's mind.

We have been led to make these remarks on the style which in a degree marks the book before us, from a persuasion, that this mode of writing has been particularly injurious to religion, and to rational religion. It has crept into sermons perhaps more than into any other compositions, and has imbued them with that soporific quality, which they have sometimes been found to possess in an eminent degree. How many hearers have been soothed by a smooth, watery flow of words, a regular chime of sentences, and elegantly rocked into repose! We are aware, that preachers, above all writers, are excusable for this style, because it is the easiest; and, having too much work to do, they must do it of course in the readiest way. But we mourn the necessity, and mourn still more the effect.—It gives us great pleasure to say, that, in this particular, we think we perceive an improvement taking place in this region. Preaching is becoming more direct, aims more at impression, and seeks the nearest way to men's hearts and consciences. We often hear from the pulpit strong thought in plain and strong language. It is hoped, from the state of society, that we shall not fly from one extreme to another, and degenerate into coarseness; but perhaps even this is a less evil than tameness and insipidity.

To return; the principal argument against Calvinism, in the General View of Christian Doctrines, is the *moral argument*, or that which is drawn from the inconsistency of the system with the divine perfections. It is plain, that a doctrine, which contradicts our best ideas of goodness and justice, cannot come from the just and good God, or be a true representation of his character. This moral argument has always been powerful to the pulling down of the strongholds of Calvinism. Even in the dark period, when this system was shaped and finished at Geneva, its advocates often writhed under the weight of it; and we cannot but deem it a mark of the progress of society, that Calvinists are more and more troubled with the palpable repugnance of their doctrines to God's nature, and accordingly labor to soften and explain them, until in many cases the name only is retained. If the stern reformer of Geneva could lift up his head, and hear the mitigated tone, in which some of his professed followers dispense his fearful doctrines, we fear, that he could not lie down in peace, until he had poured out his displeasure on their cowardice and degeneracy. He would tell them, with a frown, that *moderate Calvinism* was a solecism, a contradiction in terms, and would bid them in scorn to join their real friend, Arminius. Such is the power of public opinion and of an improved state of society on creeds, that naked, undisguised Calvinism is not very fond of showing itself, and many of consequence know imperfectly what it means. What then is the system against which the View of Christian Doctrines is directed?

Calvinism teaches, that, in consequence of Adam's sin in eating the forbidden fruit, God brings into life all his posterity with a nature wholly corrupt, so that they are utterly indisposed, disabled, and made opposite to all that is spiritually good, and wholly inclined to all evil, and that continually. It teaches, that all mankind, having fallen in Adam, are under God's wrath and curse, and so made liable to all miseries in this life, to death itself, and to the pains of hell for ever. It teaches, that, from this ruined race, God, out of his mere good pleasure, has elected a certain number to be saved by Christ, not induced to this choice by any foresight of their faith or good works, but wholly by his free grace and love; and that, having thus predestinated them to eternal life, he renews and sanctifies them by his almighty and special agency, and brings them into a state of grace, from which they cannot fall and perish. It teaches, that the rest of mankind he is pleased to pass over, and to ordain them to dishonor and wrath for their sins, to the honor of his justice and power; in other words, he leaves the rest to the corruption in which they were born, withholds the grace which is necessary to their recovery, and condemns them to "most grievous torments in soul and body without intermission in hell-fire for ever." Such is Calvinism, as gathered from the most authentic records of the doctrine. Whoever will consult the famous Assembly's Cathechisms and Confession, will see the peculiarities of the system in all their length and breadth of deformity. A man of plain sense, whose spirit has not been broken to this creed by education or terror, will think that it is not necessary for us to travel to heathen countries, to learn how mournfully the human mind may misrepresent the Deity.

The moral argument against Calvinism, of which we have spoken, must seem irresistible to common and unperverted minds, after attending to the brief statement now given. It will be asked with astonishment, How is it possible that men can hold these doctrines and yet maintain God's goodness and equity? What principles can be more contradictory?—To remove the objection to Calvinism, which is drawn from its repugnance to the Divine perfections, recourse has been had, as before observed, to the distinction between natural and moral inability, and to other like subtilties. But a more common reply, we conceive, has been drawn from the weakness and imperfection of the human mind, and from its incapacity of comprehending God. Calvinists will tell us, that, because a doctrine opposes our convictions of rectitude, it is not necessarily false; that apparent are not always real inconsistencies; that God is an infinite and incomprehensible being, and not to be tried by *our* ideas of fitness and morality; that we bring their system to an incompetent tribunal, when we submit it to the decision of human reason and conscience; that we are weak judges of what is right and wrong, good and evil, in the Deity; that the happiness of the universe may require an administration of human affairs which is very offensive to limited understandings; that we must follow revelation, not reason or moral feeling, and must consider doctrines, which shock us in revelation, as awful mysteries, which are dark through our ignorance, and which time will enlighten. How little, it is added, can man explain or understand God's ways. How inconsistent the miseries of life appear with goodness in the Creator. How prone, too, have men always been to confound good and evil, to call the just, unjust. How presumptuous is it in such a being, to sit in judgment upon God, and to question the rectitude of the divine administration, because it shocks *his* sense of rectitude. Such we conceive to be a fair statement of the manner in which the Calvinist frequently meets the objection, that his system is at war with God's attributes. Such the reasoning by which the voice of conscience and nature is stifled, and men are reconciled to doctrines, which, if tried by the established principles of morality, would be rejected with horror. On this reasoning we purpose to offer some remarks; and we shall avail ourselves of the opportunity, to give our views of *the confidence which is due to our rational and moral faculties in religion.*

That God is infinite, and that man often errs, we affirm as strongly as our Calvinistic brethren. We desire to think humbly of ourselves, and reverently of our Creator. In the strong language of Scripture, "We now see through a glass darkly." "We cannot by searching find out God unto perfection. Clouds and darkness are round about him. His judgments are a great deep."[3] God is great and good beyond utterance or thought. We have no disposition to idolize our own powers, or to penetrate the secret counsels of the Deity. But, on the other hand, we think it ungrateful to disparage the powers which our Creator has given us, or to question the certainty or importance of the knowledge, which he has seen fit to place within our reach. There is an affected humility, we think, as dangerous as pride. We may rate our faculties too meanly, as well as too boastingly. The worst error in religion, after all, is that of the skeptic, who records triumphantly the weaknesses and wanderings of the human intellect, and maintains, that no trust is due to the decisions of this erring reason. We by no means conceive, that man's greatest danger springs from pride of understanding, though we think as badly of this vice as other Christians. Ths history of the church proves, that men may trust their faculties too little as well as too much, and that the timidity, which shrinks from investigation, has injured the mind, and betrayed the interests of Christianity, as much as an irreverent boldness of thought.

It is an important truth, which, we apprehend, has not been sufficiently developed, that the ultimate reliance of a human being is and must be on his own mind. To confide in God, we must first confide in the faculties by which He is apprehended, and by which the proofs of his existence are weighed. A trust in our ability to distinguish between truth and falsehood is implied in every act of belief; for to question this ability would of necessity unsettle all belief. We cannot take a step in reasoning or action without a secret reliance on our own minds. Religion in particular implies, that we have understandings endowed and qualified for the highest employments of intellect. In affirming the existence and perfections of God, we suppose and affirm the existence in ourselves of faculties which correspond to these sublime objects, and which are fitted to discern them. Religion is a conviction and an act of the human soul, so that, in denying confidence to the one, we subvert the truth and claims of the other. Nothing is gained to piety by degrading human nature, for in the competency of this nature to know and judge of God all piety has its foundation. Our proneness to err instructs us indeed to use our powers with great caution, but not to contemn and neglect them. The occasional abuse of our faculties, be it ever so enormous, does not prove them unfit for their highest end, which is, to form clear and consistent views of God. Because our eyes sometimes fail or deceive us, would a wise man pluck them out, or cover them with a bandage, and choose to walk and work in the dark? or, because they cannot distinguish distant objects, can they discern nothing clearly in their proper sphere, and is sight to be pronounced a fallacious guide? Men who, to support a creed, would shake our trust in the calm, deliberate, and distinct decisions of our rational and moral powers, endanger religion more than its open foes, and forge the deadliest weapon for the infidel.

It is true that God is an infinite being, and also true, that his powers and perfections, his purposes and operations, his ends and means, being unlimited, are *incomprehensible*. In other words, they cannot be *wholly taken in* or *embraced* by the human mind. In the strong and figurative language of Scripture, we "know nothing" of God's ways;[4] that is, we know *very few* of them. But this is just as true of the most advanced archangel as of man. In comparison with the vastness of God's system, the range of the highest created intellect is narrow; and, in this particular, man's lot does not differ from that of his elder brethren in heaven. We are both confined in our observation and experience to a little spot in the creation. But are an angel's faculties worthy of no trust, or is his knowledge uncertain, because he learns and reasons from a small part of God's works? or are his judgments respecting the Creator to be charged with presumption, because his views do not spread through the whole extent of the universe? We grant that our understandings cannot stretch beyond a very narrow sphere. But still the lessons, which we learn within this sphere, are just as sure, as if it were indefinitely enlarged. Because much is unexplored, we are not to suspect what we have actually discovered. Knowledge is not the less real, because confined. The man, who has never set foot beyond his native village, knows its scenery and inhabitants as undoubtingly, as if he had travelled to the poles. We indeed see very little; but that little is as true, as if every thing else were seen; and our future discoveries must agree with and support it. Should the whole order and purposes of the universe be opened to us, it is certain that nothing would be disclosed, which would in any degree shake our persuasion, that the earth is inhabited by rational and moral beings, who are authorized to expect from their Creator the most benevolent and equitable government. No extent of observation can unsettle those primary and fundamental principles of moral truth, which we derive from our highest faculties operating in the relations in which God has fixed us. In every region and period of the universe, it will be as true as it is now on the earth, that knowledge and power are the measures of responsibility, and that natural incapacity absolves from guilt. These and other moral verities, which are among our clearest perceptions, would, if possible, be strengthened, in proportion as our powers should be enlarged; because harmony and consistency are the characters of God's administration, and all our researches into the universe only serve to manifest its unity, and to show a wider operation of the laws which we witness and experience on earth.

We grant that God is *incomprehensible*, in the sense already given. But he is not therefore *unintelligible*; and this distinction we conceive to be important. We do not pretend to know the *whole* nature and properties of God, but still we can form some *clear ideas* of him, and can reason from these ideas as justly as from any other. The truth is, that we cannot be said to comprehend any being whatever, not the simplest plant or animal. All have hidden properties. Our knowledge of all is limited. But have we therefore no distinct ideas of the objects around us, and is all our reasoning about them unworthy of trust? Because God is infinite, his name is not therefore a mere sound. It is a representative of some distinct conceptions of our Creator; and these conceptions are as sure, and important, and as proper materials for the reasoning faculty, as they would be if our views were indefinitely enlarged. We cannot indeed trace God's goodness and rectitude through the whole field of his operations; but we know the essential nature of these attributes, and therefore can often judge what accords with and opposes them. God's goodness, because infinite, does not cease to be goodness, or essentially differ from the same attribute in man; nor does justice change its nature, so that it cannot be understood, because it is seated in an unbounded mind. There have indeed been philosophers, "falsely so called," who have argued from the unlimited nature of God, that we cannot ascribe to him justice and other moral attributes, in any proper or definite sense of those words; and the inference is plain, that all religion or worship, wanting an intelligible object, must be a misplaced, wasted offering. This doctrine from the infidel we reject with abhorrence; but something, not very different, too often reaches us from the mistaken Christian, who, to save his creed, shrouds the Creator in utter darkness. In opposition to both, we maintain that God's attributes are intelligible, and that we can conceive as truly of his goodness and justice, as of these qualities in men. In fact, these qualities are essentially the same in God and man, though differing in degree, in purity, and in extent of operation. We know not and we cannot conceive of any other justice or goodness, than we learn from our own nature; and if God have not these, he is altogether unknown to us as a moral being; he offers nothing for esteem and love to rest upon; the objection of the infidel is just, that worship is wasted; "We worship we know not what."[5]

It is asked, On what authority do we ascribe to God goodness and rectitude, in the sense in which these attributes belong to men, or how can we judge of the nature of attributes in the mind of the Creator? We answer by asking, How is it that we become acquainted with the mind of a fellow-creature? The last is as invisible, as removed from *immediate* inspection, as the first. Still we do not hesitate to speak of the justice and goodness of a neighbour; and how do we gain our knowledge? We answer, by witnessing the effects, operations, and expressions of these attributes. It is a law of our nature to argue from the effect to the cause, from the action to the agent, from the ends proposed and from the means of pursuing them, to the character and disposition of the being in whom we observe them. By these processes, we learn the invisible mind and character of man; and by the same we ascend to the mind of God, whose works, effects, operations, and ends are as expressive and significant of justice and goodness, as the best and most decisive actions of men. If this reasoning be sound (and all religion rests upon it,) then God's justice and goodness are intelligible attributes, agreeing essentially with the same qualities in ourselves. Their operation indeed is infinitely wider, and they are employed in accomplishing not only immediate but remote and unknown ends. Of consequence, we must expect that many parts of the divine administration will be *obscure*, that is, will not produce *immediate* good, and an *immediate* distinction between virtue and vice. But still the unbounded operation of these attributes does not change their nature. They are still the same, as if they acted in the narrowest sphere. We can still determine in many cases what does not accord with them. We are particularly sure that those essential principles of justice, which enter into and even form our conception of this attribute, must pervade every province and every period of the administration of a just being, and that to suppose the Creator in any instance to forsake them, is to charge him directly with unrighteousness, however loudly the lips may compliment his equity.

''But is it not presumptuous in man,'' it is continually said, ''to sit in judgment on God?'' We answer, that to ''sit in judgment on God'' is an ambiguous and offensive phrase, conveying to common minds the ideas of irreverence, boldness, familiarity. The question would be better stated thus; —Is it not presumptuous in man to judge concerning God, and concerning what agrees or disagrees with his attributes? We answer confidently, No; for in many cases we are competent and even bound to judge. And we plead first in our defence the Scriptures. How continually does God in his word appeal to the understanding and moral judgment of man. ''O inhabitants of Jerusalem and men of Judah, judge, I pray you, between me and my vineyard. What could have been done more to my vineyard, that I have not done in it.'' We observe, in the next place, that all religion supposes and is built on judgments passed by us on God and on his operations. Is it not, for example, our duty and a leading part of piety to *praise* God: And what is praising a being, but to adjudge and ascribe to him just and generous deeds and motives? And of what value is praise, except from those, who are capable of distinguishing between actions which exalt and actions which degrade the character? Is it presumption to call God *excellent?* And what is this, but to refer his character to a standard of excellence, to try it by the established principles of rectitude, and to pronounce its conformity to them; that is, to judge of God and his operations?

We are presumptuous, we are told, in judging of our Creator. But he himself has made this our duty, in giving us a moral faculty; and to decline it, is to violate the primary law of our nature. Conscience, the sense of right, the power of perceiving moral distinctions, the power of discerning between justice and injustice, excellence and baseness, is the highest faculty given us by God, the whole foundation of our responsibility, and our sole capacity for religion. Now we are forbidden by this faculty to love a being, who wants, or who fails to discover, moral excellence. God, in giving us conscience, has implanted a principle within us, which forbids us to prostrate ourselves before mere power, or to offer praise where we do not discover worth; a principle, which challenges our supreme homage for supreme goodness, and which absolves us from guilt, when we abhor a severe and unjust administration. Our Creator has consequently waived his own claims on our veneration and obedience, any farther than he discovers himself to us in characters of benevolence, equity, and righteousness.[6] He rests his authority on the perfect coincidence of his will and government with those great and fundamental principles of morality written on our souls. He desires no worship, but that which springs from the exercise of our moral faculties upon his character, from our discernment and persuasion of his rectitude and goodness. He asks, he accepts, no love or admiration but from those, who can understand the nature and the proofs of moral excellence.

There are two or three striking facts, which show that there is no presumption in judging of God, and of what agrees or disagrees with his attributes. The first fact is, that the most intelligent and devout men have often employed themselves in proving the existence and perfections of God, and have been honored for this service to the cause of religion. Now we ask, what is meant by the *proofs* of a divine perfection? They are certain acts, operations, and methods of government, which are proper and natural effects, signs, and expressions of this perfection, and from which, according to the established principles of reasoning, it may be inferred. To prove the divine attributes is to collect and arrange those works and ways of the Creator, which accord with these attributes, correspond to them, flow from them, and express them. Of consequence, to prove them requires and implies *the power of judging of what agrees with them,* of discerning their proper marks and expressions. All our treatises on natural theology rest on this power. Every argument in support of a divine perfection is an exercise of it. To deny it, is to overthrow all religion.

Now if such are the proofs of God's goodness and justice, and if we are capable of discerning them, then we are not necessarily presumptuous, when we say of particular measures ascribed to him, that they are inconsistent with his attributes, and cannot belong to him. There is plainly no more presumption in affirming of certain principles of administration, that they oppose God's equity and would prove him unrighteous, than to affirm of others, that they prove him upright and good. There are signs and evidences of injustice as unequivocal as those of justice; and our faculties are as adequate to the perception of the last as of the first. If they must not be trusted in deciding what would prove God unjust, they are unworthy of confidence when they gather evidences of his rectitude; and of course, the whole structure of religion must fall.

It is no slight objection to the mode of reasoning adopted by the Calvinist, that it renders the proof of the divine attributes impossible. When we object to his representations of the divine government, that they shock our clearest ideas of goodness and justice, he replies, that still they may be true, because we know very little of God, and what seems unjust to man, may be in the Creator the perfection of rectitude. Now this weapon has a double edge. If the strongest marks and expressions of injustice do not prove God unjust, then the strongest marks of the opposite character do not prove him righteous. If the first do not deserve confidence, because of our narrow views of God, neither do the last. If, when more shall be known, the first may be found consistent with perfect rectitude, so, when more shall be known, the last may be found consistent with infinite malignity and oppression. This reasoning of our opponents casts us on an ocean of awful uncertainty. Admit it, and we have no proofs of God's goodness and equity to rely upon. What we call proofs, may be mere appearances, which a wider knowledge of God may reverse. The future may show us, that the very laws and works of the Creator, from which we now infer his kindness, are consistent with the most determined purpose to spread infinite misery and guilt, and were intended, by raising hope, to add the agony of disappointment to our other woes. Why may not these anticipations, horrible as they are, be verified by the unfolding of God's system, if our reasonings about his attributes are rendered so very uncertain, as Calvinism teaches, by the infinity of his nature?

We have mentioned one fact to show that it is not presumptuous to judge of God, and of what accords with and opposes his attributes; namely, the fact that his attributes are thought susceptible of proof. Another fact, very decisive on this point, is, that Christians of all classes have concurred in resting the truth of Christianity in a great degree on its *internal* evidence, that is, on its accordance with the perfections of God. How common is it to hear from religious teachers, that Christianity is worthy of a good and righteous being, that it bears the marks of a divine original. Volumes have been written on its internal proofs, on the coincidence of its purposes and spirit with our highest conceptions of God. How common too is it, to say of other religions, that they are at war with the divine nature, with God's rectitude and goodness, and that we want no other proofs of their falsehood. And what does all this reasoning imply? Clearly this, that we are capable of determining, in many cases, what is worthy and what is unworthy of God, what accords with and what opposes his moral attributes. Deny us this capacity, and it would be no presumption against a professed revelation, that it ascribed to the Supreme Being the most detestable practices. It might still be said in support of such a system, that it is arrogant in man to determine what kind of revelation suits the character of the Creator. Christianity then leans, at least in part, and some think chiefly, on internal evidence, or on its agreeableness to God's moral attributes; and is it probable, that this religion, having this foundation, contains representations of God's government which shock our ideas of rectitude, and that it silences our objections by telling us, that we are no judges of what suits or opposes his infinite nature?

We will name one more fact to show, that it is not presumption to form these judgments of the Creator. All Christians are accustomed to reason from God's attributes, and to use them as tests of doctrines. In their controversies with one another, they spare no pains to show, that their particular views accord best with the divine perfections, and every sect labors to throw on its adversaries the odium of maintaining what is unworthy of God. Theological writings are filled with such arguments; and yet *we*, it seems, are guilty of awful presumption, when we deny of God principles of administration, against which every pure and good sentiment in our breasts rises in abhorrence.

We shall conclude this discussion with an important inquiry. If God's justice and goodness are consistent with those operations and modes of government, which Calvinism ascribes to him, of what use is our belief in these perfections? What expectations can we found upon them? If it consist with divine rectitude to consign to everlasting misery, beings who have come guilty and impotent from his hand, we beg to know what interest we have in this rectitude, what pledge of good it contains, or what evil can be imagined which may not be its natural result? If justice and goodness, when stretched to infinity, take such strange forms and appear in such unexpected and apparently inconsistent operations, how are we sure, that they will not give up the best men to ruin, and leave the universe to the powers of darkness? Such results indeed seem incompatible with these attributes, but not more so than the acts attributed to God by Calvinism. Is it said, that the divine faithfulness is pledged in the Scriptures to a happier issue of things?[7] But why should not divine faithfulness transcend our poor understandings as much as divine goodness and justice, and why may not God, consistently with this attribute, crush every hope which his word has raised? Thus all the divine perfections are lost to us as grounds of encouragement and consolation, if we maintain, that their infinity places them beyond our judgment, and that we must expect from them measures and operations entirely opposed to what seems to us most accordant with their nature.

We have thus endeavored to show, that the testimony of our rational and moral faculties against Calvinism is worthy of trust.—We know that this reasoning will be met by the question, What then becomes of Christianity? for this religion plainly teaches the doctrines you have condemned. Our answer is ready. Christianity contains no such doctrines. Christianity, reason, and conscience are perfectly harmonious on the subject under discussion. Our religion, fairly construed, gives no countenance to that system, which has arrogated to itself the distinction of Evangelical. We cannot, however, enter this field at present. We will only say, that the general spirit of Christianity affords a very strong presumption, that its records teach no such doctrines as we have opposed. This spirit is love, charity, benevolence. Christianity, we all agree, is designed to manifest God as perfect benevolence, and to bring men to love and imitate him. Now it is probable, that a religion, having this object, gives views of the Supreme Being, from which our moral convictions and benevolent sentiments shrink with horror, and which, if made our pattern, would convert us into monsters! It is plain, that, were a human parent to form himself on the universal Father, as described by Calvinism, that is, were he to bring his children into life totally depraved, and then to pursue them with endless punishment, we should charge him with a cruelty not surpassed in the annals of the world; or, were a sovereign to incapacitate his subjects in any way whatever for obeying his laws, and then to torture them in dungeons of perpetual woe, we should say, that history records no darker crime. And is it probable, that a religion, which aims to attract and assimilate us to · God, considered as love, should hold him up to us in these heart-withering characters? We may confidently expect to find in such a system the brightest views of the divine nature; and the same objections lie against interpretations of its records, which savour of cruelty and injustice, as lie against the literal sense of passages which ascribe to God bodily wants and organs. Let the Scriptures be read with a recollection of the spirit of Christianity, and with that modification of particular texts by this general spirit, which a just criticism requires, and Calvinism would no more enter the mind of the reader, than Popery, we had almost said, than Heathenism.

In the remarks now made, it will be seen, we hope, that we have aimed to expose doctrines, not to condemn their professors. It is true, that men are apt to think themselves assailed, when their system only is called to account. But we have no foe but error. We are less and less disposed to measure the piety of others by peculiarities of faith. Men's characters are determined, not by the opinions which they profess, but by those on which their thoughts habitually fasten, which recur to them most forcibly, and which color their ordinary views of God and duty. The creed of habit, imitation, or fear, may be defended stoutly, and yet have little practical influence. The mind, when compelled by education or other circumstances to receive irrational doctrines, has yet a power of keeping them, as it were, on its surface, of excluding them from its depths, of refusing to incorporate them with its own being; and, when burdened with a mixed, incongruous system, it often discovers a sagacity, which reminds us of the instinct of inferior animals, in selecting the healthful and nutritious portions, and in making them its daily food. Accordingly the real faith often corresponds little with that which is professed. It often happens, that, through the progress of the mind in light and virtue, opinions, once central, are gradually thrown outward, lose their vitality, and cease to be principles of action, whilst through habit they are defended as articles of faith. The words of the creed survive, but its advocates sympathize with it little more than its foes. These remarks are particularly applicable to the present subject. A large number, perhaps a majority of those, who surname themselves with the name of Calvin, have little more title to it than ourselves. They keep the name, and drop the principles which it signifies. They adhere to the system as a whole, but shrink from all its parts and distinguishing points. This silent but real defection from Calvinism is spreading more and more widely. The grim features of this system are softening, and its stern spirit yielding to conciliation and charity. We beg our readers to consult for themselves the two Catechisms and the Confession of the Westminster Assembly, and to compare these standards of Calvinism, with what now bears its name. They will rejoice, we doubt not, in the triumphs of truth. With these views, we have no disposition to disparage the professors of the system which we condemn, although we believe that its influence is yet so extensive and pernicious as to bind us to oppose it.

Calvinism, we are persuaded, is giving place to better views. It has passed its meridian, and is sinking, to rise no more. It has to contend with foes more formidable than theologians, with foes, from whom it cannot shield itself in mystery and metaphysical subtilties, we mean with the progress of the human mind, and with the progress of the spirit of the Gospel. Society is going forward in intelligence and charity, and of course is leaving the theology of the sixteenth century behind it. We hail this revolution of opinion as a most auspicious event to the Christian cause. We hear much at present of efforts to spread the Gospel. But Christianity is gaining more by the removal of degrading errors, than it would by armies of missionaries who should carry with them a corrupted form of the religion. We think the decline of Calvinism one of the most encouraging facts in our passing history; for this system, by outraging conscience and reason, tends to array these high faculties against revelation. Its errors are peculiarly mournful, because they relate to the character of God. It darkens and stains his pure nature; spoils his character of its sacredness, loveliness, glory; and thus quenches the central light of the universe, makes existence a curse, and the extinction of it a consummation devoutly to be wished. We now speak of the *peculiarities* of this system, and of their natural influence, when not counteracted, as they always are in a greater or less degree, by better views, derived from the spirit and plain lessons of Christianity.

We have had so much to do with our subject, that we have neglected to make the usual extracts from the book which we proposed to review. We earnestly wish, that a work, answering to the title of this, which should give us "a general view of Christian doctrines," might be undertaken by a powerful hand. Next to a good commentary on the Scriptures, it would be the best service which could be rendered to Christian truth.

Notes

1. That the book under review had been published over a decade before suggests that it served Channing as a convenient vehicle for his general attack on Calvinism. Channing's review was published in the *Christian Disciple*.

2. The five points of Calvinism evolved from the condemnation of Arminianism at the Synod of Dort (1618-19). They were generally recognized as human depravity, predestination, election to salvation, irresistible grace and the perseverance of the elect. See the article by T.C. O'Brien in the *Encyclopedic Dictionary of Religion* (Washington: Corpus, 1979), 2 (F-N): 1360. James Freeman Clarke's famous later formulation of the five points of Unitarianism was a response to the Calvinist formula. They were: the Fatherhood of God, the Brotherhood of Man, the Leadership of Jesus, Salvation by Character, and the Progress of Mankind onward and upward

forever. Clarke, *Vexed Questions in Theology* (Boston: George H. Ellis, 1886).

3. I Corinthians 13:12—"For now we see through a glass, darkly; but then face to face: now I know in part; but then shall I know even as also I am known." Job 11:7—"Canst thou find out the Almighty unto perfection?" Psalms 97:2—"Clouds and darkness *are* round about him: righteousness and judgment *are* the habitation of his throne." Psalms 36:6—"Thy righteousness *is* like the great mountains; thy judgments *are* a great deep: O Lord, thou preservest man and beast."

4. Job 8:9—("For we *are but of* yesterday, and know nothing, because our days upon earth *are* a shadow)."

5. John 4:22—"Ye worship ye know not what: we know what we worship: for salvation is of the Jews."

6. *Textual emendation:* "waived" has been substituted for "waved" in the foregoing sentence.

7. *Textual emendation:* "pledged" has been substituted for "pleged" in the foregoing sentence.

THE EVIDENCES OF REVEALED RELIGION
(1821)*

*The original text that follows this introduction is from *The Works of William E. Channing, D. D.*, 6 vols. (Boston: James Munroe, 1841-43), 3:105-136.

Channing's exposition of "revealed religion" was one of a series of such public pronouncements made possible by the 1751 bequest of Paul Dudley; Harvard's Dudleian Lectures are the oldest endowed lectures in America.[1] In his defense of the Biblical revelation, Channing argued that nature, as it is manifested in both human reason and the natural world, is not a sufficient basis for religion, and thus needs the supplement of supernatural evidence. The Biblical miracles, which had been dismissed most notably by David Hume in his 1748 essay "Of Miracles" (see note 2 to the text), were thus seen by Channing as an essential element of the Christian faith. His address is a classic delineation of the "supernatural rationalism" of eighteenth- and nineteenth-century Protestantism, which blended the rational outlook of the Age of Enlightenment with a rigorous defense of the plausibility and the necessity of the miracles and other guidance provided by scripture.[2] But there was more at work in Channing's address than tradition and expected apologetics. One young man, Ralph Waldo Emerson, caught a strain of poetry in the lecture, and found in it a confidence that he also possessed the "moral imagination" necessary to pursue a career in the ministry.[3] That reaction is important not only because of Emerson's stature

---

1. On the background of the Dudleian Lectures, see Perry Miller, "The Insecurity of Nature," in *Nature's Nation* (Cambridge: Harvard University Press, 1967), 121-33, and Conrad Wright, "Rational Religion in Eighteenth-Century America," in *The Liberal Christians: Essays on American Unitarian History* (Boston: Beacon, 1970), 1-21.

2. See Wright, "Rational Religion in Eighteenth-Century America."

3. *The Journals and Miscellaneous Notebooks of Ralph Waldo Emerson*, ed. William H. Gilman et al., 16 vols. (Cambridge: Harvard University Press, 1960-82), 2: 238.

in literary history. It is also representative of the dynamism that Channing's oratory produced among its hearers, especially the younger ones.

THE EVIDENCES OF REVEALED RELIGION.
DISCOURSE BEFORE THE UNIVERSITY
IN CAMBRIDGE, AT THE DUDLEIAN LECTURE, 14TH MARCH, 1821.

John iii. 2: "The same came to Jesus by night, and said unto him, Rabbi, we know that thou art a teacher come from God; for no man can do these miracles that thou doest, except God be with him."

The evidences of revealed religion are the subject of this lecture, a subject of great extent, as well as of vast importance. In discussing it, an immense variety of learning has been employed, and all the powers of the intellect been called forth. History, metaphysics, ancient learning, criticism, ethical science, and the science of human nature, have been summoned to the controversy, and have brought important contributions to the Christian cause. To condense into one discourse what scholars and great men have written on this point, is impossible, even if it were desirable; and I have stated the extent of speculation into which our subject has led, not because I propose to give an abstract of others' labors, but because I wish you to understand, that the topic is one not easily despatched, and because I would invite you to follow me in a discussion, which will require concentrated and continued attention. A subject more worthy of attention, than the claims of that religion which was impressed on our childhood, and which is acknowledged to be the only firm foundation of the hope of immortality, cannot be presented; and our minds must want the ordinary seriousness of human nature, if it cannot arrest us.

That Christianity has been opposed, is a fact, implied in the establishment of this lecture. That it has had adversaries of no mean intellect, you know. I propose in this discourse to make some remarks on what seems to me the great objection to Christianity, on the general principle on which its evidences rest, and on some of its particular evidences.

The great objection to Christianity, the only one which has much influence at the present day, meets us at the very threshold. We cannot, if we would, evade it, for it is founded on a primary and essential attribute of this religion. The objection is oftener felt than expressed, and amounts to this, that miracles are incredible, and that the supernatural character of an alleged fact is proof enough of its falsehood. So strong is this propensity to doubt of departures from the order of nature, that there are sincere Christians, who incline to rest their religion wholly on its internal evidence, and to overlook the outward extraordinary interposition of God, by which it was at first established. But the difficulty cannot in this way be evaded; for Christianity is not only confirmed by miracles, but is in itself, in its very essence, a miraculous religion. It is not a system which the human mind might have gathered, in the ordinary exercise of its powers, from the ordinary course of nature. Its doctrines, especially those which relate to its founder, claim for it the distinction of being a supernatural provision for the recovery of the human race. So that the objection which I have stated still presses upon us, and, if it be well grounded, it is fatal to Christianity.

It is proper, then, to begin the discussion with inquiring, whence the disposition to discredit miracles springs, and how far it is rational. A preliminary remark of some importance is, that this disposition is not a necessary part or principle of our mental constitution, like the disposition to trace effects to adequate causes. We are indeed so framed, as to expect a continuance of that order of nature which we have uniformly experienced; but not so framed as to revolt at alleged violations of that order, and to account them impossible or absurd. On the contrary, men at large discover a strong and incurable propensity to believe in miracles. Almost all histories, until within the two last centuries, reported seriously supernatural facts. Skepticism as to miracles is comparatively a new thing, if we except the Epicurean or Atheistical sect among the ancients; and so far from being founded in human nature, it is resisted by an almost infinite preponderance of belief on the other side.

Whence, then, has this skepticism sprung? It may be explained by two principal causes. 1. It is now an acknowledged fact, among enlightened men, that in past times and in our own, a strong disposition has existed and still exists to admit miracles without examination. Human credulity is found to have devoured nothing more eagerly than reports of prodigies. Now it is argued, that we discover here a principle of human nature, namely, the love of the supernatural and marvellous, which accounts sufficiently for the belief of miracles, wherever we find it; and that it is, consequently, unnecessary and unphilosophical to seek for other causes, and especially to admit that most improbable one, the actual existence of miracles. This sweeping conclusion is a specimen of that rash habit of generalizing, which rather distinguishes our times, and shows that philosophical reasoning has made fewer advances than we are apt to boast. It is true, that there is a principle of credulity as to prodigies in a considerable part of society, a disposition to believe without due scrutiny. But this principle, like every other in our nature, has its limits; acts according to fixed laws; is not omnipotent; cannot make the eyes see, and the ears hear, and the understanding credit delusions, under all imaginable circumstances; but requires the concurrence of various circumstances and of other principles of our nature in order to its operation. For example, the belief of spectral appearances has been very common; but under what circumstances and in what state of mind has it occurred? Do men see ghosts in broad day, and amidst cheerful society? Or in solitary places; in grave-yards; in twilights or mists, where outward objects are so undefined, as easily to take a form from imagination; and in other circumstances favorable to terror, and associated with the delusion in question? The principle of credulity is as regular in its operation, as any other principle of the mind; and is so dependent on circumstances and so restrained and checked by other parts of human nature, that sometimes the most obstinate incredulity is found in that very class of people, whose easy belief on other occasions moves our contempt. It is well known, for example, that the efficacy of the vaccine inoculation has been encountered with much more unyielding skepticism among the vulgar, than among the improved; and in general, it may be affirmed, that the credulity of the ignorant operates under the control of their strongest passions and impressions, and that no class of society yield a slower assent to positions, which manifestly subvert their old modes of thinking and most settled prejudices. It is, then, very unphilosophical to assume this principle as an explanation of all miracles whatever. I grant that the fact, that accounts of supernatural agency so generally prove false, is a reason for looking upon them with peculiar distrust. Miracles ought on this account to be sifted more than common facts. But if we find, that a belief in a series of supernatural works, has occurred under circumstances very different from those under which false prodigies have been received, under circumstances most unfavorable to the operation of credulity; then this belief cannot be resolved into the common causes, which have blinded men in regard to supernatural agency. We must look for other causes, and if none can be found but the actual existence of the miracles, then true philosophy binds us to believe them. I close this head with observing, that the propensity of men to believe in what is strange and miraculous, though a presumption against particular miracles, is not a presumption against miracles universally, but rather the reverse; for great principles of human nature have generally a foundation in truth, and one explanation of this propensity so common to mankind is obviously this, that in the earlier ages of the human race, miraculous interpositions, suited to man's infant state, were not uncommon, and, being the most striking facts of human history, they spread through all future times a belief and expectation of miracles.

I proceed now to the second cause of the skepticism in regard to supernatural agency, which has grown up, especially among the more improved, in later times. These later times are distinguished, as you well know, by successful researches into nature; and the discoveries of science have continually added strength to that great principle, that the phenomena of the universe are regulated by general and permanent laws, or that the Author of the universe exerts his power according to an established order. Nature, the more it is explored, is found to be uniform. We observe an unbroken succession of causes and effects. Many phenomena, once denominated irregular, and ascribed to supernatural agency, are found to be connected with preceding circumstances, as regularly as the most common events. The comet, we learn, observes the same attraction as the sun and planets. When a new phenomenon now occurs, no one thinks it miraculous, but believes, that, when better understood, it may be reduced to laws already known, or is an example of a law not yet investigated.

Now this increasing acquaintance with the uniformity of nature begets a distrust of alleged violations of it, and a rational distrust too; for, while many causes of mistake in regard to alleged miracles may be assigned, there is but one adequate cause of real miracles, that is, the power of God; and the regularity of nature forms a strong presumption against the miraculous exertion of this power, except in extraordinary circumstances, and for extraordinary purposes, to which the established laws of the creation are not competent. But the observation of the uniformity of nature produces, in multitudes, not merely this rational distrust of alleged violations of it, but a secret feeling, as if such violations were impossible. That attention to the powers of nature, which is implied in scientific research, tends to weaken the practical conviction of a higher power; and the laws of the creation, instead of being regarded as the modes of Divine operation, come insensibly to be considered as fetters on his agency, as too sacred to be suspended even by their Author. This secret feeling, essentially atheistical, and at war with all sound philosophy, is the chief foundation of that skepticism, which prevails in regard to miraculous agency, and deserves our particular consideration.

To a man whose belief in God is strong and practical, a miracle will appear as possible as any other effect, as the most common event in life; and the argument against miracles, drawn from the uniformity of nature, will weigh with him, only as far as this uniformity is a pledge and proof of the Creator's disposition to accomplish his purposes by a fixed order or mode of operation. Now it is freely granted, that the Creator's regard or attachment to such an order may be inferred from the steadiness with which he observes it; and a strong presumption lies against any violation of it on slight occasions, or for purposes to which the established laws of nature are adequate. But this is the utmost which the order of nature authorizes us to infer respecting its Author. It forms no presumption against miracles universally, in all imaginable cases; but may even furnish a presumption in their favor.

We are never to forget, that God's adherence to the order of the universe is not necessary and mechanical, but intelligent and voluntary. He adheres to it, not for its own sake, or because it has a sacredness which compels him to respect it, but because it is most suited to accomplish his purposes. It is a means, and not an end; and, like all other means, must give way when the end can best be promoted without it. It is the mark of a weak mind, to make an idol of order and method; to cling to established forms of business, when they clog instead of advancing it. If, then, the great purposes of the universe can best be accomplished by departing from its established laws, these laws will undoubtedly be suspended; and, though broken in the letter, they will be observed in their spirit, for the ends for which they were first instituted will be advanced by their violation. Now the question arises, For what purposes were nature and its order appointed? and there is no presumption in saying, that the highest of these is the improvement of intelligent beings. Mind (by which we mean both moral and intellectual powers) is God's first end. The great purpose for which an order of nature is fixed, is plainly the formation of Mind. In a creation without order, where events would follow without any regular succession, it is obvious, that Mind must be kept in perpetual infancy; for, in such a universe, there could be no reasoning from effects to causes, no induction to establish general truths, no adaptation of means to ends; that is, no science relating to God, or matter, or mind; no action; no virtue. The great purpose of God, then, I repeat it, in establishing the order of nature, is to form and advance the mind; and if the case should occur, in which the interests of the mind could best be advanced by departing from this order, or by miraculous agency, then the great purpose of the creation, the great end of its laws and regularity, would demand such departure; and miracles, instead of warring against, would concur with nature.

Now, we Christians maintain, that such a case has existed. We affirm, that, when Jesus Christ came into the world, nature had failed to communicate instructions to men, in which, as intelligent beings, they had the deepest concern, and on which the full development of their highest faculties essentially depended; and we affirm, that there was no prospect of relief from nature; so that an exigence had occurred, in which additional communications, supernatural lights, might rationally be expected from the Father of spirits. Let me state two particulars, out of many, in which men needed intellectual aids not given by nature. I refer to the doctrine of one God and Father, on which all piety rests;[1] and to the doctrine of Immortality, which is the great spring of virtuous effort. Had I time to enlarge on the history of that period, I might show you under what heaps of rubbish and superstition these doctrines were buried. But I should repeat only what you know familiarly. The works of ancient genius, which form your studies, carry on their front the brand of polytheism, and of debasing error on subjects of the first and deepest concern. It is more important to observe, that the very unformity of nature had some tendency to obscure the doctrines which I have named, or at least to impair their practical power, so that a departure from this uniformity was needed to fasten them on men's minds.

That a fixed order of nature, though a proof of the One God to reflecting and enlarged understandings, has yet a tendency to hide him from men in general, will appear, if we consider, first, that, as the human mind is constituted, what is regular and of constant occurrence, excites it feebly; and benefits flowing to it through fixed, unchanging laws, seem to come by a kind of necessity, and are apt to be traced up to natural causes alone. Accordingly, religious convictions and feelings, even in the present advanced condition of society, are excited, not so much by the ordinary course of God's providence, as by sudden, unexpected events, which rouse and startle the mind, and speak of a power higher than nature.—There is another way, in which a fixed order of nature seems unfavorable to just impressions respecting its Author. It discovers to us in the Creator, a regard to general good rather than an affection to individuals. The laws of nature, operating, as they do, with an inflexible steadiness, never varying to meet the cases and wants of individuals, and inflicting much private suffering in their stern administration for the general weal, give the idea of a distant, reserved sovereign, much more than of a tender parent; and yet this last view of God is the only effectual security from superstition and idolatry. Nature, then, we fear, would not have brought back the world to its Creator.—And as to the doctrine of Immortality, the order of the natural world had little tendency to teach this, at least with clearness and energy. The natural world contains no provisions or arrangements for reviving the dead. The sun and the rain, which cover the tomb with verdure, send no vital influences to the mouldering body. The researches of science detect no secret processes for restoring the lost powers of life. If man is to live again, he is not to live through any known laws of nature, but by a power higher than nature; and how, then, can we be assured of this truth, but by a manifestation of this power, that is, by miraculous agency, confirming a future life?

I have labored in these remarks to show, that the uniformity of nature is no presumption against miraculous agency, when employed in confirmation of such a religion as Christianity. Nature, on the contrary, furnishes a presumption in its favor. Nature clearly shows to us a power above itself, so that it proves miracles to be possible. Nature reveals purposes and attributes in its Author, with which Christianity remarkably agrees. Nature too has deficiencies, which show that it was not intended by its Author to be his whole method of instructing mankind; and in this way it gives great confirmation to Christianity, which meets its wants, supplies its chasms, explains its mysteries, and lightens its heart-oppressing cares and sorrows.

Before quitting the general consideration of miracles, I ought to take some notice of Hume's celebrated argument on this subject;[2] not that it merits the attention which it has received, but because it is specious, and has derived weight from the name of its author. The argument is briefly this,—"that belief is founded upon and regulated by experience. Now we often experience testimony to be false, but never witness a departure from the order of nature. That men may deceive us when they testify to miracles, is therefore more accordant with experience, than that nature should be irregular; and hence there is a balance of proof against miracles, a presumption so strong as to outweigh the strongest testimony." The usual replies to this argument I have not time to repeat. Dr. Campbell's work,[3] which is accessible to all, will show you that it rests on an equivocal use of terms, and will furnish you with many fine remarks on testimony and on the conditions or qualities which give it validity. I will only add a few remarks which seem to me worthy of attention.

1. This argument affirms, that the credibility of facts or statements is to be decided by their accordance with the established order of nature, and by this standard only. Now, if nature comprehended all existences and all powers, this position might be admitted. But if there is a Being higher than nature, the origin of all its powers and motions, and whose character falls under our notice and experience as truly as the creation, then there is an additional standard to which facts and statements are to be referred; and works which violate nature's order, will still be credible, if they agree with the known properties and attributes of its author; because for such works we can assign an adequate cause and sufficient reasons, and these are the qualities and conditions on which credibility depends.

2. This argument of Hume proves too much, and therefore proves nothing. It proves too much; for if I am to reject the strongest testimony to miracles, because testimony has often deceived me, whilst nature's order has never been found to fail, then I ought to re-

ject a miracle, even if I should see it with my own eyes, and if all my senses should attest it; for all my senses have sometimes given false reports, whilst nature has never gone astray; and, therefore, be the circumstances ever so decisive or inconsistent with deception, still I must not believe what I see, and hear, and touch, what my senses, exercised according to the most deliberate judgment, declare to be true. All this the argument requires; and it proves too much; for disbelief, in the case supposed, is out of our power, and is instinctively pronounced absurd; and what is more, it would subvert that very order of nature on which the argument rests; for this order of nature is learned only by the exercise of my senses and judgment, and if these fail me, in the most unexceptionable circumstances, then their testimony to nature is of little worth.

Once more; this argument is built on an ignorance of the nature of testimony. Testimony, we are told, cannot prove a miracle. Now the truth is, that testimony of itself and immediately, proves no facts whatever, not even the most common. Testimony can do nothing more than show us the state of another's mind in regard to a given fact. It can only show us, that the testifier has a belief, a conviction, that a certain phenomenon or event has occurred. Here testimony stops; and the reality of the event is to be judged altogether from the nature and degree of this conviction, and from the circumstances under which it exists. This conviction is an effect, which must have a cause, and needs to be explained; and if no cause can be found but the real occurrence of the event, then this occurrence is admitted as true. Such is the extent of testimony. Now a man, who affirms a miraculous phenomenon or event, may give us just as decisive proofs, by his character and conduct, of the strength and depth of his conviction, as if he were affirming a common occurrence. Testimony, then, does just as much in the case of miracles, as of common events; that is, it discloses to us the conviction of another's mind. Now this conviction in the case of miracles requires a cause, an explanation, as much as in every other; and if the circumstances be such, that it could not have sprung up and been established but by the reality of the alleged miracle, then that great and fundamental principle of human belief, namely, that every effect must have a cause, compels us to admit the miracle.

It may be observed of Hume and of other philosophical opposers of our religion, that they are much more inclined to argue against miracles in general, than against the particular miracles on which Christianity rests. And the reason is obvious. Miracles, when considered in a general, abstract manner, that is, when divested of all circumstances, and supposed to occur as disconnected facts, to stand alone in history, to have no explanations or reasons in preceding events, and no influence on those which follow, are indeed open to great objection, as wanton and useless violations of nature's order; and it is accordingly against miracles, considered in this naked, general form, that the arguments of infidelity are chiefly urged. But it is great disingenuity to class under this head the miracles of Christianity. They are palpably different. They do not stand alone in history; but are most intimately incorporated with it. They were demanded by the state of the world which preceded them, and they have left deep traces on all subsequent ages. In fact, the history of the whole civilized world, since their alleged occurrence, has been swayed and colored by them, and is wholly inexplicable without them. Now, such miracles are not to be met and disposed of by general reasonings, which apply only to insulated, unimportant, uninfluential prodigies.

I have thus considered the objections to miracles in general; and I would close this head with observing, that these objections will lose their weight, just in proportion as we strengthen our conviction of God's power over nature and of his parental interest in his creatures. The great repugnance to the belief of miraculous agency is founded in a lurking atheism, which ascribes supremacy to nature, and which, whilst it professes to believe in God, questions his tender concern for the improvement of men. To a man, who cherishes a sense of God, the great difficulty is, not to account for miracles, but to account for their rare occurrence. One of the mysteries of the universe is this, that its Author retires so continually behind the veil of his works, that the great and good Father does not manifest himself more distinctly to his creatures. There is something like coldness and repulsiveness in instructing us only by fixed, inflexible laws of nature. The intercourse of God with Adam and the patriarchs suits our best conceptions of the relation which he bears to the human race, and ought not to surprise us more, than the expression of a human parent's tenderness and concern towards his offspring.

After the remarks now made to remove the objection to revelation in general, I proceed to consider the evidences of the Christian religion in particular; and these are so numerous, that should I attempt to compress them into the short space which now remains, I could give but a syllabus, a dry and uninteresting index. It will be more useful to state to you, with some distinctness, the general principle into which all Christian evidences may be resolved, and on which the whole religion rests, and then to illustrate it in a few striking particulars.

All the evidences of Christianity may be traced to this great principle,—that every effect must have an adequate cause. We claim for our religion a divine original, because no adequate cause for it can be found in the powers or passions of human nature, or in the circumstances under which it appeared; because it can only be accounted for by the interposition of that Being, to whom its first preachers universally ascribed it, and with whose nature it perfectly agrees.

Christianity, by which we mean not merely the doctrines of the religion, but every thing relating to it, its rise, its progress, the character of its author, the conduct of its propagators,—Christianity, in this broad sense, can only be accounted for in two ways. It either sprung from the principles of human nature, under the excitements, motives, impulses of the age in which it was first preached; or it had its origin in a higher and supernatural agency. To which of these causes the religion should be referred, is not a question beyond our reach; for being partakers of human nature, and knowing more of it than of any other part of creation, we can judge with sufficient accuracy of the operation of its principles, and of the effects to which they are competent. It is indeed true, that human powers are not exactly defined, nor can we state precisely the bounds beyond which they cannot pass; but still, the disproportion between human nature and an effect ascribed to it, may be so vast and palpable, as to satisfy us at once, that the effect is inexplicable by human power. I know not precisely what advances may be made by the intellect of an unassisted savage; but that a savage in the woods could not compose the "Principia" of Newton,[4] is about as plain as that he could not create the world. I know not the point at which bodily strength must stop; but that a man cannot carry Atlas or Andes on his shoulders, is a safe position. The question, therefore, whether the principles of human nature, under the circumstances in which it was placed at Christ's birth, will explain his religion, is one to which we are competent, and is the great question on which the whole controversy turns.

Now we maintain, that a great variety of facts belonging to this religion,—such as the character of its Founder; its peculiar principles; the style and character of its records; its progress; the conduct, circumstances, and sufferings of its first propagators; the reception of it from the first on the ground of miraculous attestations; the prophecies which it fulfilled and which it contains; its influence on society, and other circumstances connected with it; are utterly inexplicable by human powers and principles, but accord with, and are fully explained by, the power and perfections of God.

These various particulars I cannot attempt to unfold. One or two may be illustrated to show you the mode of applying the principles which I have laid down. I will take first the character of Jesus Christ. How is this to be explained by the principles of human nature?—We are immediately struck with this peculiarity in the Author of Christianity, that, whilst all other men are formed in a measure by the spirit of the age, we can discover in Jesus no impression of the period in which he lived. We know with considerable accuracy the state of society, the modes of thinking, the hopes and expectations of the country in which Jesus was born and grew up; and he is as free from them, and as exalted above them, as if he had lived in another world, or with every sense shut on the objects around him. His character has in it nothing local or temporary. It can be explained by nothing around him. His history shows him to us a solitary being, living for purposes which none but himself comprehended, and enjoying not so much as the sympathy of a single mind. His Apostles, his chosen companions, brought to him the spirit of the age; and nothing shows its strength more strikingly, than the slowness with which it yielded in these honest men to the instructions of Jesus.

Jesus came to a nation expecting a Messiah; and he claimed this character. But instead of conforming to the opinions which prevailed in regard to the Messiah, he resisted them wholly and without reserve. To a people anticipating a triumphant leader, under whom vengeance as well as ambition was to be glutted by the prostration of their oppressors, he came as a spiritual leader, teaching humility and peace. This undisguised hostility to the dearest hopes and prejudices of his nation; this disdain of the usual compliances, by which ambition and imposture conciliate adherents; this deliberate exposure of himself to rejection and hatred, cannot easily be explained by the common principles of human nature, and excludes the possibility of selfish aims in the Author of Christianity.

One striking peculiarity in Jesus is the extent, the vastness, of his views. Whilst all around him looked for a Messiah to liberate God's ancient people, whilst to every other Jew, Judea was the exclusive object of pride and hope, Jesus came, declaring himself to be the deliverer and light of the world, and in his whole teaching and life, you see a consciousness, which never forsakes him, of a relation to the whole human race. This idea of blessing mankind, of spreading a universal religion, was the most magnificent which had ever entered man's mind. All previous religions had been given to particular nations. No conqueror, legislator, philosopher, in the extravagance of ambition, had ever dreamed of subjecting all nations to a common faith.

This conception of a universal religion, intended alike for Jew and Gentile, for all nations and climes, is wholly inexplicable by the circumstances of Jesus. He was a Jew, and the first and deepest and most constant impression on a Jew's mind, was that of the superiority conferred on his people and himself by the national religion introduced by Moses. The wall between the Jew and the Gentile seemed to reach to heaven. The abolition of the peculiarity of Moses, the prostration of the temple on Mount Zion, the erection of a new religion, in which all men would meet as brethren, and which would be the common and equal property of Jew and Gentile, these were of all ideas the last to spring up in Judea, the last for enthusiasm or imposture to originate.

Compare next these views of Christ with his station in life. He was of humble birth and education, with nothing in his lot, with no extensive means, no rank, or wealth, or patronage, to infuse vast thoughts and extravagant plans. The shop of a carpenter, the village of Nazareth, were not spots for ripening a scheme more aspiring and extensive than had ever been formed. It is a principle of human nature, that, except in case of insanity, some proportion is observed between the power of an individual, and his plans and hopes. The purpose, to which Jesus devoted himself, was as ill suited to his con-

dition as an attempt to change the seasons, or to make the sun rise in
the west. That a young man, in obscure life, belonging to an oppressed nation, should seriously think of subverting the time-hallowed and deep-rooted religions of the world, is a strange fact; but
with this purpose we see the mind of Jesus thoroughly imbued; and,
sublime as it is, he never falls below it in his language or conduct,
but speaks and acts with a consciousness of superiority, with a dignity and authority, becoming this unparalleled destination.

In this connexion, I cannot but add another striking circumstance in Jesus, and that is, the calm confidence with which he always looked forward to the accomplishment of his design. He fully
knew the strength of the passions and powers which were arrayed
against him, and was perfectly aware that his life was to be short-
ened by violence; yet not a word escapes him implying a doubt of the
ultimate triumphs of his religion. One of the beauties of the Gospels,
and one of the proofs of their genuineness, is found in our Saviour's
indirect and obscure allusions to his approaching sufferings, and to
the glory which was to follow; allusions showing us the workings of
a mind, thoroughly conscious of being appointed to accomplish infinite good through great calamity. This entire and patient relin-
quishment of immediate success, this ever present persuasion, that
he was to perish before his religion would advance, and this calm,
unshaken anticipation of distant and unbounded triumphs, are remarkable traits, throwing a tender and solemn grandeur over our
Lord, and wholly inexplicable by human principles, or by the circumstances in which he was placed.

The views hitherto taken of Christ relate to his public character
and office. If we pass to what may be called his private character, we
shall receive the same impression of inexplicable excellence. The
most striking trait in Jesus was, undoubtedly, benevolence; and, although this virtue had existed before, yet it had not been manifested
in the same form and extent. Christ's benevolence was distinguished
first by its expansiveness. At that age, an unconfined philanthropy,
proposing and toiling to do good without distinction of country or
rank, was unknown. Love to man as man, love comprehending the
hated Samaritan and the despised publican, was a feature which separated Jesus from the best men of his nation and of the world. Another characteristic of the benevolence of Jesus, was its gentleness
and tenderness, forming a strong contrast with the hardness and fe-

rocity of the spirit and manners which then prevailed, and with that sternness and inflexibility, which the purest philosophy of Greece and Rome inculcated as the perfection of virtue. But its most distinguishing trait was its superiority to injury. Revenge was one of the recognised rights of the age in which he lived; and though a few sages, who had seen its inconsistency with man's dignity, had condemned it, yet none had inculcated the duty of regarding one's worst enemies with that kindness which God manifests to sinful men, and of returning curses with blessings and prayers. This form of benevolence, the most disinterested and divine form, was, as you well know, manifested by Jesus Christ in infinite strength, amidst injuries and indignities which cannot be surpassed. Now this singular eminence of goodness, this superiority to the degrading influences of the ages, under which all other men suffered, needs to be explained; and one thing it demonstrates, that Jesus Christ was not an unprincipled deceiver, exposing not only his own life but the lives of confiding friends, in an enterprise next to desperate.

I cannot enlarge on other traits of the character of Christ. I will only observe, that it had one distinction, which more than any thing, forms a perfect character. It was made up of contrasts; in other words, it was a union of excellences which are not easily reconciled, which seem at first sight incongruous, but which, when blended and duly proportioned, constitute moral harmony, and attract, with equal power, love and veneration. For example, we discover in Jesus Christ an unparalleled dignity of character, a consciousness of greatness, never discovered or approached by any other individual in history; and yet this was blended with a condescension, lowliness, and unostentatious simplicity, which had never before been thought consistent with greatness. In like manner, he united an utter superiority to the world, to its pleasures and ordinary interests, with suavity of manners and freedom from austerity. He joined strong feeling and self-possession; an indignant sensibility to sin, and compassion to the sinner; an intense devotion to his work, and calmness under opposition and ill success; a universal philanthropy, and a susceptibility of private attachments; the authority which became the Saviour of the world, and the tenderness and gratitude of a son. Such was the author of our religion. And is his character to be explained by imposture or insane enthusiasm? Does it not bear the unambiguous marks of a heavenly origin?

Perhaps it may be said, this character never existed. Then the invention of it is to be explained, and the reception which this fiction met with; and these perhaps are as difficult of explanation on natural principles, as its real existence. Christ's history bears all the marks of reality; a more frank, simple, unlabored, unostentatious narrative was never penned. Besides, his character, if invented, must have been an invention of singular difficulty, because no models existed on which to frame it. He stands alone in the records of time. The conception of a being, proposing such new and exalted ends, and governed by higher principles than the progress of society had developed, implies singular intellectual power. That several individuals should join in equally vivid conceptions of this character; and should not merely describe in general terms the fictitious being to whom it was attributed, but should introduce him into real life, should place him in a great variety of circumstances, in connexion with various ranks of men, with friends and foes, and should in all preserve his identity, show the same great and singular mind always acting in harmony with itself; this is a supposition hardly credible, and, when the circumstances of the writers of the New Testament are considered, seems to be as inexplicable on human principles, as what I before suggested, the composition of Newton's ''Principia'' by a savage. The character of Christ, though delineated in an age of great moral darkness, has stood the scrutiny of ages; and, in proportion as men's moral sentiments have been refined, its beauty has been more seen and felt. To suppose it invented, is to suppose that its authors, outstripping their age, had attained to a singular delicacy and elevation of moral perception and feeling. But these attainments are not very reconcilable with the character of its authors, supposing it to be a fiction; that is, with the character of habitual liars and impious deceivers.

But we are not only unable to discover powers adequate to this invention. There must have been motives for it; for men do not make great efforts, without strong motives; and, in the whole compass of human incitements, we challenge the infidel to suggest any, which could have prompted to the work now to be explained.

Once more, it must be recollected, that this invention, if it were one, was received as real, at a period so near to the time ascribed to Christ's appearance, that the means of detecting it were infinite. That men should send out such a forgery, and that it should prevail and triumph, are circumstances not easily reconcilable with the principles of our nature.

The character of Christ, then, was real. Its reality is the only explanation of the mighty revolution produced by his religion. And how can you account for it, but by that cause to which he always referred it,—a mission from the Father?

Next to the character of Christ, his religion might be shown to abound in circumstances which contradict and repel the idea of a human origin. For example, its representations of the paternal character of God; its inculcation of a universal charity; the stress which it lays on inward purity; its substitution of a spiritual worship for the forms and ceremonies, which everywhere had usurped the name and extinguished the life of religion; its preference of humility, and of the mild, unostentatious, passive virtues, to the dazzling qualities which had monopolized men's admiration; its consistent and bright discoveries of immortality; its adaptation to the wants of man as a sinner; its adaptation to all the conditions, capacities, and sufferings of human nature; its pure, sublime, yet practicable morality; its high and generous motives; and its fitness to form a character, which plainly prepares for a higher life than the present; these are peculiarities of Christianity, which will strike us more and more, in proportion as we understand distinctly the circumstances of the age and country in which this religion appeared, and for which no adequate human cause has been or can be assigned.

Passing over these topics, each of which might be enlarged into a discourse, I will make but one remark on this religion, which strikes my own mind very forcibly. Since its introduction, human nature has made great progress, and society experienced great changes; and in this advanced condition of the world, Christianity, instead of losing its application and importance, is found to be more and more congenial and adapted to man's nature and wants. Men have outgrown the other institutions of that period when Christianity appeared, its philosophy, its modes of warfare, its policy, its public and private economy; but Christianity has never shrunk as intellect has opened, but has always kept in advance of men's faculties, and unfolded nobler views in proportion as they have ascended. The highest powers and affections, which our nature has developed, find more than adequate objects in this religion. Christianity is indeed peculiarly fitted to the more improved stages of society, to the more delicate sensibilities of refined minds, and especially to that dissatisfaction with the present state, which always grows with the growth of our moral powers and affections. As men advance in civilization, they become susceptible of mental sufferings, to which ruder ages are strangers; and these Christianity is fitted to assuage. Imagination and intellect become more restless; and Christianity brings them tranquillity, by the eternal and magnificent truths, the solemn and unbounded prospects, which it unfolds. This fitness of our religion to more advanced stages of society than that in which it was introduced, to wants of human nature not then developed, seems to me very striking. The religion bears the marks of having come from a being who perfectly understood the human mind, and had power to provide for its progress. This feature of Christianity is of the nature of prophecy. It was an anticipation of future and distant ages; and, when we consider among whom our religion sprung, where, but in God, can we find an explanation of this peculiarity?

I have now offered a few hints on the character of Christ, and on the character of his religion; and, before quitting these topics, I would observe, that they form a strong presumption in favor of the miraculous facts of the Christian history. These miracles were not wrought by a man, whose character, in other respects, was ordinary. They were acts of a being, whose mind was as singular as his works, who spoke and acted with more than human authority, whose moral qualities and sublime purposes were in accordance with superhuman powers. Christ's miracles are in unison with his whole character, and bear a proportion to it, like that which we observe in the most harmonious productions of nature; and in this way they receive from it great confirmation. And the same presumption in their favor arises from his religon. That a religion, carrying in itself such marks of divinity, and so inexplicable on human principles, should receive outward confirmations from Omnipotence, is not surprising. The extraordinary character of the religion accords with and seems to demand extraordinary interpositions in its behalf. Its miracles are not solitary, naked, unexplained, disconnected events, but are bound up with a system, which is worthy of God, and impressed with God; which occupies a large space, and is operating, with great and increasing energy, in human affairs.

As yet I have not touched on what seem to many writers the

strongest proofs of Christianity, I mean the direct evidences of its miracles; by which we mean the testimony borne to them, including the character, conduct, and condition of the witnesses. These I have not time to unfold; nor is this labor needed; for Paley's inestimable work, which is one of your classical books, has stated these proofs with great clearness and power.[5] I would only observe, that they may all be resolved into this single principle, namely, that the Christian miracles were originally believed under such circumstances, that this belief can only be explained by their actual occurrence. That Christianity was received at first on the ground of miracles, and that its first preachers and converts proved the depth and strength of their conviction of these facts, by attesting them in sufferings and in death, we know from the most ancient records which relate to this religion, both Christian and Heathen; and, in fact, this conviction can alone explain their adherence to Christianity. Now, that this conviction could only have sprung from the reality of the miracles, we infer from the known circumstances of these witnesses, whose passions, interests, and strongest prejudices were originally hostile to the new religion; whose motives for examining with care the facts on which it rested, were as urgent and solemn, and whose means and opportunities of ascertaining their truth were as ample and unfailing, as can be conceived to conspire; so that the supposition of their falsehood cannot be admitted, without subverting our trust in human judgment and human testimony under the most favorable circumstances for discovering truth; that is, without introducing universal skepticism.

There is one class of Christian evidences, to which I have but slightly referred, but which has struck with peculiar force men of reflecting minds. I refer to the marks of truth and reality, which are found in the Christian Records; to the internal proofs, which the books of the New Testament carry with them, of having been written by men who lived in the first age of Christianity, who believed and felt its truth, who bore a part in the labors and conflicts which attended its establishment, and who wrote from personal knowledge and deep conviction. A few remarks to illustrate the nature and power of these internal proofs, which are furnished by the books of the New Testament, I will now subjoin.

The New Testament consists of histories and epistles. The his-

torical books, namely, the Gospels and the Acts, are a continued
narrative, embracing many years, and professing to give the history
of the rise and progress of the religion. Now it is worthy of observation, that these writings completely answer their end; that they
completely solve the problem, how this peculiar religion grew up
and established itself in the world; that they furnish precise and adequate causes for this stupendous revolution in human affairs. It is
also worthy of remark, that they relate a series of facts, which are not
only connected with one another, but are intimately linked with the
long series which has followed them, and agree accurately with subsequent history, so as to account for and sustain it. Now, that a collection of fictitious narratives, coming from different hands,
comprehending many years, and spreading over many countries,
should not only form a consistent whole, when taken by themselves;
but should also connect and interweave themselves with real history
so naturally and intimately, as to furnish no clue for detection, as to
exclude the appearance of incongruity and discordance, and as to
give an adequate explanation and the only explanation of acknowledged events, of the most important revolution in society; this is a
supposition from which an intelligent man at once revolts, and
which, if admitted, would shake a principal foundation of history.

I have before spoken of the unity and consistency of Christ's
character as developed in the Gospels, and of the agreement of the
different writers in giving us the singular features of his mind. Now
there are the same marks of truth running through the whole of these
narratives. For example, the effects produced by Jesus on the various classes of society; the different feelings of admiration, attachment, and envy, which he called forth; the various expressions of
these feelings; the prejudices, mistakes, and gradual illumination of
his disciples; these are all given to us with such marks of truth and
reality as could not easily be counterfeited. The whole history is precisely such, as might be expected from the actual appearance of such
a person as Jesus Christ, in such a state of society as then existed.

The Epistles, if possible, abound in marks of truth and reality
even more than the Gospels. They are imbued thoroughly with the
spirit of the first age of Christianity. They bear all the marks of having come from men plunged in the conflicts which the new religion
excited, alive to its interests, identified with its fortunes. They betray the very state of mind which must have been generated by the

peculiar condition of the first propagators of the religion. They are letters written on real business, intended for immediate effects, designed to meet prejudices and passions, which such a religion must at first have awakened. They contain not a trace of the circumstances of a later age, or of the feelings, impressions, and modes of thinking by which later times were characterized, and from which later writers could not easily have escaped. The letters of Paul have a remarkable agreement with his history. They are precisely such as might be expected from a man of a vehement mind, who had been brought up in the schools of Jewish literature, who had been converted by a sudden, overwhelming miracle, who had been intrusted with the preaching of the new religion to the Gentiles, and who was everywhere met by the prejudices and persecuting spirit of his own nation. They are full of obscurities growing out of these points of Paul's history and character, and out of the circumstances of the infant church, and which nothing but an intimate acquaintance with that early period can illustrate. This remarkable infusion of the spirit of the first age into the Christian Records, cannot easily be explained but by the fact, that they were written in that age by the real and zealous propagators of Christianity, and that they are records of real convictions and of actual events.

There is another evidence of Christianity, still more internal than any on which I have yet dwelt, an evidence to be felt rather than described, but not less real because founded on feeling. I refer to that conviction of the divine original of our religion, which springs up and continually gains strength, in those who apply it habitually to their tempers and lives, and who imbibe its spirit and hopes. In such men, there is a consciousness of the adaptation of Christianity to their noblest faculties; a consciousness of its exalting and consoling influences, of its power to confer the true happiness of human nature, to give that peace which the world cannot give; which assures them, that it is not of earthly origin, but a ray from the Everlasting Light, a stream from the Fountain of Heavenly Wisdom and Love. This is the evidence which sustains the faith of thousands, who never read and cannot understand the learned books of Christian apologists, who want, perhaps, words to explain the ground of their belief, but whose faith is of adamantine firmness, who hold the Gospel with a conviction more intimate and unwavering than mere argument ever produced.

But I must tear myself from a subject, which opens upon me continually as I proceed.—Imperfect as this discussion is, the conclusion, I trust, is placed beyond doubt, that Christianity is true. And, my hearers, if true, it is the greatest of all truths, deserving and demanding our reverent attention and fervent gratitude. This religion must never be confounded with our common blessings. It is a revelation of pardon, which, as sinners, we all need. Still more, it is a revelation of human immortality; a doctrine, which, however undervalued amidst the bright anticipations of inexperienced youth, is found to be our strength and consolation, and the only effectual spring of persevering and victorious virtue, when the realities of life have scattered our visionary hopes; when pain, disappointment, and temptation press upon us; when this world's enjoyments are found unable to quench that deep thirst of happiness which burns in every breast; when friends, whom we love as our own souls, die; and our own graves open before us.—To all who hear me, and especially to my young hearers, I would say, let the truth of this religion be the strongest conviction of your understandings; let its motives and precepts sway with an absolute power your characters and lives.

Notes

1. Channing's phrase "the doctrine of one God and Father" refers not only to monotheistic religion as opposed to paganism, but to Unitarianism as opposed to Trinitarianism. In "Unitarian Christianity" he had argued that the doctrine of the trinity was a departure from a belief in the unity of God.

2. Channing refers to David Hume's "Of Miracles" in *Philosophical Essays Concerning Human Understanding* (London, 1748), later titled *An Enquiry Concerning Human Understanding*.

3. Channing refers to George Campbell, *A Dissertation on Miracles* (Edinburgh, 1762).

4. Channing refers to Isaac Newton, *Philosophiae Naturalis Principia Mathematica* (London, 1686).

5. Channing refers to William Paley, *A View of the Evidences of Christianity* (London, 1794).

LIKENESS TO GOD (1828)*

*The original text that follows this introduction is from *The Works of William E. Channing, D.D.*, 6 vols. (Boston: James Munroe, 1841–43), 3:227–55.

To understand the remarkable influence of "Likeness to God" we must remember how controversial, even heretical, the suggestion of a human similarity to God seemed to many in the 1820's. The whole conception of "a kindred nature with God" violated the dogma of original sin which was central to Calvinism and an important part of many of the emerging non-Calvinist evangelical sects. It seemed, further, to compromise the un-approachable purity of a God who was conceived as wholly other from human nature. It is therefore not surprising to find beneath the surface of the text Channing's wary recognition of the controversial ground he was entering. In this context, his appeal for "calm and pure zeal" in pursuing the idea is understandable. It was this direction of Channing's thinking, the stress on the potential divinity of human nature and an immediate access to the divine, which appealed most strongly to the generation of religious radicals who followed Channing, the Transcendentalists. For Perry Miller, who excerpted the sermon for his influential anthology The Transcendentalists *(1950)*, the sermon represented Channing at his most "transcendental." Yet the sermon, though Channing's most influential, may not have been his most representative. It indicated the direction which his most famous disciples would take, but it was less a summary of his theology than a condensation of his abhorrence of the doctrine of original sin. Even here, Channing is careful to stress that this "likeness" to God is potential—it can be as easily destroyed as cultivated. Typically, then, this sermon is as much a program for action—the culture of the potential of the self—as a statement of philosophy.

LIKENESS TO GOD.
DISCOURSE AT THE ORDINATION
OF THE REV. F. A. FARLEY.
PROVIDENCE, R.I. 1828.

Ephesians v. 1: "Be ye therefore followers of God, as
dear children."

To promote true religion is the purpose of the Christian ministry. For this it was ordained. On the present occasion, therefore,
when a new teacher is to be given to the church, a discourse on the
character of true religion will not be inappropriate. I do not mean,
that I shall attempt, in the limits to which I am now confined, to set
before you all its properties, signs, and operations; for in so doing I
should burden your memories with divisions and vague generalities,
as uninteresting as they would be unprofitable. My purpose is, to select one view of the subject, which seems to me of primary dignity
and importance; and I select this, because it is greatly neglected, and
because I attribute to this neglect much of the inefficacy, and many
of the corruptions, of religion.

The text calls us to follow or imitate God, to seek accordance
with or likeness to him, and to do this, not fearfully and faintly, but
with the spirit and hope of beloved children. The doctrine which I
propose to illustrate, is derived immediately from these words, and
is incorporated with the whole New Testament. I affirm, and would
maintain, that true religion consists in proposing, as our great end, a
growing likeness to the Supreme Being. Its noblest influence consists in making us more and more partakers of the Divinity. For this
it is to be preached. Religious instruction should aim chiefly to turn
men's aspirations and efforts to that perfection of the soul, which
constitutes it a bright image of God. Such is the topic now to be discussed; and I implore Him, whose glory I seek, to aid me in unfolding and enforcing it with simplicity and clearness, with a calm and
pure zeal, and with unfeigned charity.

I begin with observing, what all indeed will understand, that the
likeness to God, of which I propose to speak, belongs to man's
higher or spiritual nature. It has its foundation in the original and essential capacities of the mind. In proportion as these are unfolded by
right and vigorous exertion, it is extended and brightened. In pro-

portion as these lie dormant, it is obscured. In proportion as they are perverted and overpowered by the appetites and passions, it is blotted out. In truth, moral evil, if unresisted and habitual, may so blight and lay waste these capacities, that the image of God in man may seem to be wholly destroyed.

The importance of this assimilation to our Creator, is a topic which needs no labored discussion. All men, of whatever name, or sect, or opinion, will meet me on this ground. All, I presume, will allow, that no good in the compass of the universe, or within the gift of omnipotence, can be compared to a resemblance of God, or to a participation of his attributes. I fear no contradiction here. Likeness to God is the supreme gift. He can communicate nothing so precious, glorious, blessed, as himself. To hold intellectual and moral affinity with the Supreme Being, to partake his spirit, to be his children by derivations of kindred excellence, to bear a growing conformity to the perfection which we adore, this is a felicity which obscures and annihilates all other good.

It is only in proportion to this likeness, that we can enjoy either God or the universe. That God can be known and enjoyed only through sympathy or kindred attributes, is a doctrine which even Gentile philosophy discerned. That the pure in heart can alone see and commune with the pure Divinity, was the sublime instruction of ancient sages as well as of inspired prophets. It is indeed the lesson of daily experience. To understand a great and good being, we must have the seeds of the same excellence. How quickly, by what an instinct, do accordant minds recognise one another! No attraction is so powerful as that which subsists between the truly wise and good; whilst the brightest excellence is lost on those who have nothing congenial in their own breasts. God becomes a real being to us, in proportion as his own nature is unfolded within us. To a man who is growing in the likeness of God, faith begins even here to change into vision. He carries within himself a proof of a Deity, which can only be understood by experience. He more than believes, he feels the Divine presence; and gradually rises to an intercourse with his Maker, to which it is not irreverent to apply the name of friendship and intimacy. The Apostle John intended to express this truth, when he tells us, that he, in whom a principle of divine charity or benevolence has become a habit and life, "dwells in God and God in him."[1]

It is plain, too, that likeness to God is the true and only preparation for the enjoyment of the universe. In proportion as we approach and resemble the mind of God, we are brought into harmony with the creation; for, in that proportion, we possess the principles from which the universe sprung; we carry within ourselves the perfections, of which its beauty, magnificence, order, benevolent adaptations, and boundless purposes, are the results and manifestations. God unfolds himself in his works to a kindred mind. It is possible, that the brevity of these hints may expose to the charge of mysticism, what seems to me the calmest and clearest truth. I think, however, that every reflecting man will feel, that likeness to God must be a principle of sympathy or accordance with his creation; for the creation is a birth and shining forth of the Divine Mind, a work through which his spirit breathes. In proportion as we receive this spirit, we possess within ourselves the explanation of what we see. We discern more and more of God in every thing, from the frail flower to the everlasting stars. Even in evil, that dark cloud which hangs over the creation, we discern rays of light and hope, and gradually come to see, in suffering and temptation, proofs and instruments of the sublimest purposes of Wisdom and Love.

I have offered these very imperfect views, that I may show the great importance of the doctrine which I am solicitous to enforce. I would teach, that likeness to God is a good so unutterably surpassing all other good, that whoever admits it as attainable, must acknowledge it to be the chief aim of life. I would show, that the highest and happiest office of religion is, to bring the mind into growing accordance with God; and that by the tendency of religious systems to this end, their truth and worth are to be chiefly tried.

I am aware that it may be said, that the Scriptures, in speaking of man as made in the image of God, and in calling us to imitate him, use bold and figurative language. It may be said, that there is danger from too literal an interpretation; that God is an unapproachable being; that I am not warranted in ascribing to man a like nature to the Divine; that we and all things illustrate the Creator by contrast, not by resemblance; that religion manifests itself chiefly in convictions and acknowledgments of utter worthlessness; and that to talk of the greatness and divinity of the human soul, is to inflate that pride through which Satan fell, and through which man involves himself in that fallen spirit's ruin.

I answer, that, to me, Scripture and reason hold a different language. In Christianity particularly, I meet perpetual testimonies to the divinity of human nature. This whole religion expresses an infinite concern of God for the human soul, and teaches that he deems no methods too expensive for its recovery and exaltation. Christianity, with one voice, calls me to turn my regards and care to the spirit within me, as of more worth than the whole outward world. It calls us to "be perfect as our Father in heaven is perfect;"[2] and everywhere, in the sublimity of its precepts, it implies and recognises the sublime capacities of the being to whom they are addressed. It assures us that human virtue is "in the sight of God of great price,"[3] and speaks of the return of a human being to virtue as an event which increases the joy of heaven. In the New Testament, Jesus Christ, the Son of God, the brightness of his glory, the express and unsullied image of the Divinity, is seen mingling with men as a friend and brother, offering himself as their example, and promising to his true followers a share in all his splendors and joys. In the New Testament, God is said to communicate his own spirit, and all his fulness to the human soul. In the New Testament man is exhorted to aspire after "honor, glory, and immortality";[4] and Heaven, a word expressing the nearest approach to God, and a divine happiness, is everywhere proposed as the end of his being. In truth, the very essence of Christian faith is, that we trust in God's mercy, as revealed in Jesus Christ, for a state of celestial purity, in which we shall grow for ever in the likeness, and knowledge, and enjoyment of the Infinite Father. Lofty views of the nature of man are bound up and interwoven with the whole Christian system. Say not, that these are at war with humility; for who was ever humbler than Jesus, and yet who ever possessed such a consciousness of greatness and divinity? Say not that man's business is to think of his sin, and not of his dignity; for great sin implies a great capacity; it is the abuse of a noble nature; and no man can be deeply and rationally contrite, but he who feels, that in wrong-doing he has resisted a divine voice, and warred against a divine principle, in his own soul.—I need not, I trust, pursue the argument from revelation. There is an argument from nature and reason, which seems to me so convincing, and is at the same time so fitted to explain what I mean by man's possession of a like nature to God, that I shall pass at once to its exposition.

That man has a kindred nature with God, and may bear most important and ennobling relations to him, seems to me to be established by a striking proof. This proof you will understand, by considering, for a moment, how we obtain our ideas of God. Whence come the conceptions which we include under that august name? Whence do we derive our knowledge of the attributes and perfections which constitute the Supreme Being? I answer, we derive them from our own souls. The divine attributes are first developed in ourselves, and thence transferred to our Creator. The idea of God, sublime and awful as it is, is the idea of our own spiritual nature, purified and enlarged to infinity. In ourselves are the elements of the Divinity. God, then, does not sustain a figurative resemblance to man. It is the resemblance of a parent to a child, the likeness of a kindred nature.

We call God a Mind. He has revealed himself as a Spirit. But what do we know of mind, but through the unfolding of this principle in our own breasts? That unbounded spiritual energy which we call God, is conceived by us only through consciousness, through the knowledge of ourselves.—We ascribe thought or intelligence to the Deity, as one of his most glorious attributes. And what means this language? These terms we have framed to express operations or faculties of our own souls. The Infinite Light would be for ever hidden from us, did not kindred rays dawn and brighten within us. God is another name for human intelligence raised above all error and imperfection, and extended to all possible truth.

The same is true of God's goodness. How do we understand this, but by the principle of love implanted in the human breast? Whence is it, that this divine attribute is so faintly comprehended, but from the feeble developement of it in the multitude of men? Who can understand the strength, purity, fulness, and extent of divine philanthropy; but he in whom selfishness has been swallowed up in love?

The same is true of all the moral perfections of the Deity. These are comprehended by us, only through our own moral nature. It is conscience within us, which, by its approving and condemning voice, interprets to us God's love of virtue and hatred of sin; and without conscience, these glorious conceptions would never have opened on the mind. It is the lawgiver in our own breasts, which gives us the idea of divine authority, and binds us to obey it. The soul, by its sense of right, or its perception of moral distinctions, is clothed with sovereignty over itself, and through this alone, it understands and recognises the Sovereign of the Universe. Men, as by a natural inspiration, have agreed to speak of conscience as the voice of God, as the Divinity within us. This principle, reverently obeyed, makes us more and more partakers of the moral perfection of the Supreme Being, of that very excellence, which constitutes the rightfulness of his sceptre, and enthrones him over the universe. Without this inward law, we should be as incapable of receiving a law from Heaven, as the brute. Without this, the thunders of Sinai might startle the outward ear, but would have no meaning, no authority to the mind. I have expressed here a great truth. Nothing teaches so encouragingly our relation and resemblance to God; for the glory of the Supreme Being is eminently moral. We blind ourselves to his chief splendor, if we think only or mainly of his power, and overlook those attributes of rectitude and goodness, to which he subjects his omnipotence, and which are the foundations and very substance of his universal and immutable Law. And are these attributes revealed to us through the principles and convictions of our own souls? Do we understand through sympathy God's perception of the right, the good, the holy, the just? Then with what propriety is it said, that in his own image he made man!

I am aware, that it may be objected to these views, that we receive our idea of God from the universe, from his works, and not so exclusively from our own souls. The universe, I know, is full of God. The heavens and earth declare his glory. In other words, the effects and signs of power, wisdom, and goodness, are apparent through the whole creation. But apparent to what? Not to the outward eye; not to the acutest organs of sense; but to a kindred mind, which interprets the universe by itself. It is only through that energy of thought, by which we adapt various and complicated means to distant ends, and give harmony and a common bearing to multiplied exertions, that we understand the creative intelligence which has established the order, dependencies, and harmony of nature. We see God around us, because he dwells within us. It is by a kindred wisdom, that we discern his wisdom in his works. The brute, with an eye as piercing as ours, looks on the universe; and the page, which to us is radiant with characters of greatness and goodness, is to him a blank. In truth, the beauty and glory of God's works, are revealed to the mind by a light beaming from itself. We discern the impress of God's attributes in the universe, by accordance of nature, and enjoy them through sympathy.—I hardly need observe, that these remarks in relation to the universe apply with equal, if not greater force, to revelation.

I shall now be met by another objection, which to many may seem strong. It will be said, that these various attributes of which I have spoken, exist in God in Infinite Perfection, and that this destroys all affinity between the human and the Divine mind. To this I have two replies. In the first place, an attribute, by becoming perfect, does not part with its essence. Love, wisdom, power, and purity do not change their nature by enlargement. If they did, we should lose the Supreme Being through his very infinity. Our ideas of him would fade away into mere sounds. For example, if wisdom in God, because unbounded, have no affinity with that attribute in man, why apply to him that term? It must signify nothing. Let me ask what we mean, when we say that we discern the marks of intelligence in the universe? We mean, that we meet there the proofs of a mind like our own. We certainly discern proofs of no other; so that to deny this doctrine would be to deny the evidences of a God, and utterly to subvert the foundations of religious belief. What man can examine the structure of a plant or an animal, and see the adaptation of its parts to each other and to common ends, and not feel, that it is the work of an intelligence akin to his own, and that he traces these marks of design by the same spiritual energy in which they had their origin?

But I would offer another answer to this objection, that God's infinity places him beyond the resemblance and approach of man. I affirm, and trust that I do not speak too strongly, that there are traces of infinity in the human mind; and that, in this very respect, it bears a likeness to God. The very conception of infinity, is the mark of a nature to which no limit can be prescribed. This thought, indeed, comes to us, not so much from abroad, as from our own souls. We ascribe this attribute to God, because we possess capacities and wants, which only an unbounded being can fill, and because we are conscious of a tendency in spiritual faculties to unlimited expansion. We believe in the Divine infinity, through something congenial with it in our own breasts. I hope I speak clearly, and if not, I would ask those to whom I am obscure, to pause before they condemn. To me it seems, that the soul, in all its higher actions, in original thought, in the creations of genius, in the soarings of imagination, in its love of beauty and grandeur, in its aspirations after a pure and unknown joy, and especially in disinterestedness, in the spirit of self-sacrifice, and in enlightened devotion, has a character of infinity.[5] There is often a depth in human love, which may be strictly called unfathomable. There is sometimes a lofty strength in moral principle, which all the power of the outward universe cannot overcome. There seems a might within, which can more than balance all might without. There is, too, a piety, which swells into a transport too vast for utterance, and into an immeasurable joy. I am speaking, indeed, of what is uncommon, but still of realities. We see, however, the tendency of the soul to the infinite, in more familiar and ordinary forms. Take, for example, the delight which we find in the vast scenes of nature, in prospects which spread around us without limits, in the immensity of the heavens and the ocean, and especially in the rush and roar of mighty winds, waves, and torrents, when, amidst our deep awe, a power within seems to respond to the omnipotence around us. The same principle is seen in the delight ministered to us by works of fiction or of imaginative art, in which our own nature is set before us in more than human beauty and power. In truth, the soul is always bursting its limits. It thirsts continually for wider knowledge. It rushes forward to untried happiness. It has deep wants, which nothing limited can appease. Its true element and end is an unbounded good. Thus, God's infinity has its image in the soul; and through the soul, much more than through the universe, we arrive at this conception of the Deity.

In these remarks I have spoken strongly. But I have no fear of expressing too strongly the connexion between the Divine and the human mind. My only fear is, that I shall dishonor the great subject. The danger to which we are most exposed, is that of severing the Creator from his creatures. The propensity of human sovereigns to cut off communication between themselves and their subjects, and to disclaim a common nature with their inferiors, has led the multitude of men, who think of God chiefly under the character of a king, to conceive of him as a being who places his glory in multiplying distinctions between himself and all other beings. The truth is, that the union between the Creator and the creature surpasses all other bonds in strength and intimacy. He penetrates all things, and delights to irradiate all with his glory. Nature, in all its lowest and inanimate forms, is pervaded by his power; and, when quickened by the mysterious property of life, how wonderfully does it show forth the perfections of its Author! How much of God may be seen in the structure of a single leaf, which, though so frail as to tremble in every wind, yet holds connexions and living communications with the earth, the air, the clouds, and the distant sun, and, through these sympathies with the universe, is itself a revelation of an omnipotent mind! God delights to diffuse himself everywhere. Through his energy, unconscious matter clothes itself with proportions, powers, and beauties, which reflect his wisdom and love. How much more must he delight to frame conscious and happy recipients of his perfections, in whom his wisdom and love may substantially dwell, with whom he may form spiritual ties, and to whom he may be an everlasting spring of moral energy and happiness! How far the Supreme Being may communicate his attributes to his intelligent offspring, I stop not to inquire. But that his almighty goodness will impart to them powers and glories, of which the material universe is but a faint emblem, I cannot doubt. That the soul, if true to itself and its Maker, will be filled with God, and will manifest him, more than the sun, I cannot doubt. Who can doubt it, that believes and understands the doctrine of human immortality?

The views which I have given in this discourse, respecting man's participation of the Divine nature, seem to me to receive strong confirmation, from the title or relation most frequently applied to God in the New Testament; and I have reserved this as the last corroboration of this doctrine, because, to my own mind, it is singularly affecting. In the New Testament God is made known to us as a Father; and a brighter feature of that book cannot be named. Our worship is to be directed to him as our Father. Our whole religion is to take its character from this view of the Divinity. In this he is to rise always to our minds. And what is it to be a Father? It is to communicate one's own nature, to give life to kindred beings; and the highest function of a Father is to educate the mind of the child, and to impart to it what is noblest and happiest in his own mind. God is our Father, not merely because he created us, or because he gives us enjoyment; for he created the flower and the insect, yet we call him not their Father. This bond is a spiritual one. This name belongs to God, because he frames spirits like himself, and delights to give them what is most glorious and blessed in his own nature. Accordingly, Christianity is said, with special propriety, to reveal God as the Father, because it reveals him as sending his Son to cleanse the mind from every stain, and to replenish it for ever with the spirit and moral attributes of its Author. Separate from God this idea of his creating and training up beings after his own likeness, and you rob him of the paternal character. This relation vanishes, and with it vanishes the glory of the Gospel, and the dearest hopes of the human soul.

The greatest use which I would make of the principles laid down in this discourse, is to derive from them just and clear views of the nature of religion. What, then, is religion? I answer; it is not the adoration of a God with whom we have no common properties; of a distinct, foreign, separate being; but of an all-communicating Parent. It recognises and adores God, as a being whom we know through our own souls, who has made man in his own image, who is the perfection of our own spiritual nature, who has sympathies with us as kindred beings, who is near us, not in place only like this all-surrounding atmosphere, but by spiritual influence and love, who looks on us with parental interest, and whose great design it is to communicate to us for ever, and in freer and fuller streams, his own power, goodness, and joy. The conviction of this near and ennobling relation of God to the soul, and of his great purposes towards it, belongs to the very essence of true religion; and true religion manifests itself chiefly and most conspicuously in desires, hopes, and efforts corresponding to this truth. It desires and seeks supremely the assimilation of the mind to God, or the perpetual unfolding and enlargement of those powers and virtues by which it is constituted his glorious image. The mind, in proportion as it is enlightened and penetrated by true religion, thirsts and labors for a godlike elevation. What else, indeed, can it seek, if this good be placed within its reach? If I am capable of receiving and reflecting the intellectual and moral glory of my Creator, what else in comparison shall I desire? Shall I deem a property in the outward universe as the highest good, when I may become partaker of the very mind from which it springs, of the prompting love, the disposing wisdom, the quickening power, through which its order, beauty, and beneficent influences subsist?

True religion is known by these high aspirations, hopes, and efforts. And this is the religion which most truly honors God. To honor him, is not to tremble before him as an unapproachable sovereign, not to utter barren praise which leaves us as it found us. It is to become what we praise. It is to approach God as an inexhaustible Fountain of light, power, and purity. It is to feel the quickening and transforming energy of his perfections. It is to thirst for the growth and invigoration of the divine principle within us. It is to seek the very spirit of God. It is to trust in, to bless, to thank him for that rich grace, mercy, love, which was revealed and proffered by Jesus Christ, and which proposes as its great end the perfection of the human soul.

I regard this view of religion as infinitely important. It does more than all things to make our connexion with our Creator ennobling and happy; and, in proportion as we want it, there is danger that the thought of God may itself become the instrument of our degradation. That religion has been so dispensed as to depress the human mind, I need not tell you; and it is a truth which ought to be known, that the greatness of the Deity, when separated in our thoughts from his parental character, especially tends to crush human energy and hope. To a frail, dependent creature, an omnipotent Creator easily becomes a terror, and his worship easily degenerates into servility, flattery, self-contempt, and selfish calculation. Religion only ennobles us, in as far as it reveals to us the tender and intimate connexion of God with his creatures, and teaches us to see in the very greatness which might give alarm, the source of great and glorious communications to the human soul. You cannot, my hearers, think too highly of the majesty of God. But let not this majesty sever him from you. Remember, that his greatness is the infinity of attributes which yourselves possess. Adore his infinite wisdom; but remember that this wisdom rejoices to diffuse itself, and let an exhilarating hope spring up, at the thought of the immeasurable intelligence which such a Father must communicate to his children. In like manner adore his power. Let the boundless creation fill you with awe and admiration of the energy which sustains it. But remember that God has a nobler work than the outward creation, even the spirit within yourselves; and that it is his purpose to replenish this with his own energy, and to crown it with growing power and triumphs over the material universe. Above all, adore his unutterable goodness.

But remember, that this attribute is particularly proposed to you as your model; that God calls you, both by nature and revelation, to a fellowship in his philanthropy; that he has placed you in social relations, for the very end of rendering you ministers and representatives of his benevolence; that he even summons you to espouse and to advance the sublimest purpose of his goodness, the redemption of the human race, by extending the knowledge and power of Christian truth. It is through such views, that religion raises up the soul, and binds man by ennobling bonds to his Maker.

To complete my views of this topic, I beg to add an important caution. I have said that the great work of religion is, to conform ourselves to God, or to unfold the divine likeness within us. Let none infer from this language, that I place religion in unnatural effort, in straining after excitements which do not belong to the present state, or in any thing separate from the clear and simple duties of life. I exhort you to no extravagance. I reverence human nature too much to do it violence. I see too much divinity in its ordinary operations, to urge on it a forced and vehement virtue. To grow in the likeness of God, we need not cease to be men. This likeness does not consist in extraordinary or miraculous gifts, in supernatural additions to the soul, or in any thing foreign to our original constitution; but in our essential faculties, unfolded by vigorous and conscientious exertion in the ordinary circumstances assigned by God. To resemble our Creator, we need not fly from society, and entrance ourselves in lonely contemplation and prayer. Such processes might give a feverish strength to one class of emotions, but would result in disproportion, distortion, and sickliness of mind. Our proper work is to approach God by the free and natural unfolding of our highest powers, of understanding, conscience, love, and the moral will.[6]

Shall I be told that, by such language, I ascribe to nature the effects which can only be wrought in the soul by the Holy Spirit? I anticipate this objection, and wish to meet it by a simple exposition of my views. I would on no account disparage the gracious aids and influences which God imparts to the human soul. The promise of the Holy Spirit is among the most precious in the Sacred Volume. Worlds could not tempt me to part with the doctrine of God's intimate connexion with the mind, and of his free and full communications to it. But these views are in no respect at variance with what I have taught, of the method by which we are to grow in the likeness of God. Scripture and experience concur in teaching, that, by the Holy Spirit, we are to understand a divine assistance adapted to our moral freedom, and accordant with the fundamental truth, that virtue is the mind's own. work. By the Holy Spirit, I understand an aid, which must be gained and made effectual by our own activity; an aid, which no more interferes with our faculties, than the assistance which we receive from our fellow-beings; an aid, which silently mingles and conspires with all other helps and means of goodness; an aid, by which we unfold our natural powers in a natural order, and by which we are strengthened to understand and apply the resources derived from our munificent Creator. This aid we cannot prize too much, or pray for too earnestly. But wherein, let me ask, does it war with the doctrine, that God is to be approached by the exercise and unfolding of our highest powers and affections, in the ordinary circumstances of human life?

I repeat it, to resemble our Maker we need not quarrel with our nature or our lot. Our present state, made up, as it is, of aids and trials, is worthy of God, and may be used throughout to assimilate us to him. For example, our domestic ties, the relations of neighbourhood and country, the daily interchanges of thoughts and feelings, the daily occasions of kindness, the daily claims of want and suffering, these and the other circumstances of our social state, form the best sphere and school for that benevolence, which is God's brightest attribute; and we should make a sad exhange, by substituting for these natural aids, any self-invented artificial means of sanctity. Christianity, our great guide to God, never leads us away from the path of nature, and never wars with the unsophisticated dictates of conscience. We approach our Creator by every right exertion of the powers he gives us. Whenever we invigorate the understanding by honestly and resolutely seeking truth, and by withstanding whatever might warp the judgment; whenever we invigorate the conscience by following it in opposition to the passions; whenever we receive a blessing gratefully, bear a trial patiently, or encounter peril or scorn with moral courage; whenever we perform a disinterested deed; whenever we lift up the heart in true adoration to God; whenever we war against a habit or desire which is strengthening itself against our higher principles; whenever we think, speak, or act, with moral energy, and resolute devotion to duty, be the occasion ever so humble, obscure, familiar; then the divinity is growing within us, and we are ascending towards our Author. True religion thus blends itself with common life. We are thus to draw nigh to God, without forsaking men. We are thus, without parting with our human nature, to clothe ourselves with the divine.

My views on the great subject of this discourse have now been given. I shall close with a brief consideration of a few objections, in the course of which I shall offer some views of the Christian ministry, which this occasion and the state of the world, seem to me to demand.—I anticipate from some an objection to this discourse, drawn as they will say from experience. I may be told, that, I have talked of the godlike capacities of human nature, and have spoken of man as a divinity; and where, it will be asked, are the warrants of this high estimate of our race? I may be told that I dream, and that I have peopled the world with the creatures of my lonely imagination. What! Is it only in dreams, that beauty and loveliness have beamed on me from the human countenance, that I have heard tones of kindness, which have thrilled through my heart, that I have found sympathy in suffering, and a sacred joy in friendship? Are all the great and good men of past ages only dreams? Are such names as Moses, Socrates, Paul, Alfred, Milton, only the fictions of my disturbed slumbers? Are the great deeds of history, the discoveries of philosophy, the creations of genius, only visions? O! no. I do not dream when I speak of the divine capacities of human nature. It is a real page in which I read of patriots and martyrs, of Fenelon and Howard, of Hampden and Washington.[7] And tell me not that these were prodigies, miracles, immeasurably separated from their race; for the very reverence, which has treasured up and hallowed their memories, the very sentiments of admiration and love with which their names are now heard, show that the principles of their greatness are diffused through all your breasts. The germs of sublime virtue are scattered liberally on our earth. How often have I seen in the obscurity of domestic life, a strength of love, of endurance, of pious trust, of virtuous resolution, which in a public sphere would have attracted public homage. I cannot but pity the man, who recognises nothing godlike in his own nature. I see the marks of God in the heavens and the earth, but how much more in a liberal intellect, in magnanimity, in unconquerable rectitude, in a philanthropy which forgives every wrong, and which never despairs of the cause of Christ and human virtue. I do and I must reverence human nature. Neither the sneers of a worldly skepticism, nor the groans of a gloomy theology, disturb my faith in its godlike powers and tendencies. I know how it is despised, how it has been oppressed, how civil and religious establishments have for ages conspired to crush it. I know its history. I shut my eyes on none of its weaknesses and crimes. I understand the proofs, by which despotism demonstrates, that man is a wild beast, in want of a master, and only safe in chains. But, injured, trampled on, and scorned as our nature is, I still turn to it with intense sympathy and strong hope. The signatures of its origin and its end are impressed too deeply to be ever wholly effaced. I bless it for its kind affections, for its strong and tender love. I honor it for its struggles against oppression, for its growth and progress under the weight of so many chains and prejudices, for its achievements in science and art, and still more for its examples of heroic and saintly virtue. These are marks of a divine origin and the pledges of a celestial inheritance; and I thank God that my own lot is bound up with that of the human race.

But another objection starts up. It may be said, "Allow these views to be true; are they fitted for the pulpit? fitted to act on common minds? They may be prized by men of cultivated intellect and taste; but can the multitude understand them? Will the multitude feel them? On whom has a minister to act? On men immersed in business, and buried in the flesh; on men, whose whole power of thought has been spent on pleasure or gain; on men chained by habit and wedded to sin. Sooner may adamant be riven by a child's touch, than the human heart be pierced by refined and elevated sentiment. Gross instruments will alone act on gross minds. Men sleep, and nothing but thunder, nothing but flashes from the everlasting fire of hell, will thoroughly wake them."

I have all along felt that such objections would be made to the views I have urged. But they do not move me. I answer, that I think these views singularly adapted to the pulpit, and I think them full of power. The objection is that they are refined. But I see God accomplishing his noblest purposes by what may be called refined means. All the great agents of nature, attraction, heat, and the principle of life, are refined, spiritual, invisible, acting gently, silently, imperceptibly; and yet brute matter feels their power, and is transformed by them into surpassing beauty. The electric fluid, unseen, unfelt, and everywhere diffused, is infinitely more efficient, and ministers to infinitely nobler productions, than when it breaks forth in thunder. Much less can I believe, that in the moral world, noise, menace, and violent appeals to gross passions, to fear and selfishness, are God's chosen means of calling forth spiritual life, beauty, and greatness. It is seldom that human nature throws off all susceptibility of grateful and generous impressions, all sympathy with superior virtue; and here are springs and principles to which a generous teaching, if simple, sincere, and fresh from the soul, may confidently appeal.

It is said, men cannot understand the views which seem to me so precious. This objection I am anxious to repel, for the common intellect has been grievously kept down and wronged through the belief of its incapacity. The pulpit would do more good, were not the mass of men looked upon and treated as children. Happily for the race, the time is passing away, in which intellect was thought the monopoly of a few, and the majority were given over to hopeless ignorance. Science is leaving her solitudes to enlighten the multitude. How much more may religious teachers take courage to speak to men on subjects, which are nearer to them than the properties and laws of matter, I mean their own souls. The multitude, you say, want capacity to receive great truths relating to their spiritual nature. But what, let me ask you, is the Christian religion? A spiritual system, intended to turn men's minds upon themselves, to frame them to watchfulness over thought, imagination, and passion, to establish them in an intimacy with their own souls. What are all the Christian virtues, which men are exhorted to love and seek? I answer, pure and high motions or determinations of the mind. That refinement of thought, which, I am told, transcends the common intellect, belongs to the very essence of Christianity. In confirmation of these views, the human mind seems to me to be turning itself more and more inward, and to be growing more alive to its own worth, and its capacities of progress. The spirit of education shows this, and so does the spirit of freedom. There is a spreading conviction that man was made for a higher purpose than to be a beast of burden, or a creature of sense. The divinity is stirring within the human breast, and demanding a culture and a liberty worthy of the child of God. Let religious teaching correspond to this advancement of the mind. Let it rise above the technical, obscure, and frigid theology which has come down to us from times of ignorance, superstition, and slavery.

Let it penetrate the human soul, and reveal it to itself. No preaching, I believe, is so intelligible, as that which is true to human nature, and helps men to read their own spirits.

But the objection which I have stated not only represents men as incapable of understanding, but still more of being moved, quickened, sanctified, and saved, by such views as I have given. If by this objection nothing more is meant, than that these views are not alone or of themselves sufficient, I shall not dispute it; for true and glorious as they are, they do not constitute the whole truth, and I do not expect great moral effects from narrow and partial views of our nature. I have spoken of the godlike capacities of the soul. But other and very different elements enter into the human being. Man has animal propensities as well as intellectual and moral powers. He has a body as well as mind. He has passions to war with reason, and self-love with conscience. He is a free being, and a tempted being, and thus constituted he may and does sin, and often sins grievously. To such a being, religion, or virtue, is a conflict, requiring great spiritual effort, put forth in habitual watchfulness and prayer; and all the motives are needed, by which force and constancy may be communicated to the will. I exhort not the preacher, to talk perpetually of man as "made but a little lower than the angels."[8] I would not narrow him to any class of topics. Let him adapt himself to our whole and various nature. Let him summon to his aid all the powers of this world, and the world to come. Let him bring to bear on the conscience and the heart, God's milder and more awful attributes, the promises and threatenings of the divine word, the lessons of history, the warnings of experience. Let the wages of sin here and hereafter be taught clearly and earnestly. But amidst the various motives to spiritual effort, which belong to the minister, none are more quickening than those drawn from the soul itself, and from God's desire and purpose to exalt it, by every aid consistent with its freedom. These views I conceive are to mix with all others, and without them all others fail to promote a generous virtue. Is it said, that the minister's proper work is, to preach Christ, and not the dignity of human nature? I answer, that Christ's greatness is manifested in the greatness of the nature which he was sent to redeem; and that his chief glory consists in this, that he came to restore God's image where it was obscured or effaced, and to give an everlasting impulse and life to what is divine within us. Is it said, that the malignity of sin is to be the minister's great theme? I answer, that this malignity can only be understood and felt, when sin is viewed as the ruin of God's noblest work, as darkening a light brighter than the sun, as carrying discord, bondage, disease, and death into a mind framed for perpetual progress towards its Author. Is it said, that terror is the chief instrument of saving the soul? I answer, that if by terror, be meant a rational and moral fear, a conviction and dread of the unutterable evil incurred by a mind which wrongs, betrays, and destroys itself, then I am the last to deny its importance. But a fear like this, which regards the debasement of the soul as the greatest of evils, is plainly founded upon and proportioned to our conceptions of the greatness of our nature. The more common terror, excited by vivid images of torture and bodily pain, is a very questionable means of virtue. When strongly awakened, it generally injures the character, breaks men into cowards and slaves, brings the intellect to cringe before human authority, makes man abject before his Maker, and, by a natural reaction of the mind, often terminates in a presumptuous confidence, altogether distinct from virtuous self-respect, and singularly hostile to the unassuming, charitable spirit of Christianity. The preacher should rather strive to fortify the soul against physical pains, than to bow it to their mastery, teaching it to dread nothing in comparison with sin, and to dread sin as the ruin of a noble nature.

Men, I repeat it, are to be quickened and raised by appeals to their highest principles. Even the convicts of a prison may be touched by kindness, generosity, and especially by a tone, look, and address, expressing hope and respect for their nature. I know, that the doctrine of ages has been, that terror, restraint, and bondage are the chief safeguards of human virtue and peace. But we have begun to learn, that affection, confidence, respect, and freedom are mightier as well as nobler agents. Men can be wrought upon by generous influences. I would that this truth were better understood by religious teachers. From the pulpit, generous influences too seldom proceed. In the church, men too seldom hear a voice to quicken and exalt them. Religion, speaking through her public organs, seems often to forget her natural tone of elevation. The character of God, the principles of his government, his relations to the human family, the purposes for which he brought us into being, the nature which he has given us, and the condition in which he has placed us, these and the like topics, though the sublimest which can enter the mind, are not unfrequently so set forth as to narrow and degrade the hearers, disheartening and oppressing with gloom the timid and sensitive, and infecting coarser minds with the unhallowed spirit of intolerance, presumption, and exclusive pretension to the favor of God. I know, and rejoice to know, that preaching in its worst forms does good; for so bright and piercing is the light of Christianity, that it penetrates in a measure the thickest clouds in which men contrive to involve it. But that evil mixes with the good, I also know; and I should be unfaithful to my deep convictions, did I not say, that human nature requires for its elevation, more generous treatment from the teachers of religion.

I conclude with saying, let the minister cherish a reverence for his own nature. Let him never despise it even in its most forbidding forms. Let him delight in its beautiful and lofty manifestations. Let him hold fast as one of the great qualifications for his office, a faith in the greatness of the human soul, that faith, which looks beneath the perishing body, beneath the sweat of the laborer, beneath the rags and ignorance of the poor, beneath the vices of the sensual and selfish, and discerns in the depths of the soul a divine principle, a ray of the Infinite Light, which may yet break forth and "shine as the sun"9 in the kingdom of God. Let him strive to awaken in men a consciousness of the heavenly treasure within them, a consciousness of possessing what is more worth than the outward universe. Let hope give life to all his labors. Let him speak to men, as to beings liberally gifted, and made for God. Let him always look round on a congregation with the encouraging trust, that he has hearers prepared to respond to the simple, unaffected utterance of great truths, and to the noblest workings of his own mind. Let him feel deeply for those, in whom the divine nature is overwhelmed by the passions. Let him sympathize tenderly with those, in whom it begins to struggle, to mourn for sin, to thirst for a new life. Let him guide and animate to higher and diviner virtue, those in whom it has gained strength. Let him strive to infuse courage, enterprise, devout trust, and an inflexible will, into men's labors for their own perfection. In one word, let him cherish an unfaltering and growing faith in God as the Father and quickener of the human mind, and in Christ as its triumphant and immortal friend. That by such preaching he is to work miracles, I do not say. That he will rival in sudden and outward effects what is wrought by the preachers of a low and terrifying theology, I do not expect or desire. That all will be made better, I am far from believing. His office is, to act on free beings, who, after all, must determine themselves; who have power to withstand all foreign agency; who are to be saved, not by mere preaching, but by their own prayers and toil. Still I believe that such a minister will be a benefactor beyond all praise to the human soul. I believe, and know, that, on those who will admit his influence, he will work deeply, powerfully, gloriously. His function is the sublimest under heaven; and his reward will be, a growing power of spreading truth, virtue, moral strength, love, and happiness, without limit and without end.

Notes

1. John 6:56—"He that eateth my flesh, and drinketh my blood, dwelleth in me, and I in him."

2. Matthew 5:48—"Be ye therefore perfect, even as your Father which is in heaven is perfect."

3. I Peter 3:4—"But *let it be* the hidden man of the heart, in that which is not corruptible, *even the ornament* of a meek and quiet spirit, which is in the sight of God of great price."

4. Romans 2:7—"To them who by patient continuance in well doing seek for glory and honour and immortality, eternal life."

5. Channing's stress on "disinterestedness" as a sign of divinity has its roots in his reading of Francis Hutcheson. See the discussion in the introduction to this volume.

6. Channing's opposition to extreme emotion as a manifestation of religion is characteristic of the general liberal opposition to evangelical emotionalism in revivals, beginning with Charles Chauncy's critique of the Great Awakening in the 1740's.

7. Channing refers to François de Salignac de la Mothe Fenelon (1651–1715), a religious philosopher and Archbishop of Cambrai, and the subject of an essay by Channing; John Howard (1726–1790), an English prison reformer; John Hampden (c. 1595–1643), a leader of the English revolution; and George Washington (1732–1799), the first president of the United States.

8. Psalms 8:5—"For thou hast made him a little lower than the angels, and hast crowned him with glory and honour."

9. Matthew 13:43—"Then shall the righteous shine forth as the sun in the Kingdom of their Father. Who hath ears to hear, let him hear."

REMARKS ON NATIONAL LITERATURE
(1830)*

*The original text that follows this introduction is from *The Works of William E. Channing, D. D.*, 6 vols. (Boston: James Munroe, 1841–43), 1:243–80.

America's political independence preceded its cultural independence, and the sense of the young nation's intellectual subservience to Europe, and especially to England, hung oppressively over American intellectuals of the early nineteenth century. Not only was there resentment of the sneering deprecation of American literature among English critics, but worse, a suspicion that the English critics were right. Channing's essay on "National Literature," published in the Christian Examiner *in 1830, was one of the most important early articulations of this crisis in the nation's intellect, notable both for its frank condemnation of America's lack and its confident appeal for change. With this essay, and several which had preceded it, notably the essay on Milton, Channing had begun to contribute to the momentum for change. He was an important precursor to the "American Renaissance" of the 1840's and 1850's. Even though Channing himself had his share of abuse from English critics, he was generally accorded a place with James Fenimore Cooper and Washington Irving as one of the three most important American authors, and his essays were extensively reviewed abroad. Robert E. Spiller commented in 1930 that Channing's "historical position in American literary history" was "underestimated" and the last half-century does not seem to have altered that situation.*[1] *Channing's misfortune, at least for his modern literary reputation, was that he worked in the medium of the genial, wide-ranging essay, a form which with a few exceptions has lacked historical longevity. Nevertheless, it spoke to his own age, and especially to his countrymen who aspired to a richer literary culture for the nation.*

1. Robert E. Spiller, "A Case for W. E. Channing," *New England Quarterly* 3 (January 1930): 55–81.

REMARKS ON
NATIONAL LITERATURE.

Review of a Discourse concerning the Influence of America on the Mind; being the Annual Oration delivered before the American Philosophical Society, at the University in Philadelphia, October 18, 1823. By C. J. Ingersoll.

We shall use the work prefixed to this article, as ministers are sometimes said to use their texts. We shall make it a point to start from, not the subject of our remarks. Our purpose is to treat of the importance and means of a National Literature. The topic seems to us a great one, and to have intimate connexions with morals and religion, as well as with all our public interests. Our views will be given with great freedom, and, if they serve no other purpose than to recommend the subject to more general attention, one of our principal objects will be accomplished.

We begin with stating what we mean by national literature. We mean the expression of a nation's mind in writing. We mean the production among a people of important works in philosophy, and in the departments of imagination and taste. We mean the contributions of new truths to the stock of human knowledge. We mean the thoughts of profound and original minds, elaborated by the toil of composition, and fixed and made immortal in books. We mean the manifestation of a nation's intellect in the only forms by which it can multiply itself at home, and send itself abroad. We mean that a nation shall take a place, by its authors, among the lights of the world. It will be seen, that we include under literature all the writings of superior minds, be the subjects what they may. We are aware that the term is often confined to compositions which relate to human nature, and human life; that it is not generally extended to physical science; that mind, not matter, is regarded as its main subject and sphere. But the worlds of matter and mind are too intimately connected to admit of exact partition. All the objects of human thought flow into one another. Moral and physical truths have many bonds and analogies, and, whilst the former are the chosen and noblest themes of literature, we are not anxious to divorce them from the latter, or to shut them up in a separate department. The expression of superior mind in writing, we regard, then, as a nation's literature. We regard its gifted men, whether devoted to the exact sciences, to mental and ethical philosophy, to history and legislation, or to fiction and poetry, as forming a noble intellectual brotherhood, and it is for the purpose of quickening all to join their labors for the public good, that we offer the present plea in behalf of a national literature.

To show the importance which we attach to the subject, we begin with some remarks on what we deem the distinction which a nation should most earnestly covet. We believe, that more distinct apprehensions on this point are needed, and that, for want of them, the work of improvement is carried on with less energy, consistency, and wisdom, than may and should be brought to bear upon it. The great distinction of a country, then, is, that it produces superior men. Its natural advantages are not to be disdained. But they are of secondary importance. No matter what races of animals a country breeds. The great question is, Does it breed a noble race of men? No matter what its soil may be. The great question is, How far is it prolific of moral and intellectual power? No matter how stern its climate is, if it nourish force of thought and virtuous purpose. These are the products by which a country is to be tried, and institutions have value only by the impulse which they give to the mind. It has sometimes been said, that the noblest men grow where nothing else will grow. This we do not believe, for mind is not the creature of climate or soil. But were it true, we should say, that it were better to live among rocks and sands, than in the most genial and productive region on the face of the earth.

As yet, the great distinction of a nation on which we have insisted, has been scarcely recognised. The idea of forming a superior race of men has entered little into schemes of policy. Invention and effort have been expended on matter, much more than on mind. Lofty piles have been reared; the earth has groaned under pyramids and palaces. The thought of building up a nobler order of intellect and character, has hardly crossed the most adventurous statesman. We beg that we may not be misapprehended. We offer these remarks to correct what we deem a disproportioned attention to physical good, and not at all to condemn the expenditure of ingenuity and strength on the outward world. There is a harmony between all our great interests, between inward and outward improvements; and, by establishing among them a wise order, all will be secured. We have no desire to shut up man in his own spiritual nature. The mind was made to act on matter, and it grows by expressing itself in material forms. We believe, too, that, in proportion as it shall gain intellectual and moral power, it will exert itself with increased energy and delight on the outward creation; will pour itself forth more freely in useful and ornamental arts; will rear more magnificent structures, and will call forth new beauties in nature. An intelligent and resolute spirit in a community, perpetually extends its triumphs over matter. It can even subject to itself the most unpromising region. Holland, diked from the ocean,—Venice, rising amidst the waves,—and New England, bleak and rock-bound New England, converted by a few generations from a wilderness into smiling fields and opulent cities,—point us to the mind as the great source of physical good, and teach us, that, in making the culture of man our highest end, we shall not retard, but advance, the cultivation of nature.

The question which we most solicitously ask about this country is, what race of men it is likely to produce. We consider its liberty of value only as far as it favors the growth of men. What is liberty? The removal of restraint from human powers. Its benefit is, that it opens new fields for action, and a wider range for the mind. The only freedom worth possessing, is that which gives enlargement to a people's energy, intellect, and virtues. The savage makes his boast of freedom. But what is its worth? Free as he is, he continues for ages in the same ignorance, leads the same comfortless life, sees the same untamed wilderness spread around him. He is indeed free from what he calls the yoke of civil institutions. But other and worse chains bind him. The very privation of civil government is in effect a chain; for, by withholding protection from property, it virtually shackles the arm of industry, and forbids exertion for the melioration of his lot. Progress, the growth of power, is the end and boon of liberty; and, without this, a people may have the name, but want the substance and spirit of freedom.

We are the more earnest in enlarging on these views, because we feel that our attachment to our country must be very much proportioned to what we deem its tendency to form a generous race of men. We pretend not to have thrown off national feeling; but we have some stronger feelings. We love our country much, but mankind more. As men and Christians, our first desire is to see the improvement of human nature. We desire to see the soul of man wiser, firmer, nobler, more conscious of its imperishable treasures, more beneficent and powerful, more alive to its connexion with God, more able to use pleasure and prosperity aright, and more victorious over poverty, adversity, and pain. In our survey of our own and other countries, the great question which comes to us is this, Where and under what institutions are men most likely to advance? Where are the soundest minds and the purest hearts formed? What nation possesses, in its history, its traditions, its government, its religion, its manners, its pursuits, its relations to other communities, and especially in its private and public means of education, the instruments and pledges of a more resolute virtue and devotion to truth, than we now witness? Such a nation, be it where it may, will engage our warmest interest. We love our country, but not blindly. In all nations we recognise one great family, and our chief wish for our native land is, that it may take the first rank among the lights and benefactors of the human race.

These views will explain the vast importance which we attach to a national literature. By this, as we have said, we understand the expression of a nation's mind in writing. It is the action of the most gifted understandings on the community. It throws into circulation through a wide sphere the most quickening and beautiful thoughts, which have grown up in men of laborious study or creative genius. It is a much higher work than the communication of a gifted intellect in discourse. It is the mind giving to multitudes whom no voice can reach, its compressed and selected thoughts, in the most lucid order and attractive forms which it is capable of inventing. In other words, literature is the concentration of intellect for the purpose of spreading itself abroad and multiplying its energy.

Such being the nature of literature, it is plainly among the most powerful methods of exalting the character of a nation, of forming a better race of men; in truth, we apprehend that it may claim the first rank among the means of improvement. We know nothing so fitted to the advancement of society, as to bring its higher minds to bear upon the multitude; as to establish close connexions between the more and less gifted; as to spread far and wide the light which springs up in meditative, profound, and sublime understandings. It is the ordinance of God, and one of his most benevolent laws, that the human race should be carried forward by impulses which originate in a few minds, perhaps in an individual; and in this way the most interesting relations and dependencies of life are framed. When a great truth is to be revealed, it does not flash at once on the race, but dawns and brightens on a superior understanding, from which it is to emanate and to illumine future ages. On the faithfulness of great minds to this awful function, the progress and happiness of men chiefly depend. The most illustrious benefactors of the race have been men, who, having risen to great truths, have held them as a sacred trust for their kind, and have borne witness to them amidst general darkness, under scorn and persecution, perhaps in the face of death. Such men, indeed, have not always made contributions to literature, for their condition has not allowed them to be authors; but we owe the transmission, perpetuity, and immortal power of their new and high thoughts, to kindred spirits, which have concentrated and fixed them in books.

The quickening influences of literature need not be urged on those who are familiar with the history of modern Europe, and who of course know the spring given to the human mind by the revival of ancient learning. Through their writings, the great men of antiquity have exercised a sovereignty over these later ages, not enjoyed in their own. It is more important to observe, that the influence of literature is perpetually increasing; for, through the press and the spread of education, its sphere is indefinitely enlarged. Reading, once the privilege of a few, is now the occupation of multitudes, and is to become one of the chief gratifications of all. Books penetrate everywhere, and some of the works of genius find their way to obscure dwellings, which, a little while ago, seemed barred against all intellectual light. Writing is now the mightiest instrument on earth. Through this, the mind has acquired a kind of omnipresence. To literature we then look, as the chief means of forming a better race of human beings. To superior minds, which may act through this, we look for the impulses, by which their country is to be carried forward. We would teach them, that they are the depositaries of the highest power on earth, and that on them the best hopes of society rest.

We are aware that some may think, that we are exalting intellectual above moral and religious influence. They may tell us that the teaching of moral and religious truth, not by philosophers and boasters of wisdom, but by the comparatively weak and foolish, is the great means of renovating the world. This truth we indeed regard as "the power of God unto salvation."[1] But let none imagine that its chosen temple is an uncultivated mind, and that it selects, as its chief organs, the lips of the unlearned. Religious and moral truth is indeed appointed to carry forward mankind; but not as conceived and expounded by narrow minds, not as darkened by the ignorant, not as debased by the superstitious, not as subtilized by the visionary, not as thundered out by the intolerant fanatic, not as turned into a drivelling cant by the hypocrite. Like all other truths, it requires for its full reception and powerful communication, a free and vigorous intellect. Indeed, its grandeur and infinite connexions demand a more earnest and various use of our faculties than any other subject. As a single illustration of this remark, we may observe, that all moral and religious truth may be reduced to one great and central thought, Perfection of Mind; a thought which comprehends all that is glorious in the Divine nature, and which reveals to us the end and happiness of our own existence. This perfection has as yet only dawned on the most gifted human beings, and the great purpose of our present and future existence is, to enlarge our conceptions of it without end, and to embody and make them manifest in character and life. And is this sublime thought to grow within us, to refine itself from error and impure mixture, to receive perpetual accessions of brightness from the study of God, man, and nature, and especially to be communicated powerfully to others, without the vigorous exertion of our intellectual nature? Religion has been wronged by nothing more, than by being separated from intellect; than by being removed from the province of reason and free research, into that of mystery and authority, of impulse and feeling. Hence it is, that the prevalent forms or exhibitions of Christianity are comparatively inert, and that most which is written on the subject is of little or no worth. Christianity was given, not to contradict and degrade the rational nature, but to call it forth, to enlarge its range and its powers. It admits of endless developement. It is the last truth which should remain stationary. It ought to be so explored and so expressed, as to take the highest place in a nation's literature, as to exalt and purify all other literature. From these remarks it will be seen, that the efficacy which we have ascribed to literary or intellectual influence in the work of human improvement, is consistent with the supreme importance of moral and religious truth.

If we have succeeded in conveying the impressions which we have aimed to make, our readers are now prepared to inquire with interest into the condition and prospects of literature among ourselves. Do we possess, indeed, what may be called a national literature? Have we produced eminent writers in the various departments of intellectual effort? Are our chief resources of instruction and literary enjoyment furnished from ourselves? We regret that the reply to these questions is so obvious. The few standard works which we have produced, and which promise to live, can hardly, by any courtesy, be denominated a national literature. On this point, if marks and proofs of our real condition were needed, we should find them in the current apologies for our deficiencies. Our writers are accustomed to plead in our excuse, our youth, the necessities of a newly settled country, and the direction of our best talents to practical life. Be the pleas sufficient or not, one thing they prove, and that is, our consciousness of having failed to make important contributions to the interests of the intellect. We have few names to place by the side of the great names in science and literature on the other side of the ocean. We want those lights which make a country conspicuous at a distance. Let it not be said, that European envy denies our just claims.[2] In an age like this, when the literary world forms a great family, and the products of mind are circulated more rapidly than those of machinery, it is a nation's own fault, if its name be not pronounced with honor beyond itself. We have ourselves heard, and delighted to hear, beyond the Alps, our country designated as the land of Franklin. This name had scaled that mighty barrier, and made us known where our institutions and modes of life were hardly better understood than those of the natives of our forests.

We are accustomed to console ourselves for the absence of a commanding literature, by urging our superiority to other nations in our institutions for the diffusion of elementary knowledge through all classes of the community. We have here just cause for boasting, though perhaps less than we imagine. That there are gross deficiencies in our common schools, and that the amount of knowledge which they communicate, when compared with the time spent in its acquisition, is lamentably small, the community begin to feel. There is a crying need for a higher and more quickening kind of instruction than the laboring part of society have yet received, and we rejoice that the cry begins to be heard. But, allowing our elementary institutions to be ever so perfect, we confess that they do not satisfy us. We want something more. A dead level of intellect, even if it should rise above what is common in other nations, would not answer our wishes and hopes for our country. We want great minds to be formed among us, minds which shall be felt afar, and through which we may act on the world. We want the human intellect to do its utmost here. We want this people to obtain a claim on the gratitude of the human race, by adding strength to the foundation, and fulness and splendor to the developement of moral and religious truth; by originality of thought, by discoveries of science, and by contributions to the refining pleasures of taste and imagination.

With these views we do and must lament, that, however we surpass other nations in providing for, and spreading elementary instruction, we fall behind many in provision for the liberal training of the intellect, for forming great scholars, for communicating that profound knowledge, and that thirst for higher truths, which can alone originate a commanding literature. The truth ought to be known. There is among us much superficial knowledge, but little severe, persevering research; little of that consuming passion for new truth, which makes outward things worthless; little resolute devotion to a high intellectual culture. There is nowhere a literary atmosphere, or such an accumulation of literary influences, as determines the whole strength of the mind to its own enlargement, and to the manifestation of itself in enduring forms. Few among us can be said to have followed out any great subject of thought patiently, laboriously, so as to know thoroughly what others have discovered and taught concerning it, and thus to occupy a ground from which new views may be gained. Of course, exceptions are to be found. This country has produced original and profound thinkers. We have named Franklin, and we may name Edwards, one of the greatest men of his age, though unhappily his mind was lost, in a great degree, to literature, and we fear to religion, by vassalage to a false theology. His work on the Will throws, indeed, no light on human nature, and, notwithstanding the nobleness of the subject, gives no great or elevated thoughts; but, as a specimen of logical acuteness and controversial power, it certainly ranks in the very highest class of metaphysical writings.[3] We might also name living authors who do honor to their country. Still, we may say, we chiefly prize what has been done among us, as a promise of higher and more extensive effort. Patriotism, as well as virtue, forbids us to burn incense to national vanity. The truth should be seen and felt. In an age of great intellectual activity, we rely chiefly for intellectual excitement and enjoyment on foreign minds, nor is our own mind felt abroad. Whilst clamoring against dependence on European manufactures, we contentedly rely on Europe for the nobler and more important fabrics of the intellect. We boast of our political institutions, and receive our chief teachings, books, impressions, from the school of monarchy. True, we labor under disadvantages. But, if our liberty deserves the praise which it receives, it is more than a balance for these. We believe that it is. We believe that it does open to us an indefinite intellectual progress. Did we not so regard it, we should value it little. If hereditary governments minister most to the growth of the mind, it were better to restore them than to cling to a barren freedom. Let us not expose liberty to this reproach. Let us prove, by more generous provisions for the diffusion of elementary knowledge, for the training of great minds, and for the joint culture of the moral and intellectual powers, that we are more and more instructed, by freedom, in the worth and greatness of human nature, and in the obligation of contributing to its strength and glory.

We have spoken of the condition of our literature. We now proceed to the consideration of the causes which obstruct its advancement; and we are immediately struck by one so prevalent, as to deserve distinct notice. We refer to the common doctrine, that we need, in this country, useful knowledge, rather than profound, extensive, and elegant literature, and that this last, if we covet it, may be imported from abroad in such variety and abundance, as to save us the necessity of producing it among ourselves. How far are these opinions just? This question we purpose to answer.

That useful knowledge should receive our first and chief care, we mean not to dispute. But in our views of utility, we may differ from some who take this position. There are those who confine this term to the necessaries and comforts of life, and to the means of producing them. And is it true, that we need no knowledge, but that which clothes and feeds us? Is it true, that all studies may be dispensed with, but such as teach us to act on matter, and to turn it to our use? Happily, human nature is too stubborn to yield to this narrow utility. It is interesting to observe how the very mechanical arts, which are especially designed to minister to the necessities and comforts of life, are perpetually passing these limits; how they disdain to stop at mere convenience. A large and increasing proportion of mechanical labor is given to the gratification of an elegant taste. How simple would be the art of building, if it limited itself to the construction of a comfortable shelter! How many ships should we dismantle, and how many busy trades put to rest, were dress and furniture reduced to the standard of convenience! This "utility" would work a great change in town and country, would level to the dust the wonders of architecture, would annihilate the fine arts, and blot out innumerable beauties, which the hand of taste has spread over the face of the earth. Happily, human nature is too strong for the utilitarian. It cannot satisfy itself with the convenient. No passion unfolds itself sooner than the love of the ornamental. The savage decorates his person, and the child is more struck with the beauty than the uses of its raiment. So far from limiting ourselves to convenient food and raiment, we enjoy but little a repast which is not arranged with some degree of order and taste; and a man who should consult comfort alone in his wardrobe, would find himself an unwelcome guest in circles which he would very reluctantly forego. We are aware that the propensity to which we have referred, often breaks out in extravagance and ruinous luxury. We know that the love of ornament is often vitiated by vanity, and that, when so perverted, it impairs, sometimes destroys, the soundness and simplicity of the mind and the relish for true glory. Still it teaches, even in its excesses, that the idea of beauty is an indestructible principle of our nature, and this single truth is enough to put us on our guard against vulgar notions of utility.

We have said that we prize, as highly as any, useful knowledge. But by this we mean knowledge which answers and ministers to our complex and various nature; we mean that which is useful, not only to the animal man, but to the intellectual, moral, and religious man; useful to a being of spiritual faculties, whose happiness is to be found in their free and harmonious exercise. We grant, that there is primary necessity for that information and skill by which subsistence is earned, and life is preserved; for it is plain that we must live, in order to act and improve. But life is the means; action and improvement the end; and who will deny that the noblest utility belongs to that knowledge, by which the chief purpose of our creation is accomplished? According to these views, a people should honor and cultivate, as unspeakably useful, that literature which corresponds to, and calls forth, the highest faculties; which expresses and communicates energy of thought, fruitfulness of invention, force of moral purpose, a thirst for the true, and a delight in the beautiful. According to these views, we attach special importance to those branches of literature which relate to human nature, and which give it a consciousness of its own powers. History has a noble use, for it shows us human beings in various and opposite conditions, in their strength and weakness, in their progress and relapses, and thus reveals the causes and means by which the happiness and virtue of the race may be enlarged. Poetry is useful, by touching deep springs in the human soul; by giving voice to its more delicate feelings; by breathing out, and making more intelligible, the sympathy which subsists between the mind and the outward universe; by creating beautiful forms of manifestations for great moral truths. Above all, that higher philosophy, which treats of the intellectual and moral constitution of man, of the foundation of knowledge, of duty, of perfection, of our relations to the spiritual world, and especially to God; this has a usefulness so peculiar as to throw other departments of knowledge into obscurity; and a people, among whom this does not find honor, has little ground to boast of its superiority to uncivilized tribes. It will be seen from these remarks, that utility, with us, has a broad meaning. In truth, we are slow to condemn as useless, any researches or discoveries of original and strong minds, even when we discern in them no bearing on any interests of mankind; for all truth is of a prolific nature, and has connexions not immediately perceived; and it may be, that what we call vain speculations, may, at no distant period, link themselves with some new facts or theories, and guide a profound thinker to the most important results. The ancient mathematician, when absorbed in solitary thought, little imagined that his theorems, after the lapse of ages, were to be applied by the mind of Newton to the solution of the mysteries of the universe, and not only to guide the astronomer through the heavens, but the navigator through the pathless ocean. For ourselves, we incline to hope much from truths, which are particularly decried as useless; for the noblest and most useful truth is of an abstract or universal nature; and yet the abstract, though susceptible of infinite application, is generally, as we know, opposed to the practical.

We maintain, that a people, which has any serious purpose of taking a place among improved communities, should studiously promote within itself every variety of intellectual exertion. It should resolve strenuously to be surpassed by none. It should feel that mind is the creative power, through which all the resources of nature are to be turned to account, and by which a people is to spread its influence, and establish the noblest form of empire. It should train within itself men able to understand and to use whatever is thought and discovered over the whole earth. The whole mass of human knowledge should exist among a people, not in neglected libraries, but in its higher minds. Among its most cherished institutions, should be those, which will ensure to it ripe scholars, explorers of ancient learning, profound historians and mathematicians, intellectual laborers devoted to physical and moral science, and to the creation of a refined and beautiful literature.

Let us not be misunderstood. We have no desire to rear in our country a race of pedants, of solemn triflers, of laborious commentators on the mysteries of a Greek accent or a rusty coin. We would have men explore antiquity, not to bury themselves in its dust, but to learn its spirit, and so to commune with its superior minds, as to accumulate on the present age, the influences of whatever was great and wise in former times. What we want is, that those among us, whom God has gifted to comprehend whatever is now known, and to rise to new truths, may find aids and institutions to fit them for their high calling, and may become at once springs of a higher intellectual life to their own country, and joint workers with the great of all nations and times in carrying forward their race.

We know that it will be said, that foreign scholars, bred under institutions which this country cannot support, may do our intellectual work, and send us books and learning to meet our wants. To this we have much to answer. In the first place, we reply, that, to avail ourselves of the higher literature of other nations, we must place ourselves on a level with them. The products of foreign machinery we can use, without any portion of the skill that produced them. But works of taste and genius, and profound investigations of philosophy, can only be estimated and enjoyed through a culture and power corresponding to that from which they sprung.

In the next place, we maintain, that it is an immense gain to a people, to have in its own bosom, among its own sons, men of distinguished intellect. Such men give a spring and life to a community by their presence, their society, their fame; and what deserves remark, such men are nowhere so felt as in a republic like our own; for here the different classes of society flow together and act powerfully on each other, and a free communication, elsewhere unknown, is established between the gifted few and the many. It is one of the many good fruits of liberty, that it increases the diffusiveness of intellect; and accordingly a free country is, above all others, false to itself, in withholding from its superior minds the means of enlargement.

We next observe, and we think the observation important, that the facility with which we receive the literature of foreign countries, instead of being a reason for neglecting our own, is a strong motive for its cultivation. We mean not to be paradoxical, but we believe that it would be better to admit no books from abroad, than to make them substitutes for our own intellectual activity. The more we receive from other countries, the greater the need of an original literature. A people, into whose minds the thoughts of foreigners are poured perpetually, needs an energy within itself to resist, to modify this mighty influence, and, without it, will inevitably sink under the worst bondage, will become intellectually tame and enslaved.[4] We have certainly no desire to complete our restrictive system, by adding to it a literary non-intercourse law.[5] We rejoice in the increasing intellectual connexion between this country and the old world. But sooner would we rupture it, than see our country sitting passively at the feet of foreign teachers. It were better to have no literature, than form ourselves unresistingly on a foreign one. The true sovereigns of a country are those who determine its mind, its modes of thinking, its tastes, its principles; and we cannot consent to lodge this sovereignty in the hands of strangers. A country, like an individual, has dignity and power only in proportion as it is self-formed. There is a great stir to secure to ourselves the manufacturing of our own clothing. We say, let others spin and weave for us, but let them not think for us. A people, whose government and laws are nothing but the embodying of public opinion, should jealously guard this opinion against foreign dictation. We need a literature to counteract, and to use wisely the literature which we import. We need an inward power proportionate to that which is exerted on us, as the means of self-subsistence. It is particularly true of a people, whose institutions demand for their support a free and bold spirit, that they should be able to subject to a manly and independent criticism, whatever comes from abroad. These views seem to us to deserve serious attention. We are more and more a reading people. Books are already among the most powerful influences here. The question is, shall Europe, through these, fashion us after its pleasure? Shall America be only an echo of what is thought and written under the aristocracies beyond the ocean?

Another view of the subject is this. A foreign literature will always, in a measure, be foreign. It has sprung from the soul of another people, which, however like, is still not our own soul. Every people has much in its own character and feelings, which can only be embodied by its own writers, and which, when transfused through literature, makes it touching and true, like the voice of our earliest friend.

We now proceed to an argument in favor of native literature, which, if less obvious, is, we believe, not less sound than those now already adduced. We have hitherto spoken of literature as the expression, the communication, of the higher minds in a community. We now add, that it does much more than is commonly supposed, to *form* such minds, so that, without it, a people wants one of the chief means of educating or perfecting talent and genius.[6] One of the great laws of our nature, and a law singularly important to social beings, is, that the intellect enlarges and strengthens itself by expressing worthily its best views. In this, as in other respects, it is more blessed to give than to receive. Superior minds are formed, not merely by solitary thought, but almost as much by communication. Great thoughts are never fully possessed, till he who has conceived them has given them fit utterance. One of the noblest and most invigorating labors of genius is, to clothe its conceptions in clear and glorious forms, to give them existence in other souls. Thus literature creates, as well as manifests, intellectual power, and, without it, the highest minds will never be summoned to the most invigorating action.

We doubt whether a man ever brings his faculties to bear with their whole force on a subject, until he writes upon it for the instruction or gratification of others. To place it clearly before others, he feels the necessity of viewing it more vividly himself. By attempting to seize his thoughts, and fix them in an enduring form, he finds them vague and unsatisfactory, to a degree which he did not suspect, and toils for a precision and harmony of views, of which he never before felt the need. He places his subject in new lights; submits it to a searching analysis; compares and connects with it his various knowledge; seeks for it new illustrations and analogies; weighs objections; and, through these processes, often arrives at higher truths than he at first aimed to illustrate. Dim conceptions grow bright. Glorious thoughts, which had darted as meteors through the mind, are arrested, and gradually shine with a sunlike splendor, with prolific energy, on the intellect and heart. It is one of the chief distinctions of a great mind, that it is prone to rush into twilight regions, and to catch faint glimmerings of distant and unbounded prospects; and nothing perhaps aids it more to pierce the shadows which surround it, than the labor to unfold to other minds the indistinct conceptions which have dawned on its own. Even where composition yields no such fruits, it is still a great intellectual help. It always favors comprehensive and systematical views. The laborious distribution of a great subject, so as to assign to each part or topic its just position and due proportion, is singularly fitted to give compass and persevering force of thought.

If we confine ourselves simply to the consideration of style, we shall have reason to think that a people among whom this is neglected, wants one important intellectual aid. In this, great power is exerted, and by exertion increased. To the multitude, indeed, language seems so natural an instrument, that to use it with clearness and energy seems no great effort. It is framed, they think, to the writer's hand, and so continually employed as to need little thought or skill. But in nothing is the creative power of a gifted writer seen more than in his style. True, his words may be found in the dictionary. But there they lie disjointed and dead. What a wonderful life does he breathe into them by compacting them into his sentences! Perhaps he uses no term which has not been hackneyed by ordinary writers; and yet with these vulgar materials what miracles does he achieve! What a world of thought does he condense into a phrase! By new combinations of common words, what delicate hues or what a blaze of light does he pour over his subject! Power of style depends very little on the structure or copiousness of the language which the writer of genius employs, but chiefly, if not wholly, on his own mind. The words, arranged in his dictionary, are no more fitted to depict his thoughts, than the block of marble in the sculptor's shop, to show forth the conceptions which are dawning in his mind. Both are inert materials. The power, which pervades them, comes from the soul; and the same creative energy is manifested in the production of a noble style, as in extracting beautiful forms from lifeless stone. How unfaithful, then, is a nation to its own intellect, in which grace and force of style receive no culture.

The remarks now made on the importance of literature as a means of educating talent and genius, we are aware, do not apply equally to all subjects or kinds of knowledge. In the exact or physical sciences, a man may acquire much without composition, and may make discoveries without registering them. Even here, however, we believe, that, by a systematic developement of his views in a luminous style, he will bring great aid to his own faculties, as well as to others'. It is on the vast subjects of morals and human nature, that the mind especially strengthens itself by elaborate composition; and these, let it be remembered, form the staple of the highest literature. Moral truth, under which we include every thing relating to mind and character, is of a refined and subtile, as well as elevated nature, and requires the joint and full exercise of discrimination, invention, imagination, and sensibility, to give it effectual utterance. A writer, who would make it visible and powerful, must strive to join an austere logic to a fervent eloquence; must place it in various lights; must create for it interesting forms; must wed it to beauty; must illuminate it by similitudes and contrasts; must show its correspondence with the outward world; perhaps must frame for it a vast machinery of fiction. How invigorating are these efforts! Yet it is only in writing, in elaborate composition, that they are deliberately called forth and sustained, and without literature they would almost cease. It may be said of many truths, that greater intellectual energy is required to express them with effect, than to conceive them; so that a nation, which does not encourage this expression, impoverishes so far its own mind. Take, for example, Shakspeare's Hamlet. This is a developement of a singularly interesting view of human nature. It shows us a mind, to which life is a burden; in which the powers of meditation and feeling are disproportioned to the active powers; which sinks under its own weight, under the consciousness of wanting energies commensurate with its visions of good, with its sore trials, and with the solemn task which is laid upon it. To conceive clearly this form of human nature, shows indeed the genius of the writer. But what a new power is required to bring it out in such a drama as Shakspeare's; to give it life and action; to invent for it circumstances and subordinate characters, fitted to call it forth; to give it tones of truth and nature; to show the hues which it casts over all the objects of thought! This intellectual energy we all perceive; and this was not merely *manifested* in Shakspeare's work, but, without such a work, it would not have been awakened. His invention would have slumbered, had he not desired to give forth his mind, in a visible and enduring form. Thus literature is the nurse of genius. Through this, genius learns its own strength, and continually accumulates it; and of course, in a country without literature, genius, however liberally bestowed by the Creator, will languish, and will fail to fulfil its great duty of quickening the mass amidst which it lives.

We come now to our last, and what we deem a weighty argument in favor of a native literature. We desire and would cherish it, because we hope from it important aids to the cause of truth and human nature. We believe, that a literature, springing up in this new soil, would bear new fruits, and, in some respects, more precious fruits, than are elsewhere produced. We know that our hopes may be set down to the account of that national vanity, which, with too much reason, is placed by foreigners among our besetting sins. But we speak from calm and deliberate conviction. We are inclined to believe, that, as a people, we occupy a position, from which the great subjects of literature may be viewed more justly than from those which most other nations hold. Undoubtedly we labor under disadvantages. We want the literary apparatus of Europe; her libraries, her universities, her learned institutions, her race of professed scholars, her spots consecrated by the memory of sages, and a thousand stirring associations which hover over ancient nurseries of learning. But the mind is not a local power. Its spring is within itself, and, under the inspiration of liberal and high feeling, it may attain and worthily express nobler truth than outward helps could reveal.

The great distinction of our country is, that we enjoy some peculiar advantages for understanding our own nature. Man is the great subject of literature, and juster and profounder views of man may be expected here, than elsewhere. In Europe, political and artificial distinctions have, more or less, triumphed over and obscured our common nature. In Europe, we meet kings, nobles, priests, peasants. How much rarer is it to meet *men;* by which we mean, human beings conscious of their own nature, and conscious of the utter worthlessness of all outward distinctions, compared with what is treasured up in their own souls. Man does not value himself as man. It is for his blood, his rank, or some artificial distinction, and not for the attributes of humanity, that he holds himself in respect. The institutions of the old world all tend to throw obscurity over what we most need to know, and that is, the worth and claims of a human being. We know that great improvements in this respect are going on abroad. Still the many are too often postponed to the few. The mass of men are regarded as instruments to work with, as materials to be shaped for the use of their superiors. That consciousness of our own nature, which contains, as a germ, all nobler thoughts, which teaches us at once self-respect and respect for others, and which binds us to God by filial sentiment and hope, this has been repressed, kept down by establishments founded in force; and literature, in all its departments, bears, we think, the traces of this inward degradation. We conceive that our position favors a juster and profounder estimate of human nature. We mean not to boast, but there are fewer obstructions to that moral consciousness, that consciousness of humanity, of which we have spoken. Man is not hidden from us by so many disguises as in the old world. The essential equality of all human beings, founded on the possession of a spiritual, progressive, immortal nature, is, we hope, better understood; and nothing more than this single conviction is needed, to work the mightiest changes in every province of human life and of human thought.

We have stated what seems to us our most important distinction. But our position has other advantages. The mere circumstance of its being a new one, gives reason to hope for some new intellectual activity, some fresher views of nature and life. We are not borne down by the weight of antiquated institutions, time-hallowed abuses, and the remnants of feudal barbarism. The absence of a religious establishment is an immense gain, as far as originality of mind is in question; for an establishment, however advantageous in other respects, is, by its nature, hostile to discovery and progress. To keep the mind where it is, to fasten the notions of one age on all future time, is its aim and proper business; and if it happened, as has generally been the case, to grow up in an age of strife and passion, when, as history demonstrates, the church was overrun with error, it cannot but perpetuate darkness and mental bondage. Among us, intellect, though far from being free, has broken some of the chains of other countries, and is more likely, we conceive, to propose to itself its legitimate object, truth,—everlasting and universal truth.

We have no thought of speaking contemptuously of the literature of the old world. It is our daily nutriment. We feel our debt to be immense to the glorious company of pure and wise minds, which in foreign lands have bequeathed us in writing their choicest thoughts and holiest feelings. Still we feel, that all existing literature has been produced under influences, which have necessarily mixed with it much error and corruption; and that the whole of it ought to pass, and must pass, under rigorous review. For example, we think that the history of the human race is to be re-written. Men imbued with the prejudices which thrive under aristocracies and state religions, cannot understand it. Past ages, with their great events, and great men, are to undergo, we think, a new trial, and to yield new results. It is plain, that history is already viewed under new aspects, and we believe, that the true principles for studying and writing it are to be unfolded here, at least as rapidly as in other countries. It seems to us that in literature an immense work is yet to be done. The most interesting questions to mankind are yet in debate. Great principles are yet to be settled in criticism, in morals, in politics; and, above all, the true character of religion is to be rescued from the disguises and corruptions of ages. We want a reformation. We want a literature, in which genius will pay supreme, if not undivided homage, to truth and virtue; in which the childish admiration of what has been called greatness, will give place to a wise moral judgment; which will breathe reverence for the mind, and elevating thoughts of God. The part which this country is to bear in this great intellectual reform, we presume not to predict. We feel, however, that, if true to itself, it will have the glory and happiness of giving new impulses to the human mind. This is our cherished hope. We should have no heart to encourage native literature, did we not hope that it would become instinct with a new spirit. We cannot admit the thought, that this country is to be only a repetition of the old world. We delight to believe that God, in the fulness of time, has brought a new continent to light, in order that the human mind should move here with a new freedom, should frame new social institutions, should explore new paths, and reap new harvests. We are accustomed to estimate nations by their creative energies, and we shall blush for our country, if, in circumstances so peculiar, original, and creative, it shall satisfy itself with a passive reception and mechanical reiteration of the thoughts of strangers.

We have now completed our remarks on the importance of a native literature. The next great topic is, the means of producing it; and here our limits forbid us to enlarge; yet we cannot pass it over in silence. A primary and essential means of the improvement of our literature, is, that, as a people, we should feel its value, should desire it, should demand it, should encourage it, and should give it a hearty welcome. It will come if called for; and, under this conviction, we have now labored to create a want for it in the community. We say, that we must call for it; by which we mean, not merely that we must invite it by good wishes and kind words, but must make liberal provision for intellectual education. We must enlarge our literary institutions, secure more extensive and profound teaching, and furnish helps and resources to men of superior talent for continued, laborious research. As yet, intellectual labor, devoted to a thorough investigation and a full developement of great subjects, is almost unknown among us; and, without it, we shall certainly rear few lasting monuments of thought. We boast of our primary schools. We want universities worthy of the name, where a man of genius and literary zeal may possess himself of all that is yet known, and may strengthen himself by intercourse with kindred minds. We know it will be said, that we cannot afford these. But it is not so. We are rich enough for ostentation, for intemperance, for luxury. We can lavish millions on fashion, on furniture, on dress, on our palaces, on our pleasures; but we have nothing to spend for the mind. Where lies our poverty? In the purse, or in the soul?

We have spoken of improved institutions as essential to an improved literature. We beg, however, not to be misunderstood, as if these were invested with a creating power, or would necessarily yield the results which we desire. They are the means, not causes, of advancement. Literature depends on individual genius, and this, though fostered, cannot be created by outward helps. No human mechanism can produce original thought. After all the attempts to explain by education the varieties of intellect, we are compelled to believe that minds, like all the other products of nature, have original and indestructible differences; that they are not exempted from the great and beautiful law, which joins with strong resemblances as strong diversities; and, of consequence, we believe, that the men who are to be the lights of the world, bring with them their commission and power from God. Still, whilst institutions cannot create, they may and do unfold genius; and, for want of them, great minds often slumber or run to waste, whilst a still larger class, who want genius, but possess admirable powers, fail of that culture, through which they might enjoy and approach their more gifted brethren.

A people, as we have said, are to give aid to literature, by founding wise and enlarged institutions. They may do much more. They may exert a nobler patronage. By cherishing in their own breasts the love of truth, virtue, and freedom, they may do much to nurse and kindle genius in its favored possessors. There is a constant reaction between a community and the great minds which spring up within it, and they form one another. In truth, great minds are developed more by the spirit and character of the people to which they belong, than by all other causes. Thus, a free spirit, a thirst for new and higher knowledge in a community, does infinitely more for literature, than the most splendid benefactions under despotism. A nation under any powerful excitement, becomes fruitful of talent. Among a people called to discuss great questions, to contend for great interests, to make great sacrifices for the public weal, we always find new and unsuspected energies of thought brought out. A mercenary, selfish, luxurious, sensual people, toiling only to secure the pleasures of sloth, will often communicate their own softness and baseness to the superior minds which dwell among them. In this impure atmosphere, the celestial spark burns dim, and well will it be, if God's great gift of genius be not impiously prostituted to lust and crime.

In conformity with the views now stated, we believe that literature is to be carried forward, here and elsewhere, chiefly by some new and powerful impulses communicated to society; and it is a question naturally suggested by this discussion, from what impulse, principle, excitement, the highest action of the mind may now be expected. When we look back, we see that literature has been originated and modified by a variety of principles; by patriotism and national feeling, by reverence for antiquity, by the spirit of innovation, by enthusiasm, by skepticism, by the passion for fame, by romantic love, and by political and religious convulsions. Now we do not expect from these causes any higher action of the mind, than they have yet produced. Perhaps most of them have spent their force. The very improvements of society seem to forbid the manifestation of their former energy. For example, the patriotism of antiquity and the sexual love of chivalrous ages, which inspired so much of the old literature, are now seen to be feverish and vicious excesses of natural principles, and have gone, we trust, never to return.

Are we asked, then, to what impulse or power, we look for a higher literature than has yet existed? We answer, to a new action or developement of the religious principle. This remark will probably surprise not a few of our readers. It seems to us, that the energy with which this principle is to act on the intellect, is hardly suspected. Men identify religion with superstition, with fanaticism, with the common forms of Christianity; and seeing it arrayed against intellect, leagued with oppression, fettering inquiry, and incapable of being blended with the sacred dictates of reason and conscience, they see in its progress only new encroachments on free and enlightened thinking. Still, man's relation to God is the great quickening truth, throwing all other truths into insignificance, and a truth which, however obscured and paralyzed by the many errors which ignorance and fraud have hitherto linked with it, has ever been a chief spring of human improvement. We look to it as the true life of the intellect. No man can be just to himself, can comprehend his own existence, can put forth all his powers with an heroic confidence, can deserve to be the guide and inspirer of other minds, till he has risen to communion with the Supreme Mind; till he feels his filial connexion with the Universal Parent; till he regards himself as the recipient and minister of the Infinite Spirit; till he feels his consecration to the ends which religion unfolds; till he rises above human opinion, and is moved by a higher impulse than fame.

From these remarks it will be seen, that our chief hopes of an improved literature rest on our hopes of an improved religion. From the prevalent theology, which has come down to us from the dark ages, we hope nothing. It has done its best. All that can grow up under its sad shade has already been brought forth. It wraps the Divine nature and human nature in impenetrable gloom. It overlays Christianity with technical, arbitrary dogmas.[7] True faith is of another lineage. It comes from the same source with reason, conscience, and our best affections, and is in harmony with them all. True faith is essentially a moral conviction; a confidence in the reality and immutableness of moral distinctions; a confidence in disinterested virtue or in spiritual excellence as the supreme good; a confidence in God as its fountain and almighty friend, and in Jesus Christ as having lived and died to breathe it into the soul; a confidence in its power, triumphs, and immortality; a confidence, through which outward changes, obstructions, disasters, sufferings, are overcome, or rather made instruments of perfection. Such a faith, unfolded freely and powerfully, must "work mightily"[8] on the intellect as well as on practice. By revealing to us the supreme purpose of the Creator, it places us, as it were, in the centre of the universe, from which the harmonies, true relations, and brightest aspects of things are discerned. It unites calmness and enthusiasm, and the concord of these seemingly hostile elements is essential to the full and healthy action of the creative powers of the soul. It opens the eye to beauty and the heart to love. Literature, under this influence, will become more ingenuous and single-hearted; will penetrate farther into the soul; will find new interpretations of nature and life; will breathe a martyr's love of truth, tempered with a never-failing charity; and, whilst sympathizing with all human suffering, will still be pervaded by a healthful cheerfulness, and will often break forth in tones of irrepressible joy, responsive to that happiness which fills God's universe.

We cannot close our remarks on the means of an improved literature, without offering one suggestion. We earnestly recommend to our educated men a more extensive acquaintance with the intellectual labors of continental Europe. Our reading is confined too much to English books, and especially to the more recent publications of Great Britain. In this we err. We ought to know the different modes of viewing and discussing great subjects in different nations. We should be able to compare the writings of the highest minds in a great variety of circumstances. Nothing can favor more our own intellectual independence and activity. Let English literature be ever so fruitful and profound, we should still improverish ourselves by making it our sole nutriment. We fear, however, that at the present moment English books want much which we need. The intellect of that nation is turned now to what are called practical and useful subjects. Physical science goes forward, and what is very encouraging, it is spread with unexampled zeal through all classes of the community. Abuses of government, of the police, of the penal code, of charity, of poor laws, and corn laws, are laboriously explored. General education is improved. Science is applied to the arts with brilliant success. We see much good in progress. But we find little profound or fervid thinking, expressed in the higher forms of literature. The noblest subjects of the intellect receive little attention. We see an almost total indifference to intellectual and moral science. In England there is a great want of philosophy, in the true sense of that word. If we examine her reviews, in which much of the intellectual power of the nation is expended, we meet perpetually a jargon of criticism, which shows a singular want of great and general principles in estimating works of art. We have no ethical work of any living English writer to be compared with that of Degerando, entitled, *"Du Perfectionnement Moral;"*[9] and, although we have little respect for the rash generalizations of the bold and eloquent Cousin, yet the interest which his metaphysics awaken in Paris, is in our estimation a better presage than the lethargy which prevails on such topics in England.[10] In these remarks we have no desire to depreciate the literature of England, which, taken as a whole, we regard as the noblest monument of the human mind. We rejoice in our descent from England, and esteem our free access to her works of science and genius, as among our high privileges. Nor do we feel as if her strength were spent. We see no wrinkles on her brow, no decrepitude in her step. At this moment she has authors, especially in poetry and fiction, whose names are "familiar in our mouths as household words," and who can never perish but with her language. Still we think, that at present her intellect is laboring more for herself than for mankind, and that our scholars, if they would improve our literature, should cultivate an intimacy not only with that of England, but of continental Europe.

We have now finished our remarks on the importance and means of an improved literature among ourselves. Are we asked what we hope in this particular? We answer, much. We see reasons for anticipating an increased and more efficient direction of talent to this object. But on these we cannot enlarge. There is, however, one ground of expectation, to which we will call a moment's attention. We apprehend that literature is to make progress through an important change in society, which civilization and good institutions are making more and more apparent. It seems to us, that, through these causes, political life is less and less regarded as the only or chief sphere for superior minds, and that influence and honor are more and more accumulated in the hands of literary and thinking men. Of consequence, more and more of the intellect of communities is to be drawn to literature. The distinction between antiquity and the present times, in respect to the importance attached to political life, seems to us striking; and it is not an accidental difference, but founded on permanent causes which are to operate with increased power. In ancient times, every thing, abroad and at home, threw men upon the public, and generated an intense thirst for political power. On the contrary, the improvement of later periods inclines men to give importance to literature. For example, the instability of the ancient republics, the unsettled relations of different classes of society, the power of demagogues and orators, the intensity of factions, the want of moral and religious restraints, the want of some regular organ for expressing the public mind, the want of precedents and precise laws for the courts of justice, these and other circumstances gave to the ancient citizen a feeling as if revolutions and convulsions were inseparable from society, turned his mind with unremitting anxiety to public affairs, and made a participation of political power an important, if not an essential, means of personal safety.—Again, the ancient citizen had no home, in our sense of the word. He lived in the market, the forum, the place of general resort, and of course his attention was very much engrossed by affairs of state.—Again, religion, which now more than all things throws a man upon himself, was in ancient times a public concern, and turned men to political life. The religion of the heart and closet was unknown. The relation of the gods to particular states, was their most prominent attribute; and to conciliate their favor to the community, the chief end of worship. Accordingly, religion consisted chiefly in public and national rites. In Rome, the highest men in the state presided at the altar, and, adding to their other titles that of Supreme Pontiff, performed the most solemn functions of the priesthood. Thus the whole strength of the religious principle was turned into political channels. The gods were thought to sustain no higher office than a political one, and of consequence this was esteemed the most glorious for men.—Once more, in ancient times political rank was vastly more efficient, whether for good or for evil, than at present, and of consequence was the object of a more insatiable ambition. It was almost the only way of access to the multitude. The public man held a sway over opinion, over his country, perhaps over foreign states, now unknown. It is the influence of the press and of good institutions to reduce the importance of the man of office. In proportion as private individuals can act on the public mind; in proportion as a people read, think, and have the means of expressing and enforcing their opinions; in proportion as laws become fixed, known, and sanctioned by the moral sense of the community; in proportion as the interests of the state, the principles of administration, and all public measures, are subjected to free and familiar discussion, government becomes a secondary influence. The power passes into the hands of those who think, write, and spread their minds far and wide. Accordingly, literature is to become more and more the instrument of swaying men, of doing good, of achieving fame. The contrast between ancient and modern times, in the particulars now stated, is too obvious to need illustration, and our great inference is equally clear. The vast improvements, which, in the course of ages, have taken place in social order, in domestic life, in religion, in knowledge, all conspire to one result, all tend to introduce other and higher influences than political power, and to give to that form of intellectual effort, which we call literature, dominion over human affairs. Thus truth, we apprehend, is more and more felt; and from its influence, joined with our peculiar condition and free institutions, we hope for our country the happiness and glory of a pure, deep, rich, beautiful, and ennobling literature.

Notes

1. Romans 1:16—"For I am not ashamed of the Gospel of Christ: for it is the power of God unto salvation to every one that believeth; to the Jew first, and also to the Greek."

2. Channing is here referring to the tension which often surrounded the question of the reception of American books in England in the early nineteenth century. Americans both craved English attention and scorned English opinion as biased, and there was ambivalence about whether American authors should imitate the best British models or strive for complete originality.

3. Channing refers to Jonathan Edwards, *A Careful and Strict Enquiry into the Modern Prevailing Notion, of that Freedom of Will which is*

supposed to be Essential to Moral Agency, Vertue and Vice, Reward and Punishment, Praise and Blame (Boston, 1754).

4. Channing's direct plea here for an American national literature is a pioneering statement in the development of the American literary consciousness, and has been seen as a precursor to Emerson's essay "The American Scholar" (1837).

5. In 1824 a new tariff law was enacted which met with general opposition from Massachusetts. Channing's reference to "our restrictive system" and "a literary non-intercourse law" seems to be a disparaging reference to the tariff situation. See F. W. Taussig, *The Tariff History of the United States,* 8th ed. (New York and London, 1931).

6. Channing's advocacy of an educative purpose for literature places him within the parameters of the didactic critical outlook which has been described in William Charvat, *The Origins of American Critical Thought, 1810–1835* (Philadelphia, 1936).

7. The "prevalent theology" is Calvinism. See Channing's "The Moral Argument Against Calvinism" in this volume.

8. Colossians 1:20—"Whereunto I also labour, striving according to his working, which worketh in me mightily."

9. Baron Joseph Marie De Gerando, *Du Perfectionnement moral, ou de l'éducation de soi-même* (Paris, 1824). In 1830, Channing's friend and disciple Elizabeth Palmer Peabody published an English translation, *Self-Education; or, The Means and Art of Moral Progress* (Boston, 1830).

10. Victor Cousin was the founder of the school of "eclecticism" in French philosophy, and Channing's sense of his importance was confirmed by wide interest in his work in the 1830's among the Transcendentalists. See in particular George Ripley, ed., *Philosophical Miscellanies, From the French of Cousin, Jouffroy, and Benjamin Constant* (Boston, 1836).

SPIRITUAL FREEDOM (1830)*

*The original text that follows this introduction is from *The Works of William E. Channing, D.D.*, 6 vols. (Boston: James Munroe, 1841-43), 4:67-103.

The tradition of the annual Election Sermon in Massachusetts provided Channing with the opportunity to bring his vision of the primacy of the spiritual life before those who controlled political life. His bold argument was that "civil and political liberty" were worth little without a basis in the inner freedom of the spirit. Channing launched some of his most effective rhetoric in this address, notably the refrain "I call that mind free . . ." But he also offered some shrewdly perceptive arguments which were by no means designed to pamper the complaisance of any elected officials. Thus he argued that government which does not recognize the primacy of the inner nature has often become "the scourge of mankind," or that Americans put an "idolatrous trust" in free institutions, feeling that these can by some magic "secure our rights, however we enslave ourselves to evil passions." In the 1830's, because of his stand against slavery, Channing became a public figure whose opinion and political issues had weight. But as this address shows, his public life was always tinged with a profound skepticism about politics, and a refusal to recognize it as anything except secondary to the inner life.

SPIRITUAL FREEDOM.

DISCOURSE PREACHED AT THE ANNUAL ELECTION,

MAY 26, 1830.

John viii. 31, 32, 36: "Then said Jesus to those Jews which believed on him, If ye continue in my word, then are ye my disciples indeed; and ye shall know the truth, and the truth shall make you free." "If the Son therefore shall make you free, ye shall be free indeed."

Intro

The Scriptures continually borrow from nature and social life, illustrations and emblems of spiritual truth. The character, religion, and blessings of Jesus Christ, are often placed before us by sensible images. His influences on the mind are shadowed forth by the light of the sun, by the vital union of the head with the members, by the shepherd bringing back the wandering flock, by the vine which nourishes and fructifies the branches, by the foundation sustaining the edifice, by bread and wine invigorating the animal frame. In our text we have a figurative illustration of his influence or religion, peculiarly intelligible and dear to this community. He speaks of himself as giving freedom, that great good of individuals and states; and by this similitude he undoubtedly intended to place before men, in a strong and attractive light, that spiritual and inward liberty which his truth confers on its obedient disciples. Inward, spiritual liberty, this is the great gift of Jesus Christ. This will be the chief topic of the present discourse. I wish to show, that this is the supreme good of men, and that civil and political liberty has but little worth, but as it springs from and invigorates this.

From what I have now said, the general tone of this discourse may be easily anticipated. I shall maintain, that the highest interest of communities, as well as individuals, is a spiritual interest; that outward and earthly goods are of little worth, but as bearing on the mind, and tending to its liberation, strength, and glory. And I am fully aware that in taking that course, I lay myself open to objection. I shall be told, that I show my ignorance of human nature, in attempting to interest men by such refined views of society; that I am too speculative; that spirtual liberty is too unsubstantial and visionary to be proposed to statesmen as an end in legislation; that the dreams of the closet should not be obtruded on practical men; that gross and tangible realities can alone move the multitude; and that to talk to politicians of the spiritual interests of society as of supreme importance, is as idle as to try to stay with a breath the force of the whirlwind. [1]

I anticipate such objections. But they do not move me. I firmly believe, that the only truth which is to do men lasting good, is that which relates to the soul, which carries them into its depths, which reveals to them its powers and the purposes of its creation. The progress of society is retarded, by nothing more than by the low views which its leaders are accustomed to take of human nature. Man has a mind as well as a body, and this he ought to know; and till he knows it, feels it, and is deeply penetrated by it, he knows nothing aright. His body should, in a sense, vanish away before his mind; or, in the language of Christ, he should hate his animal life in comparison with the intellectual and moral life which is to endure for ever. This doctrine, however, is pronounced too refined. Useful and practical truth, according to its most improved expositors, consists in knowing that we have an animal nature, and in making this our chief care; in knowing that we have mouths to be filled, and limbs to be clothed; that we live on the earth, which it is our business to till; that we have a power of accumulating wealth, and that this power is the measure of the greatness of the community! For such doctrines I have no respect. I know no wisdom but that which reveals man to himself, and which teaches him to regard all social institutions, and his whole life, as the means of unfolding and exalting the spirit within him. All policy which does not recognise this truth, seems to me shallow. The statesman who does not look at the bearing of his measures on the mind of a nation, is unfit to touch one of men's great interests. Unhappily, statesmen have seldom understood the sacredness of human nature and human society. Hence, policy has become almost a contaminated word. Hence, government has so often been the scourge of mankind.

I mean not to disparage political science. The best constitution and the best administration of a state, are subjects worthy of the profoundest thought. But there are deeper foundations of public prosperity than these. The statesman who would substitute these for that virtue which they ought to subserve and exalt, will only add his name to the long catalogue which history preserves of baffled politicians. It is idle to hope, by our shortsighted contrivances, to insure to a people a happiness which their own character has not earned. The everlasting laws of God's moral government we cannot repeal; and parchment constitutions, however wise, will prove no shelter from the retributions which fall on a degraded community.

With these convictions, I feel that no teaching is so practical as that which impresses on a people the importance of their spiritual interests. With these convictions, I feel that I cannot better meet the demands of this occasion, than by leading you to prize, above all other rights and liberties, that inward freedom which Christ came to confer. To this topic I now solicit your attention.

And first, I may be asked what I mean by Inward, Spiritual Freedom. The common and true answer is, that it is freedom from sin. I apprehend, however, that to many, if not to most, these words are too vague to convey a full and deep sense of the greatness of the blessing. Let me, then, offer a brief explanation; and the most important remark in illustrating this freedom, is, that it is not a negative state, nor the mere absence of sin; for such a freedom may be ascribed to inferior animals, or to children before becoming moral agents. Spiritual freedom is the attribute of a mind, in which reason and conscience have begun to act, and which is free through its own energy, through fidelity to the truth, through resistance of temptation. I cannot therefore better give my views of spiritual freedom, than by saying, that it is moral energy or force of holy purpose put forth against the senses, against the passions, against the world, and thus liberating the intellect, conscience, and will, so that they may act with strength and unfold themselves for ever. The essence of spiritual freedom is power. A man liberated from sensual lusts by a palsy, would not therefore be inwardly free. He only is free, who, through self-conflict and moral resolution, sustained by trust in God, subdues the passions which have debased him, and, escaping the thraldom of low objects, binds himself to pure and lofty ones. That mind alone is free, which, looking to God as the inspirer and rewarder of virtue, adopts his law, written on the heart and in his word, as its supreme rule, and which, in obedience to this, governs itself, reveres itself, exerts faithfully its best powers, and unfolds itself by well-doing, in whatever sphere God's providence assigns.

It has pleased the All-wise Disposer to encompass us from our birth by difficulty and allurement, to place us in a world where wrong-doing is often gainful, and duty rough and perilous, where many vices oppose the dictates of the inward monitor, where the body presses as a weight on the mind, and matter, by its perpetual agency on the senses, becomes a barrier between us and the spiritual world. We are in the midst of influences, which menace the intellect and heart; and to be free, is to withstand and conquer these.

I call that mind free, which masters the senses, which protects itself against animal appetites, which contemns pleasure and pain in comparison with its own energy, which penetrates beneath the body and recognises its own reality and greatness, which passes life, not in asking what it shall eat or drink, but in hungering, thirsting, and seeking after righteousness.

I call that mind free, which escapes the bondage of matter, which, instead of stopping at the material universe and making it a prison wall, passes beyond it to its Author, and finds in the radiant signatures which it everywhere bears of the Infinite Spirit, helps to its own spiritual enlargement.

I call that mind free, which jealously guards its intellectual rights and powers, which calls no man master, which does not content itself with a passive or hereditary faith, which opens itself to light whencesoever it may come, which receives new truth as an angel from heaven, which, whilst consulting others, inquires still more of the oracle within itself, and uses instructions from abroad, not to supersede but to quicken and exalt its own energies.

I call that mind free, which sets no bounds to its love, which is not imprisoned in itself or in a sect, which recognises in all human beings the image of God and the rights of his children, which delights in virtue and sympathizes with suffering wherever they are seen, which conquers pride, anger, and sloth, and offers itself up a willing victim to the cause of mankind.

I call that mind free, which is not passively framed by outward circumstances, which is not swept away by the torrent of events, which is not the creature of accidental impulse, but which bends events to its own improvement, and acts from an inward spring, from immutable principles which it has deliberately espoused.

I call that mind free, which protects itself against the usurpations of society, which does not cower to human opinion, which feels itself accountable to a higher tribunal than man's, which respects a higher law than fashion, which respects itself too much to be the slave or tool of the many or the few.

I call that mind free, which, through confidence in God and in the power of virtue, has cast off all fear but that of wrong-doing, which no menace or peril can enthrall, which is calm in the midst of tumults, and possesses itself though all else be lost.

I call that mind free, which resists the bondage of habit, which does not mechanically repeat itself and copy the past, which does not live on its old virtues, which does not enslave itself to precise rules, but which forgets what is behind, listens for new and higher monitions of conscience, and rejoices to pour itself forth in fresh and higher exertions.

I call that mind free, which is jealous of its own freedom, which guards itself from being merged in others, which guards its empire over itself as nobler than the empire of the world.

In fine, I call that mind free, which, conscious of its affinity with God, and confiding in his promises by Jesus Christ, devotes itself faithfully to the unfolding of all its powers, which passes the bounds of time and death, which hopes to advance for ever, and which finds inexhaustible power, both for action and suffering, in the prospect of immortality.

Such is the spiritual freedom which Christ came to give. It consists in moral force, in self-control, in the enlargement of thought and affection, and in the unrestrained action of our best powers. This is the great good of Christianity, nor can we conceive a greater within the gift of God. I know that to many, this will seem too refined a good to be proposed as the great end of society and government. But our skepticism cannot change the nature of things. I know how little this freedom is understood or enjoyed, how enslaved men are to sense, and passion, and the world; and I know, too, that through this slavery they are wretched, and that while it lasts no social institution can give them happiness.

I now proceed, as I proposed, to show, that civil or political liberty is of little worth, but as it springs from, expresses, and invigorates this spiritual freedom. I account civil liberty as the chief good of states, because it accords with, and ministers to, energy and elevation of mind. Nor is this a truth so remote or obscure as to need laborious proof or illustration. For consider what civil liberty means. It consists in the removal of all restraint, but such as the public weal demands. And what is the end and benefit of removing restraint? It is that men may put forth their powers, and act from themselves. Vigorous and invigorating action is the chief fruit of all outward freedom. Why break the chains from the captive, but that he may bring into play his liberated limbs? Why open his prison, but that he may go forth, and open his eyes on a wide prospect, and exert and enjoy his various energies? Liberty, which does not minister to action and the growth of power, is only a name, is no better than slavery.

The chief benefit of free institutions is clear and unutterably precious. Their chief benefit is, that they aid freedom of mind, that they give scope to man's faculties, that they throw him on his own resources, and summon him to work out his own happiness. It is, that, by removing restraint from intellect, they favor force, originality, and enlargement of thought. It is, that, by removing restraint from worship, they favor the ascent of the soul to God. It is, that, by removing restraint from industry, they stir up invention and enterprise to explore and subdue the material world, and thus rescue the race from those sore physical wants and pains, which narrow and blight the mind. It is, that they cherish noble sentiments, frankness, courage, and self-respect.

Free institutions contribute in no small degree to freedom and force of mind, by teaching the essential equality of men, and their right and duty to govern themselves; and I cannot but consider the superiority of an elective government, as consisting very much in the testimony which it bears to these ennobling truths. It has often been said, that a good code of laws, and not the form of government, is what determines a people's happiness. But good laws, if not springing from the community, if imposed by a master, would lose much of their value. The best code is that which has its origin in the will of the people who obey it; which, whilst it speaks with authority, still recognises self-government as the primary right and duty of a rational being; and which thus cherishes in the individual, be his condition what it may, a just self-respect.

We may learn, that the chief good and the most precious fruit of civil liberty, is spiritual freedom and power, by considering what is the chief evil of tyranny. I know that tyranny does evil by invading men's outward interests, by making property and life insecure, by robbing the laborer to pamper the noble and king. But its worst influence is *within*. Its chief curse is, that it breaks and tames the spirit, sinks man in his own eyes, takes away vigor of thought and action, substitutes for conscience an outward rule, makes him abject, cowardly, a parasite and a cringing slave. This is the curse of tyranny. It wars with the soul, and thus it wars with God. We read in theologians and poets, of angels fighting against the Creator, of battles in heaven.² But God's throne in heaven is unassailable. The only war against God is against his image, against the divine principle in the soul, and this is waged by tyranny in all its forms. We here see the chief curse of tyranny; and this should teach us that civil freedom is a blessing, chiefly as it reverences the human soul, and ministers to its growth and power.

Without this inward, spiritual freedom, outward liberty is of little worth. What boots it, that I am crushed by no foreign yoke, if through ignorance and vice, through selfishness and fear, I want the command of my own mind? The worst tyrants are those which establish themselves in our own breast. The man who wants force of principle and purpose, is a slave, however free the air he breathes. The mind, after all, is our only possession, or, in other words, we possess all things through its energy and enlargement; and civil institutions are to be estimated by the free and pure minds to which they give birth.

It will be seen from these remarks, that I consider the freedom or moral strength of the individual mind, as the supreme good, and the highest end of government. I am aware that other views are often taken. It is said that government is intended for the public, for the community, not for the individual. The idea of a national interest prevails in the minds of statesmen, and to this it is thought that the individual may be sacrificed. But I would maintain, that the individual is not made for the state, so much as the state for the individual. A man is not created for political relations as his highest end, but for indefinite spiritual progress, and is placed in political relations as the means of his progress. The human soul is greater, more sacred, than the state, and must never be sacrificed to it. The human soul is to outlive all earthly institutions. The distinction of nations is to pass away. Thrones, which have stood for ages, are to meet the doom pronounced upon all man's works. But the individual mind survives, and the obscurest subject, if true to God, will rise to a power never wielded by earthly potentates.

A human being is a member of the community, not as a limb is a member of the body, or as a wheel is a part of a machine, intended only to contribute to some general, joint result. He was created, not to be merged in the whole, as a drop in the ocean, or as a particle of sand on the sea-shore, and to aid only in composing a mass. He is an ultimate being, made for his own perfection as the highest end, made to maintain an individual existence, and to serve others only as far as consists with his own virtue and progress. Hitherto governments have tended greatly to obscure this importance of the individual, to depress him in his own eyes, to give him the idea of an outward interest more important than the invisible soul, and of an outward authority more sacred than the voice of God in his own secret conscience. Rulers have called the private man the property of the state, meaning generally by the state themselves, and thus the many have been immolated to the few, and have even believed that this was their highest destination. These views cannot be too earnestly withstood. Nothing seems to me so needful as to give to the mind the consciousness, which governments have done so much to suppress, of its own separate worth. Let the individual feel, that, through his immortality, he may concentrate in his own being a greater good than that of nations. Let him feel that he is placed in the community, not to part with his individuality, or to become a tool, but that he should find a sphere for his various powers, and a preparation for immortal glory. To me, the progress of society consists in nothing more, than in bringing out the individual, in giving him a consciousness of his own being, and in quickening him to strengthen and elevate his own mind.

In thus maintaining that the individual is the end of social institutions, I may be thought to discourage public efforts and the sacrifice of private interests to the state. Far from it. No man, I affirm, will serve his fellow-beings so effectually, so fervently, as he who is not their slave; as he who, casting off every other yoke, subjects himself to the law of duty in his own mind. For this law enjoins a disinterested and generous spirit, as man's glory and likeness to his Maker. Individuality, or moral self-subsistence, is the surest foundation of an all-comprehending love. No man so multiplies his bonds with the community, as he who watches most jealously over his own perfection. There is a beautiful harmony between the good of the state and the moral freedom and dignity of the individual. Were it not so, were these interests in any case discordant, were an individual ever called to serve his country by acts debasing his own mind, he ought not to waver a moment as to the good which he should prefer. Property, life, he should joyfully surrender to the state. But his soul he must never stain or enslave. From poverty, pain, the rack, the gibbet, he should not recoil; but for no good of others ought he to part with self-control, or violate the inward law. We speak of the patriot as sacrificing himself to the public weal. Do we mean, that he sacrifices what is most properly himself, the principle of piety and virtue? Do we not feel, that, however great may be the good, which, through his sufferings, accrues to the state, a greater and purer glory redounds to himself, and that the most precious fruit of his disinterested services, is the strength of resolution and philanthropy which is accumulated in his own soul?

I have thus endeavoured to illustrate and support the doctrine, that spiritual freedom, or force and elevation of soul, is the great good to which civil freedom is subordinate, and which all social institutions should propose as their supreme end.

I proceed to point out some of the means by which this spiritual liberty may be advanced; and, passing over a great variety of topics, I shall confine myself to two:—Religion and Government.

I begin with Religion, the mightiest agent in human affairs. To this belongs preeminently the work of freeing and elevating the mind. All other means are comparatively impotent. The sense of God is the only spring, by which the crushing weight of sense, of the world, and temptation, can be withstood. Without a consciousness of our relation to God, all other relations will prove adverse to spiritual life and progress. I have spoken of the religious sentiment as the mightiest agent on earth. It has accomplished more, it has strengthened men to do and suffer more, than all other principles. It can sustain the mind against all other powers. Of all principles it is the deepest, the most ineradicable. In its perversion, indeed, it has been fruitful of crime and woe; but the very energy which it has given to the passions, when they have mixed with and corrupted it, teaches us the omnipotence with which it is imbued.

Religion gives life, strength, elevation to the mind, by connecting it with the Infinite Mind; by teaching it to regard itself as the offspring and care of the Infinite Father, who created it that he might communicate to it his own spirit and perfections, who framed it for truth and virtue, who framed it for himself, who subjects it to sore trials, that by conflict and endurance it may grow strong, and who has sent his Son to purify it from every sin, and to clothe it with immortality. It is religion alone, which nourishes patient, resolute hopes and efforts for our own souls. Without it, we can hardly es-

[handwritten marginalia: Spiritual liberty advanced thru Religion]

cape self-contempt, and the contempt of our race. Without God, our existence has no support, our life no aim, our improvements no permanence, our best labors no sure and enduring results, our spiritual weakness no power to lean upon, and our noblest aspirations and desires no pledge of being realized in a better state. Struggling virtue has no friend; suffering virtue no promise of victory. Take away God, and life becomes mean, and man poorer than the brute.—I am accustomed to speak of the greatness of human nature; but it is great only through its parentage; great, because descended from God, because connected with a goodness and power from which it is to be enriched for ever; and nothing but the consciousness of this connexion, can give that hope of elevation, through which alone the mind is to rise to true strength and liberty.

All the truths of religion conspire to one end, spiritual liberty. All the objects which it offers to our thoughts are sublime, kindling, exalting. Its fundamental truth is the existence of one God, one Infinite and Everlasting Father; and it teaches us to look on the universe as pervaded, quickened, and vitally joined into one harmonious and beneficent whole, by his ever-present and omnipotent love. By this truth it breaks the power of matter and sense, of present pleasure and pain, of anxiety and fear. It turns the mind from the visible, the outward and perishable, to the Unseen, Spiritual, and Eternal, and, allying it with pure and great objects, makes it free.

I well know, that what I now say, may seem to some to want the sanction of experience. By many, religion is perhaps regarded as the last principle to give inward energy and freedom. I may be told of its threatenings, and of the bondage which they impose. I acknowledge that religion has threatenings, and it *must* have them; for evil, misery, is necessarily and unchangeably bound up with wrong-doing, with the abuse of moral power. From the nature of things, a mind disloyal to God and duty, must suffer; and religion, in uttering this, only re-echoes the plain teaching of conscience. But let it be remembered, that the single end of the threatenings of religion, is to make us spiritually free. They are all directed against the passions which enthrall and degrade us. They are weapons given to conscience, with which to fight the good fight, and to establish its throne within us. When not thus used, they are turned from their end; and if by injudicious preaching they engender superstition, let not the fault be laid at the door of religion.

I do not indeed wonder that so many doubt the power of religion to give strength, dignity, and freedom to the mind. What bears this name too often yields no such fruits. Here, religion is a form, a round of prayers and rites, an attempt to propitiate God by flattery and fawning. There, it is terror and subjection to a minister or priest; and there, it is a violence of emotion, bearing away the mind like a whirlwind, and robbing it of self-direction. But true religion disclaims connexion with these usurpers of its name. It is a calm, deep conviction of God's paternal interest in the improvement, happiness, and honor of his creatures; a practical persuasion, that he delights in virtue and not in forms and flatteries, and that he especially delights in resolute effort to conform ourselves to the disinterested love and rectitude which constitute his own glory. It is for this religion, that I claim the honor of giving dignity and freedom to the mind.

The need of religion to accomplish this work, is in no degree superseded by what is called the progress of society. I should say that civilization, so far from being able of itself to give moral strength and elevation, includes causes of degradation, which nothing but the religious principle can withstand. It multiplies, undoubtedly, the comforts and enjoyments of life; but in these I see sore trials and perils to the soul. These minister to the sensual element in human nature, to the part of our constitution, which allies, and too often enslaves us, to the earth. Of consequence, civilization needs, that proportional aid should be given to the spiritual element in man, and I know not where it is to be found but in religion. Without this, the civilized man, with all his properties and refinements, rises little in true dignity above the savage whom he disdains. You tell me of civilization, of its arts and sciences, as the sure instruments of human elevation. You tell me, how by these man masters and bends to his use the powers of nature. I know he masters them, but it is to become in turn their slave. He explores and cultivates the earth, but it is to grow more earthly. He explores the hidden mine, but it is to forge himself chains. He visits all regions, but therefore lives a stranger to his own soul. In the very progress of civilization, I see the need of an antagonist principle to the senses, of a power to free man from matter, to recall him from the outward to the inward world; and religion alone is equal to so great a work.

The advantages of civilization have their peril. In such a state of society, opinion and law impose salutary restraint, and produce general order and security. But the power of opinion grows into a despotism, which more than all things, represses original and free thought, subverts individuality of character, reduces the community to a spiritless monotony, and chills the love of perfection. Religion, considered simply as the principle, which balances the power of human opinion, which takes man out of the grasp of custom and fashion, and teaches him to refer himself to a higher tribunal, is an infinite aid to moral strength and elevation.

An important benefit of civilization, of which we hear much from the political economist, is the division of labor, by which arts are perfected. But this, by confining the mind to an unceasing round of petty operations, tends to break it into littleness. We possess improved fabrics, but deteriorated men. Another advantage of civilization is, that manners are refined, and accomplishments multiplied; but these are continually seen to supplant simplicity of character, strength of feeling, the love of nature, the love of inward beauty and glory. Under outward courtesy, we see a cold selfishness, a spirit of calculation, and little energy of love.

I confess I look round on civilized society with many fears, and with more and more earnest desire, that a regenerating spirit from heaven, from religion, may descend upon and pervade it. I particularly fear, that various causes are acting powerfully among ourselves, to inflame and madden that enslaving and degrading principle, the passion for property. For example, the absence of hereditary distinctions in our country, gives prominence to the distinction of wealth, and holds up this as the chief prize to ambition. Add to this the epicurean, self-indulgent habits, which our prosperity has multiplied, and which crave insatiably for enlarging wealth as the only means of gratification. This peril is increased by the spirit of our times, which is a spirit of commerce, industry, internal improvements, mechanical invention, political economy, and peace. Think not that I would disparage commerce, mechanical skill, and especially pacific connexions among states. But there is danger that these blessings may by perversion issue in a slavish love of lucre. It seems to me, that some of the objects which once moved men most powerfully, are gradually losing their sway, and thus the mind is left more open to the excitement of wealth. For example, military distinction is taking the inferior place which it deserves; and the consequence will be, that the energy and ambition, which have been exhausted in war, will seek new directions; and happy shall we be if they do not flow into the channel of gain. So I think that political eminence is to be less and less coveted; and there is danger that the energies absorbed by it will be spent in seeking another kind of dominion, the dominion of property. And if such be the result, what shall we gain by what is called the progress of society? What shall we gain by national peace, if men, instead of meeting on the field of battle, wage with one another the more inglorious strife of dishonest and rapacious traffic? What shall we gain by the waning of political ambition, if the intrigues of the exchange take place of those of the cabinet, and private pomp and luxury be substituted for the splendor of public life? I am no foe to civilization. I rejoice in its progress. But I mean to say, that, without a pure religion to modify its tendencies, to inspire and refine it, we shall be corrupted, not ennobled by it. It is the excellence of the religious principle, that it aids and carries forward civilization, extends science and arts, multiplies the conveniences and ornaments of life, and at the same time spoils them of their enslaving power, and even converts them into means and ministers of that spiritual freedom, which, when left to themselves, they endanger and destroy.

In order, however, that religion should yield its full and best fruits, one thing is necessary; and the times require that I should state it with great distinctness. It is necessary that religion should be held and professed in a liberal spirit. Just as far as it assumes an intolerant, exclusive, sectarian form, it subverts, instead of strengthening, the soul's freedom, and becomes the heaviest and most galling yoke which is laid on the intellect and conscience. Religion must be viewed, not as a monopoly of priests, ministers, or sects, not as conferring on any man a right to dictate to his fellow-beings, not as an instrument by which the few may awe the many, not as bestowing on one a prerogative which is not enjoyed by all, but as the property of every human being, and as the great subject for every human mind. It must be regarded as the revelation of a common Father, to whom all have equal access, who invites all to the like immediate communion, who has no favorites, who has appointed no infallible expounders of his will, who opens his works and word to every eye, and calls upon all to read for themselves, and to follow fearlessly the best convictions of their own understandings.[3] Let religion be seized on by individuals or sects, as their special province; let them clothe themselves with God's prerogative of judgment; let them succeed in enforcing their creed by penalties of law, or penalties of opinion; let them succeed in fixing a brand on virtuous men, whose only crime is free investigation; and religion becomes the most blighting tyranny which can establish itself over the mind. You have all heard of the outward evils, which religion, when thus turned into tyranny, has inflicted; how it has dug dreary dungeons, kindled fires for the martyr, and invented instruments of exquisite torture. But to me all this is less fearful than its influence over the mind. When I see the superstitions which it has fastened on the conscience, the spiritual terrors with which it has haunted and subdued the ignorant and susceptible, the dark, appalling views of God which it has spread far and wide, the dread of inquiry which it has struck into superior understandings, and the servility of spirit which it has made to pass for piety,—when I see all this, the fire, the scaffold, and the outward inquisition, terrible as they are, seem to me inferior evils. I look with a solemn joy on the heroic spirits, who have met freely and fearlessly pain and death in the cause of truth and human rights. But there are other victims of intolerance, on whom I look with unmixed sorrow. They are those, who, spell-bound by early prejudice, or by intimidations from the pulpit and the press, dare not think; who anxiously stifle every doubt or misgiving in regard to their opinions, as if to doubt were a crime; who shrink from the seekers after truth as from infection; who deny all virtue, which does not wear the livery of their own sect; who, surrendering to others their best powers, receive unresistingly a teaching which wars against reason and conscience; and who think it a merit to impose on such as live within their influence, the grievous bondage, which they bear themselves. How much to be deplored is it, that religion, the very principle which is designed to raise men above the judgment and power of man, should become the chief instrument of usurpation over the soul.

Is it said, that in this country, where the rights of private judgment, and of speaking and writing according to our convictions, are guarantied with every solemnity by institutions and laws, religion can never degenerate into tyranny; that here its whole influence must conspire to the liberation and dignity of the mind? I answer, we discover little knowledge of human nature, if we ascribe to constitutions the power of charming to sleep the spirit of intolerance and exclusion. Almost every other bad passion may sooner be put to rest;

and for this plain reason, that intolerance always shelters itself under the name and garb of religious zeal. Because we live in a country, where the gross, outward, visible chain is broken, we must not conclude that we are necessarily free. There are chains not made of iron, which eat more deeply into the soul. An espionage of bigotry may as effectually close our lips and chill our hearts, as an armed and hundred-eyed police. There are countless ways by which men in a free country may encroach on their neighbours' rights. In religion, the instrument is ready made and always at hand. I refer to opinion, combined and organized in sects, and swayed by the clergy. We say we have no Inquisition. But a sect skilfully organized, trained to utter one cry, combined to cover with reproach whoever may differ from themselves, to drown the free expression of opinion by denunciations of heresy, and to strike terror into the multitude by joint and perpetual menace,—such a sect is as perilous and palsying to the intellect as the Inquisition. It serves the ministers as effectually as the sword. The present age is notoriously sectarian, and therefore hostile to liberty. One of the strongest features of our times, is the tendency of men to run into associations, to lose themselves in masses, to think and act in crowds, to act from the excitement of numbers, to sacrifice individuality, to identify themselves with parties and sects. At such a period, we ought to fear, and cannot too much dread, lest a host should be marshalled under some sectarian standard, so numerous and so strong, as to overawe opinion, stifle inquiry, compel dissenters to a prudent silence, and thus accomplish the end, without incurring the odium, of penal laws. We have indeed no small protection against this evil, in the multiplicity of sects. But let us not forget, that coalitions are as practicable and as perilous in church as in state; and that minor differences, as they are called, may be sunk, for the purpose of joint exertion against a common foe. Happily, the spirit of this people, in spite of all narrowing influences, is essentially liberal. Here lies our safety. The liberal spirit of the people, I trust, is more and more to temper and curb that exclusive spirit, which is the besetting sin of their religious guides.

In this connexion I may be permitted to say, and I say it with heartfelt joy, that the government of this Commonwealth has uniformly distinguished itself by the spirit of religious freedom. Intolerance, however rife abroad, has found no shelter in our halls of legislation. As yet, no sentence of proscription has been openly or

indirectly passed on any body of men for religious opinions. A wise
and righteous jealousy has watched over our religious liberties, and
been startled by the first movement, the faintest sign, of sectarian
ambition. Our Commonwealth can boast no higher glory. May none
of us live to see it fade away.

I have spoken with great freedom of the sectarian and exclusive
spirit of our age. I would earnestly recommend liberality of feeling
and judgment towards men of different opinions. But, in so doing, I
intend not to teach, that opinions are of small moment, or that we
should make no effort for spreading[4] such as we deem the truth of
God. I do mean, however, that we are to spread them by means
which will not enslave ourselves to a party, or bring others into
bondage. We must respect alike our own and others' minds. We
must not demand a uniformity in religion which exists nowhere else,
but expect, and be willing, that the religious principle, like other
principles of our nature, should manifest itself in different methods
and degrees. Let us not forget, that spiritual, like animal life, may
subsist and grow under various forms. Whilst earnestly recommending what we deem the pure and primitive faith, let us remember, that
those who differ in word or speculation, may agree in heart; that the
spirit of Christianity, though mixed and encumbered with error, is
still divine; and that sects which assign different ranks to Jesus
Christ, may still adore that godlike virtue, which constituted him the
glorious representative of his Father. Under the disguises of Papal
and Protestant Creeds, let us learn to recognise the lovely aspect of
Christianity, and rejoice to believe, that, amidst dissonant forms and
voices, the common Father discerns and accepts the same deep filial
adoration. This is true freedom and enlargement of mind, a liberty
which he who knows it would not barter for the widest dominion
which priests and sects have usurped over the human soul.

I have spoken of Religion; I pass to Government, another great
means of promoting that spiritual liberty, that moral strength and elevation, which we have seen to be our supreme good. I thus speak of
government, not because it always promotes this end, but because it
may and should thus operate. Civil institutions should be directed
chiefly to a moral or spiritual good, and, until this truth is felt, they
will continue, I fear, to be perverted into instruments of crime and
misery. Other views of their design, I am aware, prevail. We are
sometimes told, that government has no purpose but an earthly one;

that, whilst religion takes care of the soul, government is to watch over outward and bodily interests. This separation of our interests into earthly and spiritual, seems to me unfounded. There is a unity in our whole being. There is one great end for which body and mind were created, and all the relations of life were ordained; one central aim, to which our whole being should tend; and this is the unfolding of our intellectual and moral nature; and no man thoroughly understands government, but he who reverences it as a part of God's stupendous machinery for this sublime design. I do not deny that government is instituted to watch over our present interests. But still it has a spiritual or moral purpose, because present interests are, in an important sense, spiritual; that is, they are instruments and occasions of virtue, calls to duty, sources of obligation, and are only blessings when they contribute to the health of the soul. For example, property, the principal object of legislation, is the material, if I may so speak, on which justice acts, or through which this cardinal virtue is exercised and expressed; and property has no higher end than to invigorate, by calling forth, the principle of impartial rectitude.

Government is the great organ of civil society, and we should appreciate the former more justly, if we better understood the nature and foundation of the latter. I say, then, that society is throughout a moral institution. It is something very different from an assemblage of animals feeding in the same pasture. It is the combination of rational beings for the security of right. Right, a moral idea, lies at the very foundation of civil communities; and the highest happiness which they confer, is the gratification of moral affections. We are sometimes taught, that society is the creature of compact, and selfish calculation; that men agree to live together for the protection of private interests. But no. Society is of earlier and higher origin. It is God's ordinance, and answers to what is most godlike in our nature. The chief ties that hold men together in communities, are not self-interests, or compacts, or positive institutions, or force. They are invisible, refined, spiritual ties, bonds of the mind and heart. Our best powers and affections crave instinctively for society as the sphere in which they are to find their life and happiness. That men may greatly strengthen and improve society by written constitutions, I readily grant. There is, however, a constitution which precedes all of men's making, and after which all others are to be formed; a constitution, the great lines of which are drawn in our very nature; a primitive law of justice, rectitude, and philanthropy, which all other laws are bound to enforce, and from which all others derive their validity and worth.

Am I now asked, how government is to promote energy and elevation of moral principle? I answer, not by making the various virtues matters of legislation, not by preaching morals, not by establishing religion; for these are not its appropriate functions. It is to serve the cause of spiritual freedom, not by teaching or persuasion, but by action; that is, by rigidly conforming itself, in all its measures, to the moral or Christian law; by the most public and solemn manifestations of reverence for right, for justice, for the general weal, for the principles of virtue. Government is the most conspicuous of human institutions, and were moral rectitude written on its front, stamped conspicuously on all its operations, an immense power would be added to pure principle in the breasts of individuals.

To be more particular, a government may, and should, ennoble the mind of the citizen, by continually holding up to him the idea of the general good. This idea should be impressed in characters of light on all legislation; and a government directing itself resolutely and steadily to this end, becomes a minister of virtue. It teaches the citizen to attach a sanctity to the public weal, carries him beyond selfish regards, nourishes magnanimity, and the purpose of sacrificing himself, as far as virtue will allow, to the commonwealth. On the other hand, a government which wields its power for selfish interests, which sacrifices the many to a few, or the state to a party, becomes a public preacher of crime, taints the mind of the citizen, does its utmost to make him base and venal, and prepares him, by its example, to sell or betray that public interest for which he should be ready to die.

Again, on government, more than on any institution, depends that most important principle, the sense of justice in the community. To promote this, it should express, in all its laws, a reverence for right, and an equal reverence for the rights of high and low, of rich and poor. It should choose to sacrifice the most dazzling advantages, rather than break its own faith, rather than unsettle the fixed laws of property, or in any way shock the sentiment of justice in the community.

Let me add one more method by which government is to lift up and enlarge the minds of its citizens. In its relations to other governments, it should inviolably adhere to the principles of justice and philanthropy. By its moderation, sincerity, uprightness, and pacific spirit towards foreign states, by abstaining from secret arts and unfair advantages, by cultivating free and mutually beneficial intercourse, it should cherish among its citizens the ennobling consciousness of belonging to the human family, and of having a common interest with the whole human race. Government only fulfils its end, when it thus joins with Christianity in inculcating the law of universal love.

Unhappily, governments have seldom recognised as the highest duty, the obligation of strengthening pure and noble principle in the community. I fear, they are even to be numbered among the chief agents in corrupting nations. Of all the doctrines by which vice has propagated itself, I know none more pernicious than the maxim, that statesmen are exempted from the common restraints of morality, that nations are not equally bound with individuals by the eternal laws of justice and philanthropy. Through this doctrine, vice has lifted its head unblushingly in the most exalted stations. Vice has seated itself on the throne. The men who have wielded the power and riveted the gaze of nations, have lent the sanction of their greatness to crime. In the very heart of nations, in the cabinet of rulers, has been bred a moral pestilence, which has infected and contaminated all orders of the state. Through the example of rulers, private men have learned to regard the everlasting law as a temporary conventional rule, and been blinded to the supremacy of virtue.

That the prosperity of a people is intimately connected with this reverence for virtue, which I have inculcated on legislators, is most true, and cannot be too deeply felt. There is no foundation for the vulgar doctrine, that a state may flourish by arts and crimes. Nations and individuals are subjected to one law. The moral principle is the life of communities. No calamity can befall a people so great, as temporary success through a criminal policy, as the hope thus cherished of trampling with impunity on the authority of God. Sooner or later, insulted virtue avenges itself terribly on states as well as on private men. We hope, indeed, security and the quiet enjoyment of our wealth, from our laws and institutions. But civil laws find their chief sanction in the law written within by the finger of God. In proportion as a people enslave themselves to sin, the fountain of public justice becomes polluted. The most wholesome statutes, wanting the support of public opinion, grow impotent. Self-seekers, unprincipled men, by flattering bad passions, and by darkening the public mind, usurp the seat of judgment and places of power and trust, and turn free institutions into lifeless forms or instruments of oppression. I especially believe, that communities suffer sorely by that species of immorality which the herd of statesmen have industriously cherished as of signal utility, I mean, by hostile feeling towards other countries. The common doctrine has been, that prejudice and enmity towards foreign states, are means of fostering a national spirit, and of confirming union at home. But bad passions, once instilled into a people, will never exhaust themselves abroad. Vice never yields the fruits of virtue. Injustice to strangers does not breed justice to our friends. Malignity, in every form, is a fire of hell, and the policy which feeds it, is infernal. Domestic feuds and the madness of party are its natural and necessary issues; and a people hostile to others, will demonstrate in its history, that no form of inhumanity or injustice, escapes its just retribution.

Our great error as a people is, that we put an idolatrous trust in our free institutions; as if these, by some magic power, must secure our rights, however we enslave ourselves to evil passions. We need to learn that the forms of liberty are not its essence; that, whilst the letter of a free constitution is preserved, its spirit may be lost; that even its wisest provisions and most guarded powers may be made weapons of tyranny. In a country called free, a majority may become a faction, and a proscribed minority may be insulted, robbed, and oppressed. Under elective governments, a dominant party may become as truly a usurper, and as treasonably conspire against the state, as an individual who forces his way by arms to the throne.

I know that it is supposed, that political wisdom can so form institutions, as to extract from them freedom, notwithstanding a people's sins. The chief expedient for this purpose has been, to balance, as it is called, men's passions and interests against each other, to use one man's selfishness as a check against his neighbour's, to produce peace by the counteraction and equilibrium of hostile forces. This whole theory I distrust. The vices can by no management or skillful poising be made to do the work of virtue. Our own history has already proved this. Our government was founded on the doctrine of checks and balances; and what does experience teach us? It teaches, what the principles of our nature might have taught, that, whenever the country is divided into two great parties, the dominant party will possess itself of both branches of the legislature, and of the different departments of the state, and will move towards its objects with as little check, and with as determined purpose, as if all powers were concentrated in a single body. There is no substitute for virtue. Free institutions secure rights, only when secured by, and when invigorating that spiritual freedom, that moral power and elevation, which I have set before you as the supreme good of our nature.

According to these views, the first duty of a statesman is to build up the moral energy of a people. This is their first interest; and he who weakens it, inflicts an injury which no talent can repair; nor should any splendor of services, or any momentary success, avert from him the infamy which he has earned. Let public men learn to think more reverently of their function. Let them feel that they are touching more vital interests than property. Let them fear nothing so much as to sap the moral convictions of a people, by unrighteous legislation, or a selfish policy. Let them cultivate in themselves the spirit of religion and virtue, as the first requisite to public station. Let no apparent advantage to the community, any more than to themselves, seduce them to the infraction of any moral law. Let them put faith in virtue as the strength of nations. Let them not be disheartened by temporary ill success in upright exertion. Let them remember, that while they and their contemporaries live but for a day, the state is to live for ages; and that Time, the unerring arbiter, will vindicate the wisdom as well as the magnanimity of the public man, who, confiding in the power of truth, justice, and philanthropy, asserts their claims, and reverently follows their monitions, amidst general disloyalty and corruption.

I have hitherto spoken of the general influence which government should exert on the moral interests of a people, by expressing reverence for the moral law in its whole policy and legislation. It is also bound to exert a more particular and direct influence. I refer to its duty of preventing and punishing crime. This is one of the chief ends of government, but it has received as yet very little of the attention which it deserves. Government, indeed, has not been slow to punish crime, nor has society suffered for want of dungeons and gibbets. But the prevention of crime and the reformation of the offender have nowhere taken rank among the first objects of legislation. Penal codes, breathing vengeance, and too often written in blood, have been set in array against the violence of human passions, and the legislator's conscience has been satisfied with enacting these. Whether by shocking humanity he has not multiplied offenders, is a question into which he would do wisely to inquire.

On the means of preventing crime, I want time, and still more ability, to enlarge. I would only say, that this object should be kept in view through the whole of legislation. For this end, laws should be as few and as simple as may be; for an extensive and obscure code multiplies occasions of offence, and brings the citizen unnecessarily into collision with the state. Above all, let the laws bear broadly on their front the impress of justice and humanity, so that the moral sense of the community may become their sanction. Arbitrary and oppressive laws invite offence, and take from disobedience the consciousness of guilt. It is even wise to abstain from laws, which, however wise and good in themselves, have the semblance of inequality, which find no response in the heart of the citizen, and which will be evaded with little remorse. The wisdom of legislation is especially seen in grafting laws on conscience. I add, what seems to me of great importance, that the penal code should be brought to bear with the sternest impartiality on the rich and exalted, as well as on the poor and fallen. Society suffers from the crimes of the former, not less than by those of the latter. It has been truly said, that the amount of property taken by theft and forgery, is small compared with what is taken by dishonest insolvency. Yet the thief is sent to prison, and the dishonest bankrupt lives perhaps in state. The moral sentiment of the community is thus corrupted; and, for this and other solemn reasons, a reform is greatly needed in the laws which respect insolvency. I am shocked at the imprisonment of the honest debtor; and the legislation, which allows a creditor to play the tyrant over an innocent man, would disgrace, I think, a barbarous age. I am not less shocked by the impunity with which criminal insolvents continually escape, and by the lenity of the community towards these transgressors of its most essential laws.

Another means of preventing crime, is to punish it wisely; and by wise punishment, I mean that which aims to reform the offender. I know that this end of punishment has been questioned by wise and good men. But what higher or more practicable end can be proposed? You say, we must punish for example. But history shows that what is called examplary punishment cannot boast of great efficiency. Crime thrives under severe penalties, thrives on the blood of offenders. The frequent exhibition of such punishments hardens a people's heart, and produces defiance and reaction in the guilty. Until recently, government seems to have labored to harden the criminal by throwing him into a crowd of offenders, into the putrid atmosphere of a common prison. Humanity rejoices in the reform, which, in this respect, is spreading through our country. To remove the convict from bad influences is an essential step to his moral restoration. It is however but a step. To place him under the aid of good influence is equally important; and here individual exertion must come to the aid of legislative provisions. Private Christians, selected at once for their judiciousness and philanthropy, must connect themselves with the solitary prisoner, and by manifestations of a sincere fraternal interest, by conversation, books, and encouragement, must touch within him chords which have long ceased to vibrate; must awaken new hopes; must show him that all is not lost, that God, and Christ, and virtue, and the friendship of the virtuous, and honor, and immortality, may yet be secured. Of this glorious ministry of private Christianity, I do not despair. I know I shall be told of the failure of all efforts to reclaim criminals. They have not always failed. And besides, has philanthropy, has genius, has the strength of humanity, been fairly and fervently put forth in this great concern? I find in the New Testament no class of human beings whom charity is instructed to forsake. I find no exception made by Him who came to seek and save that which was lost. I must add, that the most hopeless subjects are not always to be found in prisons. That convicts are dreadfully corrupt, I know; but not more corrupt than some who walk at large, and are not excluded from our kindness. The rich man who defrauds is certainly as criminal as the poor man who steals. The rich man who drinks to excess contracts deeper guilt, than he who sinks into this vice under the pressure of want. The young man who seduces innocence, deserves more richly the House of Correction, than the unhappy female whom he allured into the path of destruction. Still more, I cannot but remember how much the guilt of the convict results from the general corruption of society. When I reflect, how much of the responsibility for crimes rests on the state, how many of the offences, which are most severely punished, are to be traced to neglected education, to early squalid want, to temptations and exposures which society might do much to relieve,—I feel that a spirit of mercy should temper legislation; that we should not sever ourselves so widely from our fallen brethren; that we should recognise in them the countenance and claims of humanity; that we should strive to win them back to God.

I have thus spoken of the obligation of government to contribute by various means to the moral elevation of a people. I close this head with expressing sorrow, that an institution, capable of such purifying influences, should so often be among the chief engines of a nation's corruption.

In this discourse I have insisted on the supreme importance of virtuous principle, of moral force, and elevation in the community; and I have thus spoken, not that I might conform to professional duty, but from deep personal conviction. I feel, as I doubt not many feel, that the great distinction of a nation, the only one worth possessing, and which brings after it all other blessings, is the prevalence of pure principle among the citizens. I wish to belong to a state, in the character and institutions of which I may find a spring of improvement, which I can speak of with an honest pride, in whose records I may meet great and honored names, and which is making the world its debtor by its discoveries of truth, and by an example of virtuous freedom. O save me from a country which worships wealth, and cares not for true glory; in which intrigue bears rule; in which patriotism borrows its zeal from the prospect of office; in which hungry sycophants besiege with supplication all the departments of state; in which public men bear the brand of vice, and the seat of government is a noisome sink of private licentiousness and political corruption. Tell me not of the honor of belonging to a free country. I ask, does our liberty bear generous fruits? Does it exalt us in manly spirit, in public virtue, above countries trodden under foot by despotism? Tell me not of the extent of our territory. I care not how large it is, if it multiply degenerate men. Speak not of our prosperity. Better be one of a poor people, plain in manners, revering God and respecting themselves, than belong to a rich country which knows no higher good than riches. Earnestly do I desire for this country, that, instead of copying Europe with an undiscerning servility, it may have a character of its own, corresponding to the freedom and equality of our institutions. One Europe is enough. One Paris is enough.

How much to be desired is it, that, separated as we are from the eastern continent by an ocean, we should be still more widely separated by simplicity of manners, by domestic purity, by inward piety, by reverence for human nature, by moral independence, by withstanding that subjection to fashion and that debilitating sensuality, which characterize the most civilized portions of the old world.

Of this country I may say with peculiar emphasis, that its happiness is bound up in its virtue. On this our union can alone stand firm. Our union is not like that of other nations, confirmed by the habits of ages, and riveted by force. It is a recent, and still more, a voluntary union. It is idle to talk of force as binding us together. Nothing can retain a member of this confederacy, when resolved on separation. The only bonds that can permanently unite us, are moral ones.[5] That there are repulsive powers, principles of discord, in these States, we all feel. The attraction which is to counteract them, is only to be found in a calm wisdom, controlling the passions, in a spirit of equity and regard to the common weal, and in virtuous patriotism, clinging to union as the only pledge of freedom and peace. The union is threatened by sectional jealousies, and collisions of local interests, which can be reconciled only by a magnanimous liberality. It is endangered by the prostitution of executive patronage, through which the public treasury is turned into a fountain of corruption, and by the lust for power, which perpetually convulses the country for the sake of throwing office into new hands; and the only remedy for these evils, is to be found in the moral indignation of the community, in a pure, lofty spirit, which will overwhelm with infamy this selfish ambition.

To the Chief Magistrate of this Commonwealth, and to those associated with him in the Executive and Legislative departments, I respectfully commend the truths which have now been delivered; and, with the simplicity becoming a minister of Jesus Christ, I would remind them of their solemn obligations to God, to their fellow creatures, and to the interests of humanity, freedom, virtue, and religion. We trust that in their high stations, they will seek, not themselves, but the public weal, and will seek it by inflexible adherence to the principles of the Constitution, and still more to the principles of God's Everlasting Law.

Notes

1. Channing's audience for the address was the political leadership of Massachusetts.

2. The "battles in heaven" are described in John Milton's *Paradise Lost*.

3. Channing's objections here are to both Roman Catholicism and New England Calvinism.

4. In the text of *The Works of William E. Channing, D.D.* (1841–43), the term "spending" is used for spreading. In the first edition of the work (1830), and in the later one-volume *The Works of William Ellery Channing* (Boston, 1875) "spreading" is used. I have emended the text to read "spreading."

5. It is interesting to note Channing's sense of the voluntary nature of the union, since this became a very controversial issue in the three decades following his address.

SELF-CULTURE (1838)*

*The original text that follows this introduction is from *The Works of William E. Channing, D.D.*, 6 vols. (Boston: James Munroe, 1841–43), 2:347–411.

"The word of ambition at the present day is Culture," Emerson wrote in 1860.[1] *His remark records accurately the large influence on American intellectual history of the cluster of ideas emanating from the protean term "culture." Channing's* Self-Culture *was perhaps the classic definition of the idea in nineteenth-century America. If works such as "Unitarian Christianity" reveal his theological influence, and his writings on slavery reveal his political influence, "Self-Culture" suggests that Channing was able to articulate more general American cultural assumptions. Perhaps more than any other work, this one makes Channing representative of American values. Yet his statement of the doctrine was not without controversy. One of its implications was that the primary focus of human energy should be on the individual rather than society, and for this Channing was criticized by Orestes Brownson. Brownson's Transcendentalism was more politically oriented, and even though he admitted the "importance" of what Channing said on self-culture in his essay "The Laboring Classes," he went on to add this critique: "Self-culture is a good thing, but it cannot abolish inequality, nor restore men to their rights."*[2] *For Brownson, self-culture could only be a "means" to eventual political and economic liberation. For Channing, it was an end in itself, a vision of life that made political and economic liberation of value. This clash of ideas summarizes very well one*

1. *The Complete Works of Ralph Waldo Emerson*, ed. Edward Waldo Emerson, Centenary Edition, 12 vols. (Boston and New York: Houghton Mifflin, 1903–4), 6:131.

2. Orestes A. Brownson, "The Laboring Classes," *Boston Quarterly Review*, 3 (July 1840):375. For a discussion of the development of the idea of self-culture in Unitarian thinking, see David Robinson, *Apostle of Culture: Emerson as Preacher and Lecturer* (Philadelphia: University of Pennsylvania Press, 1982).

221

of the deepest debates on the relation of the individual and society in nine-teenth-century American culture.

Channing's principal audience for the lectures, "those who are oc-cupied by manual labor," was not the natural constituency of a Boston Un-itarian minister. But Channing felt this limitation of his milieu, and worked hard to free his message from its Brahmin context. Thus he felt that his principal idea had the power to cut across all lines of class and condition: "He who possesses the divine powers of the soul is a great being, be his place what it may."

SELF-CULTURE.
AN ADDRESS INTRODUCTORY
TO THE FRANKLIN LECTURES,
DELIVERED AT BOSTON, SEPT., 1838

This Address was intended to make two lectures; but the author was led to abridge it and deliver it as one, partly by the apprehen-sion, that some passages were too abstract for a popular address, partly to secure the advantages of presenting the whole subject at once and in close connexion, and for other reasons which need not be named. Most of the passages which were omitted, are now pub-lished. The author respectfully submits the discourse to those for whom it was particularly intended, and to the public, in the hope, that it will at least bring a great subject before the minds of some, who may not as yet have given to it the attention it deserves.

My Respected Friends:

By the invitation of the committee of arrangements for the Franklin Lectures, I now appear before you to offer some remarks introductory to this course.[1] My principal inducement for doing so is my deep interest in those of my fellow-citizens, for whom these lec-tures are principally designed. I understood that they were to be at-tended chiefly by those who are occupied by manual labor; and, hearing this, I did not feel myself at liberty to decline the service to which I had been invited. I wished by compliance to express my sympathy with this large portion of my race. I wished to express my sense of obligation to those, from whose industry and skill I derive almost all the comforts of life. I wished still more to express my joy in the efforts they are making for their own improvement, and my firm faith in their success. These motives will give a particular character and bearing to some of my remarks. I shall speak occasionally as among those who live by the labor of their hands. But I shall not speak as one separated from them. I belong rightfully to the great fraternity of working men. Happily in this community we all are bred and born to work; and this honorable mark, set on us all, should bind together the various portions of the community.

I have expressed my strong interest in the mass of the people; and this is founded, not on their usefulness to the community, so much as on what they are in themselves. Their condition is indeed obscure; but their importance is not on this account a whit the less. The multitude of men cannot, from the nature of the case, be distinguished; for the very idea of distinction is, that a man stands out from the multitude. They make little noise and draw little notice in their narrow spheres of action; but still they have their full proportion of personal worth and even of greatness. Indeed every man, in every condition, is great. It is only our own diseased sight which makes him little. A man is great as a man, be he where or what he may. The grandeur of his nature turns to insignificance all outward distinctions. His powers of intellect, of conscience, of love, of knowing God, of perceiving the beautiful, of acting on his own mind, on outward nature, and on his fellow-creatures, these are glorious prerogatives. Through the vulgar error of undervaluing what is common, we are apt indeed to pass these by as of little worth. But as in the outward creation, so in the soul, the common is the most precious. Science and art may invent splendid modes of illuminating the apartments of the opulent; but these are all poor and worthless, compared with the common light which the sun sends into all our windows, which he pours freely, impartially over hill and valley, which kindles daily the eastern and western sky; and so the common lights of reason, and conscience, and love, are of more worth and dignity than the rare endowments which give celebrity to a few. Let us not disparage that nature which is common to all men; for no thought can measure its grandeur. It is the image of God, the image even of his infinity, for no limits can be set to its unfolding. He who possesses the divine powers of the soul is a great being, be his place what it may. You may clothe him with rags, may immure him in a dungeon, may chain him to slavish tasks. But he is still great. You may shut him out of your houses; but God opens to him heavenly mansions. He makes no show indeed in the streets of a splendid city; but a clear thought, a pure affection, a resolute act of a virtuous will, have a dignity of quite another kind and far higher than accumulations of brick and granite and plaster and stucco, however cunningly put together, or though stretching far beyond our sight. Nor is this all. If we pass over this grandeur of our common nature, and turn our thoughts to that comparative greatness, which draws chief attention, and which consists in the decided superiority of the individual to the general standard of power and character, we shall find this as free and frequent a growth among the obscure and unnoticed as in more conspicuous walks of life. The truly great are to be found everywhere, nor is it easy to say, in what condition they spring up most plentifully. Real greatness has nothing to do with a man's sphere. It does not lie in the magnitude of his outward agency, in the extent of the effects which he produces. The greatest men may do comparatively little abroad. Perhaps the greatest in our city at this moment are buried in obscurity. Grandeur of character lies wholly in force of soul, that is, in the force of thought, moral principle, and love, and this may be found in the humblest condition of life. A man brought up to an obscure trade, and hemmed in by the wants of a growing family, may, in his narrow sphere, perceive more clearly, discriminate more keenly, weigh evidence more wisely, seize on the right means more decisively, and have more presence of mind in difficulty, than another who has accumulated vast stores of knowledge by laborious study; and he has more of intellectual greatness. Many a man, who has gone but a few miles from home, understands human nature better, detects motives and weighs character more sagaciously, than another, who has travelled over the known world, and made a name by his reports of different countries. It is force of thought which measures intellectual, and so it is force of principle which measures moral greatness, that highest of human endowments, that brightest manifestation of the Divinity. The greatest man is he who chooses the Right with invincible resolution, who resists the sorest temptations from within and without, who bears the heaviest burdens cheerfully, who is calmest in storms and most fearless under menace and frowns, whose reliance on truth, on virtue, on God, is most unfaltering; and is this a greatness, which is apt to make a show, or which is most likely to abound in conspicuous station? The solemn conflicts of reason with passion; the victories of moral and religious principle over urgent and almost irresistible solicitations to self-indulgence; the hardest sacrifices of duty, those of deep-seated affection and of the heart's fondest hopes; the consolations, hopes, joys, and peace, of disappointed, persecuted, scorned, deserted virtue; these are of course unseen; so that the true greatness of human life is almost wholly out of sight. Perhaps in our presence, the most heroic deed on earth is done in some silent spirit, the loftiest purpose cherished, the most generous sacrifice made, and we do not suspect it. I believe this greatness to be most common among the multitude, whose names are never heard. Among common people will be found more of hardship borne manfully, more of unvarnished truth, more of religious trust, more of that generosity which gives what the giver needs himself, and more of a wise estimate of life and death, than among the more prosperous.—And even in regard to influence over other beings, which is thought the peculiar prerogative of distinguished station, I believe, that the difference between the conspicuous and the obscure does not amount to much. Influence is to be measured, not by the extent of surface it covers, but by its *kind*. A man may spread his mind, his feelings, and opinions, through a great extent; but if his mind be a low one, he manifests no greatness. A wretched artist may fill a city with daubs, and by a false, showy style achieve a reputation; but the man of genius, who leaves behind him one grand picture, in which immortal beauty is embodied, and which is silently to spread a true taste in his art, exerts an incomparably higher influence. Now the noblest influence on earth is that exerted on character; and he who puts forth this, does a great work, no matter how narrow or obscure his sphere. The father and mother of an unnoticed family, who, in their seclusion, awaken the mind of one child to the idea and love of perfect goodness, who awaken in him a strength of will to repel all temptation, and who send him out prepared to profit by the conflicts of life, surpass in influence a Napolean breaking the world to his sway. And not only is their work higher in kind; who knows, but that they are doing a greater work even as to extent or surface than the conqueror? Who knows, but that the being, whom they inspire with holy and disinterested principles, may communicate himself to others; and that, by a spreading agency, of which they were the silent origin, improvements may spread through a nation, through the world? In these remarks you will see why I feel and express a deep interest in the obscure, in the mass of men. The distinctions of society vanish before the light of these truths. I attach myself to the multitude, not because they are voters and have political power; but because they are men, and have within their reach the most glorious prizes of humanity.

In this country the mass of the people are distinguished by possessing means of improvement, of self-culture, possessed nowhere else. To incite them to the use of these, is to render them the best service they can receive. Accordingly I have chosen for the subject of this lecture, Self-culture, or the care which every man owes to himself, to the unfolding and perfecting of his nature. I consider this topic as particularly appropriate to the introduction of a course of lectures, in consequence of a common disposition to regard these and other like means of instruction, as able of themselves to carry forward the hearer. Lectures have their use. They stir up many, who, but for such outward appeals, might have slumbered to the end of life. But let it be remembered, that little is to be gained simply by coming to this place once a-week, and giving up the mind for an hour to be wrought upon by a teacher. Unless we are roused to act upon ourselves, unless we engage in the work of self-improvement, unless we purpose strenuously to form and elevate our own minds, unless what we hear is made a part of ourselves by conscientious reflection, very little permanent good is received.

Self-culture, I am aware, is a topic too extensive for a single discourse, and I shall be able to present but a few views which seem to me most important. My aim will be, to give first the Idea of self-culture, next its Means, and then to consider some objections to the leading views which I am now to lay before you.

Before entering on the discussion, let me offer one remark. Self-culture is something possible. It is not a dream. It has foundations in our nature. Without this conviction, the speaker will but declaim, and the hearer listen without profit. There are two powers of the human soul which make self-culture possible, the self-searching and the self-forming power. We have first the faculty of turning the mind on itself; of recalling its past, and watching its present operations; of learning its various capacities and susceptibilities; what it can do and bear, what it can enjoy and suffer; and of thus learning in general what our nature is, and what it was made for. It is worthy of observation, that we are able to discern not only what we already are, but what we may become, to see in ourselves germs and promises of a growth to which no bounds can be set, to dart beyond what we have actually gained to the idea of Perfection as the end of our being. It is by this self-comprehending power that we are distinguished from the brutes, which give no signs of looking into themselves. Without this there would be no self-culture, for we should not know the work to be done; and one reason why self-culture is so little proposed is, that so few penetrate into their own nature. To most men, their own spirits are shadowy, unreal, compared with what is outward. When they happen to cast a glance inward, they see there only a dark, vague chaos. They distinguish perhaps some violent passion, which has driven them to injurious excess; but their highest powers hardly attract a thought; and thus multitudes live and die as truly strangers to themselves, as to countries of which they have heard the name, but which human foot has never trodden.

But self-culture is possible, not only because we can enter into and search ourselves. We have a still nobler power, that of acting on, determining and forming ourselves. This is a fearful as well as glorious endowment, for it is the ground of human responsibility. We have the power not only of tracing our powers, but of guiding and impelling them; not only of watching our passions, but of controlling them; not only of seeing our faculties grow, but of applying to them means and influences to aid their growth. We can stay or change the current of thought. We can concentrate the intellect on objects which we wish to comprehend. We can fix our eyes on perfection, and make almost everything speed us toward it. This is indeed a noble prerogative of our nature. Possessing this, it matters little what or where we are now, for we can conquer a better lot, and even be happier for starting from the lowest point. Of all the discoveries which men need to make, the most important at the present moment, is that of the self-forming power treasured up in themselves. They little suspect its extent, as little as the savage apprehends the energy which the mind is created to exert on the material world. It transcends in importance all our power over outward nature. There is more of divinity in it, than in the force which impels the outward universe; and yet how little we comprehend it! How it slumbers in most men unsuspected, unused! This makes self-culture possible, and binds it on us as a solemn duty.

I. I am first to unfold the idea of self-culture; and this, in its most general form, may easily be seized. To cultivate any thing, be it a plant, an animal, a mind, is to make grow. Growth, expansion is the end. Nothing admits culture, but that which has a principle of life, capable of being expanded. He, therefore, who does what he can to unfold all his powers and capacities, especially his nobler ones, so as to become a well proportioned, vigorous, excellent, happy being, practises self-culture.

This culture, of course, has various branches corresponding to the different capacities of human nature; but, though various, they are intimately united and make progress together. The soul, which our philosophy divides into various capacities, is still one essence, one life; and it exerts at the same moment, and blends in the same act, its various energies of thought, feeling, and volition. Accordingly, in a wise self-culture, all the principles of our nature grow at once by joint, harmonious action, just as all parts of the plant are unfolded together.[2] When therefore you hear of different branches of self-improvement, you will not think of them as distinct processes going on independently of each other, and requiring each its own separate means. Still a distinct consideration of these is needed to a full comprehension of the subject, and these I shall proceed to unfold.

First, self-culture is Moral, a branch of singular importance. When a man looks into himself, he discovers two distinct orders or kinds of principles, which it behoves him especially to comprehend. He discovers desires, appetites, passions, which terminate in himself, which crave and seek his own interest, gratification, distinction; and he discovers another principle, an antagonist to these, which is Impartial, Disinterested, Universal, enjoining on him a regard to the rights and happiness of other beings, and laying on him obligations which *must* be discharged, cost what they may, or however they may clash with his particular pleasure or gain. No man, however narrowed to his own interest, however hardened by selfishness, can deny, that there springs up within him a great idea in opposition to interest, the idea of Duty, that an inward voice calls him more or less distinctly, to revere and exercise Impartial Justice, and Universal Good-will. This disinterested principle in human nature we call sometimes reason, sometimes conscience, sometimes the moral sense or faculty. But, be its name what it may, it is a real principle in each of us, and it is the supreme power within us, to be cultivated above all others, for on its culture the right developement of all others depends.[3] The passions indeed may be stronger than the conscience, may lift up a louder voice; but their clamor differs wholly from the tone of command in which the conscience speaks. They are not clothed with its authority, its binding power. In their very triumphs they are rebuked by the moral principle, and often cower before its still, deep, menacing voice. No part of self-knowledge is more important than to discern clearly these two great principles, the self-seeking and the disinterested; and the most important part of self-culture is to depress the former, and to exalt the latter, or to enthrone the sense of duty within us. There are no limits to the growth of this moral force in man, if he will cherish it faithfully. There have been men, whom no power in the universe could turn from the Right, by whom death in its most dreadful forms has been less dreaded, than transgression of the inward law of universal justice and love.

In the next place, self-culture is Religious. When we look into ourselves, we discover powers, which link us with this outward, visible, finite, ever-changing world. We have sight and other senses to discern, and limbs and various faculties to secure and appropriate the material creation. And we have, too, a power, which cannot stop at what we see and handle, at what exists within the bounds of space and time, which seeks for the Infinite, Uncreated Cause, which cannot rest till it ascend to the Eternal, All-comprehending Mind. This we call the religious principle, and its grandeur cannot be exaggerated by human language; for it marks out a being destined for higher communion than with the visible universe. To develope this, is eminently to educate ourselves. The true idea of God, unfolded clearly and livingly within us, and moving us to adore and obey him, and to aspire after likeness to him, is the noblest growth in human, and, I may add, in celestial natures. The religious principle, and the moral, are intimately connected, and grow together. The former is indeed the perfection and highest manifestation of the latter. They are both disinterested. It is the essence of true religion to recognise and adore in God the attributes of Impartial Justice and Universal Love, and to hear him commanding us in the conscience to become what we adore.

Again. Self-culture is Intellectual. We cannot look into our-

selves without discovering the intellectual principle, the power
which thinks, reasons, and judges, the power of seeking and acquiring truth. This, indeed, we are in no danger of overlooking. The intellect being the great instrument by which men compass their
wishes, it draws more attention than any of our other powers. When
we speak to men of improving themselves, the first thought which
occurs to them is, that they must cultivate their understanding, and
get knowledge and skill. By education, men mean almost exclusively intellectual training. For this, schools and colleges are instituted, and to this the moral and religious discipline of the young is
sacrificed. Now I reverence, as much as any man, the intellect; but
let us never exalt it above the moral principle. With this it is most intimately connected. In this its culture is founded, and to exalt this is
its highest aim. Whoever desires that his intellect may grow up to
soundness, to healthy vigor, must begin with moral discipline.
Reading and study are not enough to perfect the power of thought.
One thing above all is needful, and that is, the Disinterestedness
which is the very soul of virtue. To gain truth, which is the great object of the understanding, I must seek it disinterestedly. Here is the
first and grand condition of intellectual progress. I must choose to
receive the truth, no matter how it bears on myself. I must follow it,
no matter where it leads, what interests it opposes, to what persecution or loss it lays me open, from what party it severs me, or to
what party it allies. Without this fairness of mind, which is only another phrase for disinterested love of truth, great native powers of
understanding are perverted and led astray; genius runs wild; "the
light within us becomes darkness."[4] The subtilest reasoners, for
want of this, cheat themselves as well as others, and become entan-
gled in the web of their own sophistry. It is a fact well known in the
history of science and philosophy, that men, gifted by nature with
singular intelligence, have broached the grossest errors, and even
sought to undermine the grand primitive truths on which human virtue, dignity, and hope depend. And, on the other hand, I have
known instances of men of naturally moderate powers of mind, who,
by a disinterested love of truth and their fellow-creatures, have gradually risen to no small force and enlargement of thought. Some of
the most useful teachers in the pulpit and in schools, have owed their
power of enlightening others, not so much to any natural superiority,
as to the simplicity, impartiality, and disinterestedness of their

minds, to their readiness to live and die for the truth. A man, who rises above himself, looks from an eminence on nature and providence, on society and life. Thought expands, as by a natural elasticity, when the pressure of selfishness is removed. The moral and religious principles of the soul, generously cultivated, fertilize the intellect. Duty, faithfully performed, opens the mind to truth, both being of one family, alike immutable, universal, and everlasting.

I have enlarged on this subject, because the connexion between moral and intellectual culture is often overlooked, and because the former is often sacrificed to the latter. The exaltation of talent, as it is called, above virtue and religion, is the curse of the age. Education is now chiefly a stimulus to learning, and thus men acquire power without the principles which alone make it a good. Talent is worshipped; but, if divorced from rectitude, it will prove more of a demon than a god.

Intellectual culture consists, not chiefly, as many are apt to think, in accumulating information, though this is important, but in building up a force of thought which may be turned at will on any subjects, on which we are called to pass judgment. This force is manifested in the concentration of the attention, in accurate, penetrating observation, in reducing complex subjects to their elements, in diving beneath the effect to the cause, in detecting the more subtile differences and resemblances of things, in reading the future in the present, and especially in rising from particular facts to general laws or universal truths. This last exertion of the intellect, its rising to broad views and great principles, constitutes what is called the philosophical mind, and is especially worthy of culture. What it means, your own observation must have taught you. You must have taken note of two classes of men, the one always employed on details, on particular facts, and the other using these facts as foundations of higher, wider truths. The latter are philosophers. For example, men had for ages seen pieces of wood, stones, metals falling to the ground. Newton seized on these particular facts, and rose to the idea, that all matter tends, or is attracted, towards all matter, and then defined the law according to which this attraction or force acts at different distances, thus giving us a grand principle, which, we have reason to think, extends to and controls the whole outward creation. One man reads a history, and can tell you all its events, and there stops. Another combines these events, brings them under one view, and learns the great causes which are at work on this or another nation, and what are its great tendencies, whether to freedom or despotism, to one or another form of civilization. So, one man talks continually about the particular actions of this or another neighbour; whilst another looks beyond the acts to the inward principle from which they spring, and gathers from them larger views of human nature. In a word, one man sees all things apart and in fragments, whilst another strives to discover the harmony, connexion, unity of all. One of the great evils of society is, that men, occupied perpetually with petty details, want general truths, want broad and fixed principles. Hence many, not wicked, are unstable, habitually inconsistent, as if they were overgrown children rather than men. To build up that strength of mind, which apprehends and cleaves to great universal truths, is the highest intellectual self-culture; and here I wish you to observe how entirely this culture agrees with that of the moral and the religious principles of our nature, of which I have previously spoken. In each of these, the improvement of the soul consists in raising it above what is narrow, particular, individual, selfish, to the universal and unconfined. To improve a man, is to liberalize, enlarge him in thought, feeling, and purpose. Narrowness of intellect and heart, this is the degradation from which all culture aims to rescue the human being.

Again. Self-culture is social, or one of its great offices is to unfold and purify the affections, which spring up instinctively in the human breast, which bind together husband and wife, parent and child, brother and sister; which bind a man to friends and neighbours, to his country, and to the suffering who fall under his eye, wherever they belong. The culture of these is an important part of our work, and it consists in converting them from instincts into principles, from natural into spiritual attachments, in giving them a rational, moral, and holy character. For example, our affection for our children is at first instinctive; and if it continue such, it rises little above the brute's attachment to its young. But when a parent infuses into his natural love for his offspring, moral and religious principle, when he comes to regard his child as an intelligent, spiritual, immortal being, and honors him as such, and desires first of all to make him disinterested, noble, a worthy child of God and the friend of his race, then the instinct rises into a generous and holy sentiment. It resembles God's paternal love for his spiritual family. A like purity and dignity we must aim to give to all our affections.

Again. Self-culture is Practical, or it proposes, as one of its chief ends, to fit us for action, to make us efficient in whatever we undertake, to train us to firmness of purpose and to fruitfulness of resource in common life, and especially in emergencies, in times of difficulty, danger, and trial. But passing over this and other topics for which I have no time, I shall confine myself to two branches of self-culture which have been almost wholly overlooked in the education of the people, and which ought not to be so slighted.

In looking at our nature, we discover, among its admirable endowments, the sense or perception of Beauty. We see the germ of this in every human being, and there is no power which admits greater cultivation; and why should it not be cherished in all? It deserves remark, that the provision for this principle is infinite in the universe. There is but a very minute portion of the creation which we can turn into food and clothes, or gratification for the body; but the whole creation may be used to minister to the sense of beauty. Beauty is an all-pervading presence. It unfolds in the numberless flowers of the spring. It waves in the branches of the trees and the green blades of grass. It haunts the depths of the earth and sea, and gleams out in the hues of the shell and the precious stone. And not only these minute objects, but the ocean, the mountains, the clouds, the heavens, the stars, the rising and setting sun, all overflow with beauty. The universe is its temple; and those men, who are alive to it, cannot lift their eyes without feeling themselves encompassed with it on every side. Now this beauty is so precious, the enjoyments it gives are so refined and pure, so congenial with our tenderest and noble feelings, and so akin to worship, that it is painful to think of the multitude of men as living in the midst of it, and living almost as blind to it, as if, instead of this fair earth and glorious sky, they were tenants of a dungeon. An infinite joy is lost to the world by the want of culture of this spiritual endowment. Suppose that I were to visit a cottage, and to see its walls lined with the choicest pictures of Raphael, and every spare nook filled with statues of the most exquisite workmanship, and that I were to learn, that neither man, woman, nor child ever cast an eye at these miracles of art, how should I feel their privation; how should I want to open their eyes, and to help them to comprehend and feel the loveliness and grandeur which in vain courted their notice! But every husbandman is living in sight of the works of a diviner Artist; and how much would his existence be elevated, could he see the glory which shines forth in their forms, hues, proportions, and moral expression! I have spoken only of the beauty of nature, but how much of this mysterious charm is found in the elegant arts, and especially in literature? The best books have most beauty. The greatest truths are wronged if not linked with beauty, and they win their way most surely and deeply into the soul when arrayed in this their natural and fit attire. Now no man receives the true culture of a man, in whom the sensibility to the beautiful is not cherished; and I know of no condition in life from which it should be excluded. Of all luxuries, this is the cheapest and most at hand; and it seems to me to be most important to those conditions, where coarse labor tends to give a grossness to the mind. From the diffusion of the sense of beauty in ancient Greece, and of the taste for music in modern Germany, we learn that the people at large may partake of refined gratifications, which have hitherto been thought to be necessarily restricted to a few.

What beauty is, is a question which the most penetrating minds have not satisfactorily answered; nor, were I able, is this the place for discussing it. But one thing I would say; the beauty of the outward creation is intimately related to the lovely, grand, interesting attributes of the soul. It is the emblem or expression of these. Matter becomes beautiful to us, when it seems to lose its material aspect, its inertness, finiteness, and grossness, and by the etherial lightness of its forms and motions seems to approach spirit; when it images to us pure and gentle affections; when it spreads out into a vastness which is a shadow of the Infinite; or when in more awful shapes and movements it speaks of the Omnipotent. Thus outward beauty is akin to something deeper and unseen, is the reflection of spiritual attributes; and of consequence the way to see and feel it more and more keenly, is to cultivate those moral, religious, intellectual, and social principles of which I have already spoken, and which are the glory of the spiritual nature; and I name this, that you may see, what I am anxious to show, the harmony which subsists among all branches of human culture, or how each forwards and is aided by all.

There is another power, which each man should cultivate according to his ability, but which is very much neglected in the mass of the people, and that is, the power of Utterance. A man was not made to shut up his mind in itself; but to give it voice and to exchange it for other minds. Speech is one of our grand distinctions from the brute. Our power over others lies not so much in the amount of thought within us, as in the power of bringing it out. A man, of more than ordinary intellectual vigor, may, for want of expression, be a cipher, without significance, in society. And not only does a man influence others, but he greatly aids his own intellect, by giving distinct and forcible utterance to his thoughts. We undertand ourselves better, our conceptions grow clearer, by the very effort to make them clear to another. Our social rank, too, depends a good deal on our power of utterance. The principal distinction between what are called gentlemen and the vulgar lies in this, that the latter are awkward in manners, and are especially wanting in propriety, clearness, grace, and force of utterance. A man who cannot open his lips without breaking a rule of grammar, without showing in his dialect or brogue or uncouth tones his want of cultivation, or without darkening his meaning by a confused, unskilful mode of communication, cannot take the place to which, perhaps, his native good sense entitles him. To have intercourse with respectable people, we must speak their language. On this account, I am glad that grammar and a correct pronunciation are taught in the common schools of this city. These are not trifles; nor are they superfluous to any class of people. They give a man access to social advantages, on which his improvement very much depends. The power of utterance should be included by all in their plans of self-culture.

I have now given a few views of the culture, the improvement, which every man should propose to himself. I have all along gone on the principle, that a man has within him capacities of growth, which deserve and will reward intense, unrelaxing toil. I do not look on a human being as a machine, made to be kept in action by a foreign force, to accomplish an unvarying succession of motions, to do a fixed amount of work, and then to fall to pieces at death, but as a being of free spiritual powers; and I place little value on any culture, but that which aims to bring out these and to give them perpetual impulse and expansion. I am aware, that this view is far from being universal. The common notion has been, that the mass of the people need no other culture than is necessary to fit them for their various trades; and, though this error is passing away, it is far from being exploded. But the ground of a man's culture lies in his nature, not in his calling. His powers are to be unfolded on account of their inherent dignity, not their outward direction. He is to be educated, because he is a man, not because he is to make shoes, nails, or pins. A trade is plainly not the great end of his being, for his mind cannot be shut up in it; his force of thought cannot be exhausted on it. He has faculties to which it gives no action, and deep wants it cannot answer. Poems, and systems of theology and philosophy, which have made some noise in the world, have been wrought at the work-bench and amidst the toils of the field. How often, when the arms are mechanically plying a trade, does the mind, lost in reverie or daydreams, escape to the ends of the earth! How often does the pious heart of woman mingle the greatest of all thoughts, that of God, with household drudgery! Undoubtedly a man is to perfect himself in his trade, for by it he is to earn his bread and to serve the community. But bread or subsistence is not his highest good; for, if it were, his lot would be harder than that of the inferior animals, for whom nature spreads a table and weaves a wardrobe, without a care of their own. Nor was he made chiefly to minister to the wants of the community. A rational, moral being cannot, without infinite wrong, be converted into a mere instrument of others' gratification. He is necessarily an end, not a means. A mind, in which are sown the seeds of wisdom, disinterestedness, firmness of purpose, and piety, is worth more than all the outward material interests of a world. It exists for itself, for its own perfection, and must not be enslaved to its own or others' animal wants. You tell me, that a liberal culture is needed for men who are to fill high stations, but not for such as are doomed to vulgar labor. I answer, that Man is a greater name than President or King. Truth and goodness are equally precious, in whatever sphere they are found. Besides, men of all conditions sustain equally the relations, which give birth to the highest virtues and demand the highest powers. The laborer is not a mere laborer. He has close, tender, responsible connections with God and his fellow-creatures. He is a son, husband, father, friend, and Christian. He belongs to a home, a country, a church, a race; and is such a man to be cultivated only for a trade? Was he not sent into the world for a great work? To educate a child perfectly requires profounder thought, greater wisdom, than to govern a state; and for this plain reason, that the interests and wants of the latter are more superficial, coarser, and more obvious, than the spiritual capacities, the growth of thought and feeling, and the subtle laws of the mind, which must all be studied and comprehended, before the work of education can be thoroughly performed; and yet to all conditions this greatest work on earth is equally committed by God. What plainer proof do we need that a higher culture, than has yet been dreamed of, is needed by our whole race?

II. I now proceed to inquire into the Means, by which the self-culture, just described, may be promoted; and here I know not where to begin. The subject is so extensive, as well as important, that I feel myself unable to do any justice to it, especially in the limits to which I am confined. I beg you to consider me as presenting but hints, and such as have offered themselves with very little research to my own mind.

And, first, the great means of self-culture, that which includes all the rest, is to fasten on this culture as our Great End, to determine deliberately and solemnly, that we will make the most and the best of the powers which God has given us. Without this resolute purpose, the best means are worth little, and with it the poorest become mighty. You may see thousands, with every opportunity of improvement which wealth can gather, with teachers, libraries, and apparatus, bringing nothing to pass, and others, with few helps, doing wonders; and simply because the latter are in earnest, and the former not. A man in earnest finds means, or, if he cannot find, creates them. A vigorous purpose makes much out of little, breathes power into weak instruments, disarms difficulties, and even turns them into assistances. Every condition has means of progress, if we have spirit enough to use them. Some volumes have recently been published, giving examples or histories of ''knowledge acquired under difficulties''; and it is most animating to see in these what a resolute man can do for himself.[5] A great idea, like this of Self-culture, if seized on clearly and vigorously, burns like a living coal in the soul. He who deliberately adopts a great end, has, by this act, half accomplished it, has scaled the chief barrier to success.

One thing is essential to the strong purpose of self-culture now insisted on, namely, faith in the practicableness of this culture. A great object, to awaken resolute choice, must be seen to be within our reach. The truth, that progress is the very end of our being, must not be received as a tradition, but comprehended and felt as a reality. Our minds are apt to pine and starve, by being imprisoned within what we have already attained. A true faith, looking up to something better, catching glimpses of a distant perfection, prophesying to ourselves improvements proportioned to our conscientious labors, gives energy of purpose, gives wings to the soul; and this faith will continually grow, by acquainting ourselves with our own nature, and with the promises of Divine help and immortal life which abound in Revelation.

Some are discouraged from proposing to themselves improvement, by the false notion, that the study of books, which their situation denies them, is the all-important, and only sufficient means. Let such consider, that the grand volumes, of which all our books are transcripts, I mean nature, revelation, the human soul, and human life, are freely unfolded to every eye. The great sources of wisdom are experience and observation; and these are denied to none. To open and fix our eyes upon what passes without and within us, is the most fruitful study. Books are chiefly useful, as they help us to interpret what we see and experience. When they absorb men, as they sometimes do, and turn them from observation of nature and life, they generate a learned folly, for which the plain sense of the laborer could not be exchanged but at great loss. It deserves attention that the greatest men have been formed without the studies, which at present are thought by many most needful to improvement. Homer, Plato, Demosthenes, never heard the name of chemistry, and knew less of the solar system than a boy in our common schools. Not that these sciences are unimportant; but the lesson is, that human improvement never wants the means, where the purpose of it is deep and earnest in the soul.

The purpose of self-culture, this is the life and strength of all the methods we use for our own elevation. I reiterate this principle on account of its great importance; and I would add a remark to prevent its misapprehension. When I speak of the purpose of self-culture, I mean, that it should be sincere. In other words, we must make self-culture really and truly our end, or choose it for its own sake, and not merely as a means or instrument of something else. And here I touch a common and very pernicious error. Not a few persons desire to improve themselves only to get property and to rise in the world; but such do not properly choose improvement, but something outward and foreign to themselves; and so low an impulse can produce only a stinted, partial, uncertain growth. A man, as I have said, is to cultivate himself because he is a man. He is to start with the conviction, that there is something greater within him than in the whole material creation, than in all the worlds which press on the eye and ear; and that inward improvements have a worth and dignity in themselves, quite distinct from the power they give over outward things. Undoubtedly a man is to labor to better his condition, but first to better himself. If he knows no higher use of his mind than to invent and drudge for his body, his case is desperate as far as culture is concerned.

In these remarks, I do not mean to recommend to the laborer indifference to his outward lot. I hold it important, that every man in every class should possess the means of comfort, of health, of neatness in food and apparel, and of occasional retirement and leisure. These are good in themselves, to be sought for their own sakes, and still more, they are important means of the self-culture for which I am pleading. A clean, comfortable dwelling, with wholesome meals, is no small aid to intellectual and moral progress. A man living in a damp cellar or a garret open to rain and snow, breathing the foul air of a filthy room, and striving without success to appease hunger on scanty or unsavory food, is in danger of abandoning himself to a desperate, selfish recklessness. Improve then your lot. Multiply comforts, and still more get wealth if you can by honorable means, and if it do not cost too much. A true cultivation of the mind is fitted to forward you in your worldly concerns, and you ought to use it for this end. Only, beware, lest this end master you; lest your motives sink as your condition improves; lest you fall victims to the miserable passion of vying with those around you in show, luxury, and expense. Cherish a true respect for yourselves. Feel that your nature is worth more than every thing which is foreign to you. He who has not caught a glimpse of his own rational and spiritual being, of something within himself superior to the world and allied to the divinity, wants the true spring of that purpose of self-culture, on which I have insisted as the first of all the means of improvement.

I proceed to another important means of self-culture, and this is the control of the animal appetites. To raise the moral and intellectural nature, we must put down the animal. Sensuality is the abyss in which very many souls are plunged and lost. Among the most prosperous classes, what a vast amount of intellectual life is drowned in luxurious excesses! It is one great curse of wealth, that it is used to pamper the senses; and among the poorer classes, though luxury is wanting, yet a gross feeding often prevails, under which the spirit is whelmed. It is a sad sight to walk through our streets, and to see how many countenances bear marks of a lethargy and a brutal coarseness, induced by unrestrained indulgence. Whoever would cultivate the soul, must restrain the appetites. I am not an advocate for the doctrine, that animal food was not meant for man; but that this is used among us to excess; that as a people we should gain much in cheerfulness, activity, and buoyancy of mind, by less gross and stimulating food, I am strongly inclined to believe. Above all, let me urge on those, who would bring out and elevate their higher nature, to abstain from the use of spirituous liquors. This bad habit is distinguished from all others by the ravages it makes on the reason, the intellect; and this effect is produced to a mournful extent, even when drunkenness is escaped. Not a few men, called temperate, and who have thought themselves such, have learned, on abstaining from the use of ardent spirits, that for years their minds had been clouded, impaired by moderate drinking, without their suspecting the injury. Multitudes in this city are bereft of half their intellectual energy, by a degree of indulgence which passes for innocent. Of all the foes of the working class, this is the deadliest. Nothing has done more to keep down this class, to destroy their self-respect, to rob them of their just influence in the community, to render profitless the means of improvement within their reach, than the use of ardent spirits as a drink. They are called on to withstand this practice, as they regard their honor, and would take their just place in society. They are under solemn obligations to give their sanction to every effort for its suppression. They ought to regard as their worst enemies (though unintentionally such), as the enemies of their rights, dignity, and influence, the men who desire to flood city and country with distilled poison. I lately visited a flourishing village, and on expressing to one of the respected inhabitants the pleasure I felt in witnessing so many signs of progress, he replied, that one of the causes of the prosperity I witnessed, was the disuse of ardent spirits by the people. And this reformation we may be assured wrought something higher than outward prosperity. In almost every family so improved, we cannot doubt that the capacities of the parent for intellectual and moral improvement were enlarged, and the means of education made more effectual to the child. I call on working men to take hold of the cause of temperance as peculiarly *their* cause. These remarks are the more needed, in consequence of the efforts made far and wide, to annul at the present moment a recent law for the suppression of the sale of ardent spirits in such quantities as favor intemperance. I know, that there are intelligent and good men, who believe, that, in enacting this law, government transcended its limits, left its true path, and established a precedent for legislative interference with all our pursuits and pleasures. No one here looks more jealously on government than myself. But I maintain, that this is a case which stands by itself, which can be confounded with no other, and on which government from its very nature and end is peculiarly bound to act. Let it never be forgotten, that the great end of government, its highest function, is, not to make roads, grant charters, originate improvements, but to prevent or repress Crimes against individual rights and social order. For this end it ordains a penal code, erects prisons, and inflicts fearful punishments. Now if it be true, that a vast proportion of the crimes, which government is instituted to prevent and repress, have their origin in the use of ardent spirits; if our poor-houses, work-houses, jails, and penitentiaries, are tenanted in a great degree by those whose first and chief impulse to crime came from the distillery and dram-shop; if murder and theft, the most fearful outrages on property and life, are most frequently the issues and consummation of intemperance, is not government bound to restrain by legislation the vending of the stimulus to these terrible social wrongs? Is government never to act as a parent, never to remove the causes or occasions of wrong-doing? Has it but one instrument for repressing crime, namely, public, infamous punishment, an evil only inferior to crime? Is government a usurper, does it wander beyond its sphere, by imposing restraints on an article, which does no imaginable good, which can plead no benefit conferred on body or mind, which unfits the citizen for the discharge of his duty to his country, and which, above all, stirs up men to the perpetration of most of the crimes, from which it is the highest and most solemn office of government to protect society?

I come now to another important measure of self-culture, and this is, intercourse with superior minds. I have insisted on our own activity as essential to our progress; but we were not made to live or advance alone. Society is as needful to us as air or food. A child doomed to utter loneliness, growing up without sight or sound of human beings, would not put forth equal power with many brutes; and a man, never brought into contact with minds superior to his own, will probably run one and the same dull round of thought and action to the end of life.

It is chiefly through books that we enjoy intercourse with superior minds, and these invaluable means of communication are in the reach of all. In the best books, great men talk to us, give us their most precious thoughts, and pour their souls into ours. God be thanked for books. They are the voices of the distant and the dead, and make us heirs of the spiritual life of past ages. Books are the true levellers. They give to all, who will faithfully use them, the society, the spiritual presence, of the best and greatest of our race. No matter how poor I am. No matter though the prosperous of my own time will not enter my obscure dwelling. If the Sacred Writers will enter and take up their abode under my roof, if Milton will cross my threshold to sing to me of Paradise, and Shakspeare to open to me the worlds of imagination and the workings of the human heart, and Franklin to enrich me with his practical wisdom, I shall not pine for want of intellectual companionship, and I may become a cultivated man though excluded from what is called the best society in the place where I live.

To make this means of culture effectual, a man must select good books, such as have been written by right-minded and strong-minded men, real thinkers, who instead of diluting by repetition what others say, have something to say for themselves, and write to give relief to full, earnest souls; and these works must not be skimmed over for amusement, but read with fixed attention and a reverential love of truth. In selecting books, we may be aided much by those who have studied more than ourselves. But, after all, it is best to be determined in this particular a good deal by our own tastes. The best books for a man are not always those which the wise recommend, but oftener those which meet the peculiar wants, the natural thirst of his mind, and therefore awaken interest and rivet thought. And here it may be well to observe, not only in regard to books but in other respects, that self-culture must vary with the individual. All means do not equally suit us all. A man must unfold himself freely, and should respect the peculiar gifts or biases by which nature has distinguished him from others. Self-culture does not demand the sacrifice of individuality. It does not regularly apply an established machinery, for the sake of torturing every man into one rigid shape, called perfection. As the human countenance, with the same features in us all, is diversified without end in the race, and is never the same in any two individuals, so the human soul, with the same grand powers and laws, expands into an infinite variety of forms, and would be wofully stinted by modes of culture requiring all men to learn the same lesson or to bend to the same rules.

I know how hard it is to some men, especially to those who spend much time in manual labor, to fix attention on books. Let them strive to overcome the difficulty, by choosing subjects of deep interest, or by reading in company with those whom they love. Nothing can supply the place of books. They are cheering or soothing companions in solitude, illness, affliction. The wealth of both continents would not compensate for the good they impart. Let every man, if possible, gather some good books under his roof, and obtain access for himself and family to some social library. Almost any luxury should be sacrificed to this.

One of the very interesting features of our times, is the multiplication of books, and their distribution through all conditions of society. At a small expense, a man can now possess himself of the most precious treasures of English literature. Books, once confined to a few by their costliness, are now accessible to the multitude; and in this way a change of habits is going on in society, highly favorable to the culture of the people. Instead of depending on casual rumor and loose conversation for most of their knowledge and objects of thought; instead of forming their judgments in crowds, and receiving their chief excitement from the voice of neighbours, men are now learning to study and reflect alone, to follow out subjects continuously, to determine for themselves what shall engage their minds, and to call to their aid the knowledge, original views, and reasonings of men of all countries and ages; and the results must be, a deliberateness and independence of judgment, and a thoroughness and extent of information, unknown in former times. The diffusion of these silent teachers, books, through the whole community, is to work greater effects than artillery, machinery, and legislation. Its peaceful agency is to supersede stormy revolutions. The culture, which it is to spread, whilst an unspeakable good to the individual, is also to become the stability of nations.

Another important means of self-culture, is to free ourselves from the power of human opinion and example, except as far as this is sanctioned by our own deliberate judgment. We are all prone to keep the level of those we live with, to repeat their words, and dress our minds as well as bodies after their fashion; and hence the spiritless tameness of our characters and lives. Our greatest danger, is not from the grossly wicked around us, but from the worldly, unreflecting multitude, who are borne along as a stream by foreign impulse, and bear us along with them. Even the influence of superior minds may harm us, by bowing us to servile acquiescence and damping our spiritual activity. The great use of intercourse with other minds, is to stir up our own, to whet our appetite for truth, to carry our thoughts beyond their old tracks. We need connexions with great thinkers to make us thinkers too. One of the chief arts of self-culture, is to unite the childlike teachableness, which gratefully welcomes light from every human being who can give it, with manly resistance of opinions however current, of influences however generally revered, which do not approve themselves to our deliberate judgment. You ought indeed patiently and conscientiously to strengthen your reason by other men's intelligence, but you must not prostrate it before them. Especially if there springs up within you any view of God's word or universe, any sentiment or aspiration which seems to you of a higher order than what you meet abroad, give reverent heed to it; inquire into it earnestly, solemnly. Do not trust it blindly, for it may be an illusion; but it may be the Divinity moving within you, a new revelation, not supernatural but still most precious, of truth or duty; and if, after inquiry, it so appear, then let no clamor, or scorn, or desertion turn you from it. Be true to your own highest convictions. Intimations from our own souls of something more perfect than others teach, if faithfully followed, give us a consciousness of spiritual force and progress, never experienced by the vulgar of high life or low life, who march, as they are drilled, to the step of their times.

Some, I know, will wonder, that I should think the mass of the people capable of such intimations and glimpses of truth, as I have just supposed. These are commonly thought to be the prerogative of men of genius, who seem to be born to give law to the minds of the multitude. Undoubtedly nature has her nobilty, and sends forth a few to be eminently "lights of the world."[6] But it is also true that a portion of the same divine fire is given to all; for the many could not receive with a loving reverence the quickening influences of the few, were there not essentially the same spiritual life in both. The minds of the multitude are not masses of passive matter, created to receive impressions unresistingly from abroad. They are not wholly shaped by foreign instruction; but have a native force, a spring of thought in themselves. Even the child's mind outruns its lessons, and overflows in questionings which bring the wisest to a stand. Even the child starts the great problems, which philosophy has labored to solve for ages. But on this subject I cannot now enlarge. Let me only say, that the power of original thought is particularly manifested in those who thirst for progress, who are bent on unfolding their whole nature. A man who wakes up to the consciousness of having been created for progress and perfection, looks with new eyes on himself and on the world in which he lives. This great truth stirs the soul from its depths, breaks up old associations of ideas, and establishes new ones, just as a mighty agent of chemistry, brought into contact with natural substances, dissolves the old affinities which had bound their particles together, and arranges them anew. This truth particularly aids us to penetrate the mysteries of human life. By revealing to us the end of our being, it helps us to comprehend more and more the wonderful, the infinite system, to which we belong. A man in the common walks of life, who has faith in perfection, in the unfolding of the human spirit, as the great purpose of God, possesses more the secret of the universe, perceives more the harmonies or mutual adaptations of the world without and the world within him, is a wiser interpreter of Providence, and reads nobler lessons of duty in the events which pass before him, than the profoundest philosopher who wants this grand central truth. Thus illuminations, inward suggestions, are not confined to a favored few, but visit all who devote themselves to a generous self-culture.

Another means of self-culture may be found by every man in his Condition or Occupation, be it what it may. Had I time, I might go through all conditions of life, from the most conspicuous to the most obscure, and might show how each furnishes continual aids to improvement. But I will take one example, and that is, of a man living by manual labor. This may be made the means of self-culture. For instance, in almost all labor, a man exchanges his strength for an equivalent in the form of wages, purchase-money, or some other product. In other words, labor is a system of contracts, bargains, imposing mutual obligations. Now the man, who, in working, no matter in what way, strives perpetually to fulfil his obligations thoroughly, to do his whole work faithfully, to be honest not because honesty is the best policy, but for the sake of justice, and that he may render to every man his due, such a laborer is continually building up in himself one of the greatest principles of morality and religion. Every blow on the anvil, on the earth, or whatever material he works upon, contributes something to the perfection of his nature.

Nor is this all. Labor is a school of benevolence as well as justice. A man to support himself must serve others. He must do or produce something for their comfort or gratification. This is one of the beautiful ordinations of Providence, that, to get a living, a man must be useful. Now this usefulness ought to be an end in his labor as truly as to earn his living. He ought to think of the benefit of those he works for, as well as of his own; and in so doing, in desiring amidst his sweat and toil to serve others as well as himself, he is exercising and growing in benevolence, as truly as if he were distributing bounty with a large hand to the poor. Such a motive hallows and dignifies the commonest pursuit. It is strange, that laboring men do not think more of the vast usefulness of their toils, and take a benevolent pleasure in them on this account. This beautiful city, with its houses, furniture, markets, public walks, and numberless accommodations, has grown up under the hands of artisans and other laborers, and ought they not to take a disinterested joy in their work? One would think, that a carpenter or mason, on passing a house which he had reared, would say to himself, "This work of mine is giving comfort and enjoyment every day and hour to a family, and will continue to be a kindly shelter, a domestic gathering-place, an abode of affection, for a century or more after I sleep in the dust;" and ought not a generous satisfaction to spring up at the thought? It is by thus interweaving goodness with common labors, that we give it strength and make it a habit of the soul.

Again. Labor may be so performed as to be a high impulse to

the mind. Be a man's vocation what it may, his rule should be to do its duties perfectly, to do the best he can, and thus to make perpetual progress in his art. In other words, Perfection should be proposed; and this I urge not only for its usefulness to society, nor for the sincere pleasure which a man takes in seeing a work well done. This is an important means of self-culture. In this way the idea of Perfection takes root in the mind, and spreads far beyond the man's trade. He gets a tendency towards completeness in whatever he undertakes. Slack, slovenly performance in any department of life is more apt to offend him. His standard of action rises, and every thing is better done for his thoroughness in his common vocation.

There is one circumstance attending all conditions of life, which may and ought to be turned to the use of self-culture. Every condition, be it what it may, has hardships, hazards, pains. We try to escape them; we pine for a sheltered lot, for a smooth path, for cheering friends, and unbroken success. But Providence ordains storms, disasters, hostilities, sufferings; and the great question, whether we shall live to any purpose or not, whether we shall grow strong in mind and heart, or be weak and pitiable, depends on nothing so much as on our use of these adverse circumstances. Outward evils are designed to school our passions, and to rouse our faculties and virtues into intenser action. Sometimes they seem to create new powers. Difficulty is the element, and resistance the true work of a man. Self-culture never goes on so fast, as when embarrassed circumstances, the opposition of men or the elements, unexpected changes of the times, or other forms of suffering, instead of disheartening, throw us on our inward resources, turn us for strength to God, clear up to us the great purpose of life, and inspire calm resolution. No greatness or goodness is worth much, unless tried in these fires. Hardships are not on this account to be sought for. They come fast enough of themselves, and we are in more danger of sinking under, than of needing them. But when God sends them, they are noble means of self-culture, and as such, let us meet and bear them cheerfully. Thus all parts of our condition may be pressed into the service of self-improvement.

I have time to consider but one more means of self-culture. We find it in our Free Government, in our Political relations and duties. It is a great benefit of free institutions, that they do much to awaken and keep in action a nation's mind. We are told, that the education of the multitude is necessary to the support of a republic; but it is equally true, that the republic is a powerful means of educating the multitude. It is the people's University. In a free state, solemn responsibilities are imposed on every citizen; great subjects are to be discussed; great interests to be decided. The individual is called to determine measures affecting the well-being of millions and the destinies of posterity. He must consider not only the internal relations of his native land, but its connexion with foreign states, and judge of a policy which touches the whole civilized world. He is called by his participation in the national sovereignty, to cherish public spirit, a regard to the general weal. A man who purposes to discharge faithfully these obligations, is carrying on a generous self-culture. The great public questions, which divide opinion around him and provoke earnest discussion, of necessity invigorate his intellect, and accustom him to look beyond himself. He grows up to a robustness, force, enlargement of mind, unknown under despotic rule.

It may be said that I am describing what free institutions ought to do for the character of the individual, not their actual effects; and the objection, I must own, is too true. Our institutions do not cultivate us, as they might and should; and the chief cause of the failure is plain. It is the strength of party-spirit; and so blighting is its influence, so fatal to self-culture, that I feel myself bound to warn every man against it, who has any desire of improvement. I do not tell you it will destroy your country. It wages a worse war against yourselves. Truth, justice, candor, fair dealing, sound judgment, self-control, and kind affections, are its natural and perpetual prey.

I do not say, that you must take no side in politics. The parties which prevail around you differ in character, principles, and spirit, though far less than the exaggeration of passion affirms; and, as far as conscience allows, a man should support that which he thinks best. In one respect, however, all parties agree. They all foster that pestilent spirit, which I now condemn. In all of them, party-spirit rages. Associate men together for a common cause, be it good or bad, and array against them a body resolutely pledged to an opposite interest, and a new passion, quite distinct from the original sentiment which brought them together, a fierce, fiery zeal, consisting chiefly of aversion to those who differ from them, is roused within them into fearful activity. Human nature seems incapable of a stronger, more unrelenting passion. It is hard enough for an individual, when contending all alone for an interest or an opinion, to keep down his pride, wilfulness, love of victory, anger, and other personal feelings. But let him join a multitude in the same warfare, and, without singular self-control, he receives into his single breast, the vehemence, obstinacy, and vindictiveness of all. The triumph of his party becomes immeasurably dearer to him than the principle, true or false, which was the original ground of division. The conflict becomes a struggle, not for principle, but for power, for victory; and the desperateness, the wickedness of such struggles, is the great burden of history. In truth, it matters little what men divide about, whether it be a foot of land or precedence in a procession. Let them but begin to fight for it, and self-will, ill-will, the rage for victory, the dread of mortification and defeat, make the trifle as weighty as a matter of life and death. The Greek or Eastern empire was shaken to its foundation by parties, which differed only about the merits of charioteers at the amphitheatre. Party spirit is singularly hostile to moral independence. A man, in proportion as he drinks into it, sees, hears, judges by the senses and understandings of his party. He surrenders the freedom of a man, the right of using and speaking his own mind, and echoes the applauses or maledictions, with which the leaders or passionate partisans see fit that the country should ring. On all points, parties are to be distrusted; but on no one so much as on the character of opponents. These, if you may trust what you hear, are always men without principle and truth, devoured by selfishness, and thirsting for their own elevation, though on their country's ruin. When I was young, I was accustomed to hear pronounced with abhorrence, almost with execration, the names of men, who are now hailed by their former foes as the champions of grand principles, and as worthy of the highest public trusts. This lesson of early experience, which later years have corroborated, will never be forgotten.

Of our present political divisions I have of course nothing to say. But among the current topics of party, there are certain accusations and recriminations, grounded on differences of social condition, which seem to me so unfriendly to the improvement of individuals and the community, that I ask the privilege of giving them a moment's notice. On one side we are told, that the rich are disposed to trample on the poor; and on the other, that the poor look with evil eye and hostile purpose on the possessions of the rich. These outcries seem to me alike devoid of truth and alike demoralizing. As for the rich, who constitute but a handful of our population, who possess not one peculiar privilege, and, what is more, who possess comparatively little of the property of the country, it is wonderful, that they should be objects of alarm. The vast and ever-growing property of this country, where is it? Locked up in a few hands? hoarded in a few strong boxes? It is diffused like the atmosphere, and almost as variable, changing hands with the seasons, shifting from rich to poor, not by the violence but by the industry and skill of the latter class. The wealth of the rich is as a drop in the ocean; and it is a well-known fact, that those men among us, who are noted for their opulence, exert hardly any political power on the community. That the rich do their whole duty; that they adopt, as they should, the great object of the social state, which is the elevation of the people in intelligence, character, and condition, cannot be pretended; but that they feel for the physical sufferings of their brethren, that they stretch out liberal hands for the succour of the poor, and for the support of useful public institutions, cannot be denied. Among them are admirable specimens of humanity. There is no warrant for holding them up to suspicion as the people's foes.

Nor do I regard as less calumnious the outcry against the working classes, as if they were aiming at the subversion of property. When we think of the general condition and character of this part of our population, when we recollect, that they were born and have lived amidst schools and churches, that they have been brought up to profitable industry, that they enjoy many of the accommodations of life, that most of them hold a measure of property and are hoping for more, that they possess unprecedented means of bettering their lot, that they are bound to comfortable homes by strong domestic affections, that they are able to give their children an education which places within their reach the prizes of the social state, that they are trained to the habits, and familiarized to the advantages of a high civilization; when we recollect these things, can we imagine that they are so insanely blind to their interests, so deaf to the claims of justice and religion, so profligately thoughtless of the peace and safety of their families, as to be prepared to make a wreck of social order, for the sake of dividing among themselves the spoils of the rich, which would not support the community for a month? Undoubtedly there is insecurity in all stages of society, and so there must be, until communities shall be regenerated by a higher culture, reaching and quickening all classes of the people; but there is not, I believe, a spot on earth, where property is safer than here, because, nowhere else is it so equally and righteously diffused. In aristocracies, where wealth exists in enormous masses, which have been entailed for ages by a partial legislation on a favored few, and where the multitude, after the sleep of ages, are waking up to intelligence, to self-respect, and to a knowledge of their rights, property is exposed to shocks which are not to be dreaded among ourselves. Here indeed as elsewhere, among the less prosperous members of the community, there are disappointed, desperate men, ripe for tumult and civil strife; but it is also true, that the most striking and honorable distinction of this country is to be found in the intelligence, character, and condition of the great working class. To me it seems, that the great danger to property here is not from the laborer, but from those who are making haste to be rich. For example, in this commonwealth, no act has been thought by the alarmists or the conservatives so subversive of the rights of property, as a recent law, authorizing a company to construct a free bridge, in the immediate neighbourhood of another, which had been chartered by a former legislature, and which had been erected in the expectation of an exclusive right. And with whom did this alleged assault on property originate? With levellers? with needy laborers? with men bent on the prostration of the rich? No; but with men of business, who are anxious to push a more lucrative trade. Again, what occurrence among us has been so suited to destroy confidence, and to stir up the people against the moneyed class, as the late criminal mismanagement of some of our banking institutions? And whence came this? from the rich, or the poor? From the agrarian, or the man of business? Who, let me ask, carry on the work of spoliation most extensively in society? Is not more property wrested from its owners by rash or dishonest failures, than by professed highwaymen and thieves? Have not a few unprincipled speculators sometimes inflicted wider wrongs and sufferings, than all the tenants of a state prison? Thus property is in more danger from those who are aspiring after wealth, than from those who live by the sweat of their brow. I do not believe, however, that the institution is in serious danger from either. All the advances of society in industry, useful arts, commerce, knowledge, jurisprudence, fraternal union, and practical Christianity, are so many hedges around honestly acquired wealth, so many barriers against revolutionary violence and rapacity. Let us not torture ourselves with idle alarms, and still more, let us not inflame ourselves against one another by mutual calumnies. Let not class array itself against class, where all have a common interest. One way of provoking men to crime, is to suspect them of criminal designs. We do not secure our property against the poor, by accusing them of schemes of universal robbery; nor render the rich better friends of the community, by fixing on them the brand of hostility to the people. Of all parties, those founded on different social conditions are the most pernicious; and in no country on earth are they so groundless as in our own.

Among the best people, especially among the more religious, there are some, who, through disgust with the violence and frauds of parties, withdraw themselves from all political action. Such, I conceive, do wrong. God has placed them in the relations, and imposed on them the duties of citizens; and they are no more authorized to shrink from these duties than from those of sons, husbands, or fathers. They owe a great debt to their country, and must discharge it by giving support to what they deem the best men and the best measures. Nor let them say, that they can do nothing. Every good man, if faithful to his convictions, benefits his country. All parties are kept in check by the spirit of the better portion of people whom they contain. Leaders are always compelled to ask what their party will bear, and to modify their measures, so as not to shock the men of principle within their ranks. A good man, not tamely subservient to the body with which he acts, but judging it impartially, criticizing it freely, bearing testimony against its evils, and withholding his support from wrong, does good to those around him, and is cultivating generously his own mind.

I respectfully counsel those whom I address, to take part in the politics of their country. These are the true discipline of a people, and do much for their education. I counsel you to labor for a clear understanding of the subjects which agitate the community, to make them your study, instead of wasting your leisure in vague, passionate talk about them. The time thrown away by the mass of the people on the rumors of the day, might, if better spent, give them a good acquaintance with the constitution, laws, history, and interests of their country, and thus establish them in those great principles by which particular measures are to be determined. In proportion as the people thus improve themselves, they will cease to be the tools of designing politicians. Their intelligence, not their passions and jealousies, will be addressed by those who seek their votes. They will exert, not a nominal, but a real influence on the government and the destinies of the country, and at the same time will forward their own growth in truth and virtue.

I ought not to quit this subject of politics, considered as a means of self-culture, without speaking of newspapers; because these form the chief reading of the bulk of the people. They are the literature of multitudes. Unhappily, their importance is not understood; their bearing on the intellectual and moral cultivation of the community little thought of. A newspaper ought to be conducted by one of our most gifted men, and its income should be such as to enable him to secure the contributions of men as gifted as himself. But we must take newspapers as they are; and a man, anxious for self-culture, may turn them to account, if he will select the best within his reach. He should exclude from his house such as are venomous or scurrilous, as he would a pestilence. He should be swayed in his choice, not merely by the ability with which a paper is conducted, but still more by its spirit, by its justice, fairness, and steady adherence to great principles. Especially, if he would know the truth, let him hear both sides. Let him read the defence as well as the attack. Let him not give his ear to one party exclusively. We condemn ourselves, when we listen to reproaches thrown on an individual and turn away from his exculpation; and is it just to read continual, unsparing invectives against large masses of men, and refuse them the opportunity of justifying themselves?

A new class of daily papers has sprung up in our country, sometimes called cent papers, and designed for circulation among those who cannot afford costlier publications. My interest in the working class induced me some time ago to take one of these, and I was gratified to find it not wanting in useful matter. Two things however gave me pain. The advertising columns were devoted very much to patent medicines; and when I considered that a laboring man's whole fortune is his health, I could not but lament, that so much was done to seduce him to the use of articles, more fitted, I fear, to undermine than to restore his constitution. I was also shocked by accounts of trials in the police court. These were written in a style adapted to the most uncultivated minds, and intended to turn into matters of sport the most painful and humiliating events of life. Were the newspapers of the rich to attempt to extract amusement from the vices and miseries of the poor, a cry would be raised against them, and very justly. But is it not something worse, that the poorer classes themselves should seek occasions of laughter and merriment in the degradation, the crimes, the woes, the punishments of their brethren, of those who are doomed to bear like themselves the heaviest burdens of life, and who have sunk under the temptations of poverty? Better go to the hospital, and laugh over the wounds and writhings of the sick or the ravings of the insane, than amuse ourselves with brutal excesses and infernal passions, which not only expose the criminal to the crushing penalties of human laws, but incur the displeasure of Heaven, and, if not repented of, will be followed by the fearful retribution of the life to come.

One important topic remains. That great means of self-improvement, Christianity, is yet untouched, and its greatness forbids me now to approach it. I will only say, that if you study Christianity in its original records, and not in human creeds; if you consider its clear revelations of God, its life-giving promises of pardon and spiritual strength, its correspondence to man's reason, conscience, and best affections, and its adaptation to his wants, sorrows, anxieties, and fears; if you consider the strength of its proofs, the purity of its precepts, the divine greatness of the character of its author, and the immortality which it opens before us, you will feel yourselves bound to welcome it joyfully, gratefully, as affording aids and incitements to self-culture, which would vainly be sought in all other means.

I have thus presented a few of the means of self-culture. The topics, now discussed, will I hope suggest others to those who have honored me with their attention, and create an interest which will extend beyond the present hour. I owe it however to truth to make one remark. I wish to raise no unreasonable hopes. I must say, then, that the means now recommended to you, though they will richly reward every man of every age who will faithfully use them, will yet not produce their full and happiest effect, except in cases where early education has prepared the mind for future improvement. They, whose childhood has been neglected, though they may make progress in future life, can hardly repair the loss of their first years; and I say this, that we may all be excited to save our children from this loss, that we may prepare them, to the extent of our power, for an effectual use of all the means of self-culture, which adult age may bring with it. With these views, I ask you to look with favor on the recent exertions of our legislature and of private citizens, in behalf of our public schools, the chief hope of our country. The legislature has of late appointed a board of education, with a secretary, who is to devote his whole time to the improvement of public schools. An individual more fitted to his responsible office, than the gentleman who now fills it,* cannot, I believe, be found in our community; and if his labors shall be crowned with success, he will earn a title to the gratitude of the good people of this State, unsurpassed by that of any other living citizen.[7] Let me also recall to your minds a munificent individual,** who, by a generous donation, has encouraged the legislature to resolve on the establishment of one or more institutions called Normal Schools, the object of which is, to prepare accomplished teachers of youth, a work, on which the progress of education depends more than on any other measure.[8] The efficient friends of education are the true benefactors of their country, and their names deserve to be handed down to that posterity, for whose highest wants they are generously providing.

There is another mode of advancing education in our whole country, to which I ask your particular attention. You are aware of the vast extent and value of the public lands of the Union. By annual sales of these, large amounts of money are brought into the national treasury, which are applied to the current expenses of the Government. For this application there is no need. In truth, the country has received detriment from the excess of its revenues. Now, I ask, why shall not the public lands be consecrated (in whole or in part, as the case may require) to the education of the people?[9] This measure would secure at once what the country most needs, that is, able, accomplished, quickening teachers of the whole rising generation. The present poor remuneration of instructors is a dark omen, and the only real obstacle which the cause of education has to contend with. We need for our schools gifted men and women, worthy, by their intelligence and their moral power, to be intrusted with a nation's youth;

---

*Horace Mann, Esq.

**Edmund Dwight, Esq.

and, to gain these, we must pay them liberally, as well as afford other proofs of the consideration in which we hold them. In the present state of the country, when so many paths of wealth and promotion are opened, superior men cannot be won to an office so responsible and laborious as that of teaching, without stronger inducements than are now offered, except in some of our large cities. The office of instructor ought to rank and be recompensed as one of the most honorable in society; and I see not how this is to be done, at least in our day, without appropriating to it the public domain. This is the people's property, and the only part of their property which is likely to be soon devoted to the support of a high order of institutions for public education. This object, interesting to all classes of society, has peculiar claims on those whose means of improvement are restricted by narrow circumstances. The mass of the people should devote themselves to it as one man, should toil for it with one soul. Mechanics, Farmers, Laborers! let the country echo with your united cry, ''The Public Lands for Education.'' Send to the public councils men who will plead this cause with power. No party triumphs, no trades-unions, no associations, can so contribute to elevate you as the measure now proposed. Nothing but a higher education can raise you in influence and true dignity. The resources of the public domain, wisely applied for successive generations to the culture of society and of the individual, would create a new people, would awaken through this community intellectual and moral energies, such as the records of no country display, and as would command the respect and emulation of the civilized world. In this grand object, the working men of all parties, and in all divisions of the land, should join with an enthusiasm not to be withstood. They should separate it from all narrow and local strifes. They should not suffer it to be mixed up with the schemes of politicians. In it, they and their children have an infinite stake. May they be true to themselves, to posterity, to their country, to freedom, to the cause of mankind.

III. I am aware, that the whole doctrine of this discourse will meet with opposition. There are not a few who will say to me, ''What you tell us sounds well; but it is impracticable. Men, who dream in their closets, spin beautiful theories; but actual life scatters them, as the wind snaps the cobweb. You would have all men to be cultivated; but necessity wills that most men shall work; and which of the two is likely to prevail? A weak sentimentality may shrink from the truth; still it *is* true, that most men were made, not for self-culture, but for toil.''

I have put the objection into strong language, that we may all look it fairly in the face. For one I deny its validity. Reason, as well as sentiment, rises up against it. The presumption is certainly very strong, that the All-wise Father, who has given to every human being reason and conscience and affection, intended that these should be unfolded; and it is hard to believe, that He, who, by conferring this nature on all men, has made all his children, has destined the great majority to wear out a life of drudgery and unimproving toil, for the benefit of a few. God cannot have made spiritual beings to be dwarfed. In the body we see no organs created to shrivel by disuse; much less are the powers of the soul given to be locked up in perpetual lethargy.

Perhaps it will be replied, that the purpose of the Creator is to be gathered, not from theory, but from facts; and that it is a plain fact, that the order and prosperity of society, which God must be supposed to intend, require from the multitude the action of their hands, and not the improvement of their minds. I reply, that a social order, demanding the sacrifice of the mind, is very suspicious, that it cannot indeed be sanctioned by the Creator. Were I, on visiting a strange country, to see the vast majority of the people maimed, crippled, and bereft of sight, and were I told that social order required this mutilation, I should say, Perish this order. Who would not think his understanding as well as best feelings insulted, by hearing this spoken of as the intention of God? Nor ought we to look with less aversion on a social system which can only be upheld by crippling and blinding the Minds of the people.

But to come nearer to the point. Are labor and self-culture irreconcilable to each other? In the first place, we have seen that a man, in the midst of labor, may and ought to give himself to the most important improvements, that he may cultivate his sense of justice, his benevolence, and the desire of perfection. Toil is the school for these high principles; and we have here a strong presumption, that, in other respects, it does not necessarily blight the soul. Next we have seen, that the most fruitful sources of truth and wisdom are not books, precious as they are, but experience and observation; and these belong to all conditions. It is another important consideration, that almost all labor demands intellectual activity, and is best carried on by those who invigorate their minds; so that the two interests, toil and self-culture, are friends to each other. It is Mind, after all, which does the work of the world, so that the more there is of mind, the more work will be accomplished. A man, in proportion as he is intelligent, makes a given force accomplish a greater task, makes skill take the place of muscles, and, with less labor, gives a better product. Make men intelligent, and they become inventive. They find shorter processes. Their knowledge of nature helps them to turn its laws to account, to understand the substances on which they work, and to seize on useful hints, which experience continually furnishes. It is among workmen, that some of the most useful machines have been contrived. Spread education, and, as the history of this country shows, there will be no bounds to useful inventions. You think, that a man without culture will do all the better what you call the drudgery of life. Go then to the Southern plantation. There the slave is brought up to be a mere drudge. He is robbed of the rights of a man, his whole spiritual nature is starved, that he may work, and do nothing but work; and in that slovenly agriculture, in that worn-out soil, in the rude state of the mechanic arts, you may find a comment on your doctrine, that, by degrading men, you make them more productive laborers.

But it is said, that any considerable education lifts men above their work, makes them look with disgust on their trades as mean and low, makes drudgery intolerable. I reply, that a man becomes interested in labor, just in proportion as the mind works with the hands. An enlightened farmer, who understands agricultural chemistry, the laws of vegetation, the structure of plants, the properties of manures, the influences of climate, who looks intelligently on his work, and brings his knowledge to bear on exigencies, is a much more cheerful, as well as more dignified laborer, than the peasant, whose mind is akin to the clod on which he treads, and whose whole life is the same dull, unthinking, unimproving toil. But this is not all. Why is it, I ask, that we call manual labor low, that we associate with it the idea of meanness, and think that an intelligent people must scorn it? The great reason is, that, in most countries, so few intelligent people have been engaged in it. Once let cultivated men plough, and dig, and follow the commonest labors, and ploughing, digging, and trades, will cease to be mean. It is the man who determines the dignity of the occupation, not the occupation which measures the dignity of the man. Physicians and surgeons perform operations less cleanly than fall to the lot of most mechanics. I have seen a distinguished chemist covered with dust like a laborer. Still these men were not degraded. Their intelligence gave dignity to their work, and so our laborers, once educated, will give dignity to their toils.—Let me add, that I see little difference in point of dignity, between the various vocations of men. When I see a clerk, spending his days in adding figures, perhaps merely copying, or a teller of a bank counting money, or a merchant selling shoes and hides, I cannot see in these occupations greater respectableness than in making leather, shoes, or furniture. I do not see in them greater intellectual activity than in several trades. A man in the fields seems to have more chances of improvement in his work, than a man behind the counter, or a man driving the quill. It is the sign of a narrow mind, to imagine, as many seem to do, that there is a repugnance between the plain, coarse exterior of a laborer, and mental culture, especially the more refining culture. The laborer, under his dust and sweat, carries the grand elements of humanity, and he may put forth its highest powers. I doubt not, there is as genuine enthusiasm in the contemplation of nature, and in the perusal of works of genius, under a homespun garb as under finery. We have heard of a distinguished author, who never wrote so well, as when he was full dressed for company. But profound thought, and poetical inspiration, have most generally visited men, when, from narrow circumstances or negligent habits, the rent coat and shaggy face have made them quite unfit for polished saloons. A man may see truth, and may be thrilled with beauty, in one costume or dwelling as well as another; and he should respect himself the more, for the hardships under which his intellectual force has been developed.

But it will be asked, how can the laboring classes find time for self-culture? I answer, as I have already intimated, that an earnest purpose finds time or makes time. It seizes on spare moments, and turns larger fragments of leisure to golden account. A man, who follows his calling with industry and spirit, and uses his earnings economically, will always have some portion of the day at command; and it is astonishing, how fruitful of improvement a short season becomes, when eagerly seized and faithfully used. It has often been observed, that they, who have most time at their disposal, profit by it least. A single hour in the day, steadily given to the study of an interesting subject, brings unexpected accumulations of knowledge. The improvements made by well-disposed pupils, in many of our country schools, which are open but three months in the year, and in our Sunday-schools, which are kept but one or two hours in the week, show what can be brought to pass by slender means. The affections, it is said, sometimes crowd years into moments, and the intellect has something of the same power. Volumes have not only been read, but written, in flying journeys. I have known a man of vigorous intellect, who had enjoyed few advantages of early education, and whose mind was almost engrossed by the details of an extensive business, but who composed a book of much original thought, in steam-boats and on horseback, while visiting distant customers. The succession of the seasons gives to many of the working class opportunities for intellectual improvement. The winter brings leisure to the husbandman, and winter evenings to many laborers in the city. Above all, in Christian countries, the seventh day is released from toil. The seventh part of the year, no small portion of existence, may be given by almost every one to intellectual and moral culture. Why is it that Sunday is not made a more effectual means of improvement? Undoubtedly the seventh day is to have a religious character; but religion connects itself with all the great subjects of human thought, and leads to and aids the study of all. God is in nature. God is in history. Instruction in the works of the Creator, so as to reveal his perfection in their harmony, beneficence, and grandeur; instruction in the histories of the church and the world, so as to show in all events his moral government, and to bring out the great moral lessons in which human life abounds; instruction in the lives of philanthropists, of saints, of men eminent for piety and virtue; all these branches of teaching enter into religion, and are appropriate to Sunday; and, through these, a vast amount of knowledge may be given to the people. Sunday ought not to remain the dull and fruitless season that it now is to multitudes. It may be clothed with a new interest and a new sanctity. It may give a new impulse to the nation's soul.— I have thus shown, that time may be found for improvement; and the fact is, that, among our most improved people, a considerable part consists of persons, who pass the greatest portion of every day at the desk, in the countingroom, or in some other sphere, chained to tasks which have very little tendency to expand the mind. In the progress of society, with the increase of machinery, and with other aids which intelligence and philanthropy will multiply, we may expect that more and more time will be redeemed from manual labor, for intellectual and social occupations.

But some will say, "Be it granted that the working classes may find some leisure; should they not be allowed to spend it in relaxation? Is it not cruel, to summon them from toils of the hand to toils of the mind? They have earned pleasure by the day's toil, and ought to partake it." Yes, let them have pleasure. Far be it from me to dry up the fountains, to blight the spots of verdure, where they refresh themselves after life's labors. But I maintain, that self-culture multiplies and increases their pleasures, that it creates new capacities of enjoyment, that it saves their leisure from being, what it too often is, dull and wearisome, that it saves them from rushing for excitement to indulgences destructive to body and soul. It is one of the great benefits of self-improvement, that it raises a people above the gratifications of the brute, and gives them pleasures worthy of men. In consequence of the present intellectual culture of our country, imperfect as it is, a vast amount of enjoyment is communicated to men, women, and children, of all conditions, by books, an enjoyment unknown to ruder times. At this moment, a number of gifted writers are employed in multiplying entertaining works. Walter Scott,[10] a name conspicuous among the brightest of his day, poured out his inexhaustible mind in fictions, at once so sportive and thrilling, that they have taken their place among the delights of all civilized nations. How many millions have been chained to his pages! How many melancholy spirits has he steeped in forgetfulness of their cares and sorrows! What multitudes, wearied by their day's work, have owed some bright evening hours and balmier sleep to his magical creations! And not only do fictions give pleasure. In proportion as the mind is cultivated, it takes delight in history and biography, in descriptions of nature, in travels, in poetry, and even graver works. Is the laborer then defrauded of pleasure by improvement? There is another class of gratifications to which self-culture introduces the mass of the people. I refer to lectures, discussions, meetings of associations for benevolent and literary purposes, and to other like methods of passing the evening, which every year is multiplying among us. A popular address from an enlightened man, who has the tact to reach the minds of the people, is a high gratification, as well as a source of knowledge. The profound silence in our public halls, where these lectures are delivered to crowds, shows that cultivation is no foe to enjoyment.—I have a strong hope, that by the progress of intelligence, taste, and morals among all portions of society, a class of public amusements will grow up among us, bearing some resemblance to the theatre, but purified from the gross evils which degrade our present stage, and which, I trust, will seal its ruin. Dramatic performances and recitations are means of bringing the mass of the people into a quicker sympathy with a writer of genius, to a profounder comprehension of his grand, beautiful, touching conceptions, than can be effected by the reading of the closet. No commentary throws such a light on a great poem or any impassioned work of literature, as the voice of a reader or speaker, who brings to the task a deep feeling of his author and rich and various powers of expression. A crowd, electrified by a sublime thought, or softened into a humanizing sorrow, under such a voice, partake a pleasure at once exquisite and refined; and I cannot but believe, that this and other amusements, at which the delicacy of woman and the purity of the Christian can take no offence, are to grow up under a higher social culture.—Let me only add, that, in proportion as culture spreads among a people, the cheapest and commonest of all pleasures, conversation, increases in delight. This, after all, is the great amusement of life, cheering us round our hearths, often cheering our work, stirring our hearts gently, acting on us like the balmy air or the bright light of heaven, so silently and continually, that we hardly think of its influence. This source of happiness is too often lost to men of all classes, for want of knowledge, mental activity, and refinement of feeling; and do we defraud the laborer of his pleasure, by recommending to him improvements which will place the daily, hourly, blessings of conversation within his reach?

I have thus considered some of the common objections which start up when the culture of the mass of men is insisted on, as the great end of society. For myself, these objections seem worthy of little notice. The doctrine is too shocking to need refutation, that the great majority of human beings, endowed as they are with rational and immortal powers, are placed on earth, simply to toil for their own animal subsistence, and to minister to the luxury and elevation of the few. It is monstrous, it approaches impiety, to suppose that

God has placed insuperable barriers to the expansion of the free, illimitable soul. True, there are obstructions in the way of improvement. But in this country, the chief obstructions lie, not in our lot, but in ourselves, not in outward hardships, but in our worldly and sensual propensities; and one proof of this is, that a true self-culture is as little thought of on exchange as in the workshop, as little among the prosperous as among those of narrower conditions. The path to perfection is difficult to men in every lot; there is no royal road for rich or poor. But difficulties are meant to rouse, not discourage. The human spirit is to grow strong by conflict. And how much has it already overcome! Under what burdens of oppression has it made its way for ages! What mountains of difficulty has it cleared! And with all this experience, shall we say, that the progress of the mass of men is to be despaired of, that the chains of bodily necessity are too strong and ponderous to be broken by the mind, that servile, unimproving drudgery is the unalterable condition of the multitude of the human race?

I conclude with recalling to you the happiest feature of our age, and that is, the progress of the mass of the people in intelligence, self-respect, and all the comforts of life. What a contrast does the present form with past times! Not many ages ago, the nation was the property of one man, and all its interests were staked in perpetual games of war, for no end but to build up his family, or to bring new territories under his yoke. Society was divided into two classes, the high-born and the vulgar, separated from one another by a great gulf, as impassable as that between the saved and the lost. The people had no significance as individuals, but formed a mass, a machine, to be wielded at pleasure by their lords. In war, which was the great sport of the times, those brave knights, of whose prowess we hear, cased themselves and their horses in armour, so as to be almost invulnerable, whilst the common people on foot were left, without protection, to be hewn in pieces or trampled down by their betters. Who, that compares the condition of Europe a few years ago, with the present state of the world, but must bless God for the change. The grand distinction of modern times is, the emerging of the people from brutal degradation, the gradual recognition of their rights, the gradual diffusion among them of the means of improvement and happiness, the creation of a new power in the state, the power of the people. And it is worthy remark, that this revolution is due in a great degree to religion, which, in the hands of the crafty and aspiring, had bowed the multitude to the dust, but which, in the fulness of time, began to fulfil its mission of freedom. It was religion, which by teaching men their near relation to God, awakened in them the consciousness of their importance as individuals. It was the struggle for religious rights, which opened men's eyes to all their rights. It was resistance to religious usurpation, which led men to withstand political oppression. It was religious discussion, which roused the minds of all classes to free and vigorous thought. It was religion, which armed the martyr and patriot in England against arbitrary power, which braced the spirits of our fathers against the perils of the ocean and wilderness, and sent them to found here the freest and most equal state on earth.

Let us thank God for what has been gained. But let us not think every thing gained. Let the people feel that they have only started in the race. How much remains to be done! What a vast amount of ignorance, intemperance, coarseness, sensuality, may still be found in our community! What a vast amount of mind is palsied and lost! When we think, that every house might be cheered by intelligence, disinterestedness, and refinement, and then remember, in how many houses the higher powers and affections of human nature are buried as in tombs, what a darkness gathers over society! And how few of us are moved by this moral desolation? How few understand, that to raise the depressed, by a wise culture, to the dignity of men, is the highest end of the social state? Shame on us, that the worth of a fellow-creature is so little felt.

I would, that I could speak with an awakening voice to the people, of their wants, their privileges, their responsibilities. I would say to them, You cannot, without guilt and disgrace, stop where you are. The past and the present call on you to advance. Let what you have gained be an impulse to something higher. Your nature is too great to be crushed. You were not created what you are, merely to toil, eat, drink, and sleep, like the inferior animals. If you will, you can rise. No power in society, no hardship in your condition can depress you, keep you down, in knowledge, power, virtue, influence, but by your own consent. Do not be lulled to sleep by the flatteries which you hear, as if your participation in the national sovereignty made you equal to the noblest of your race. You have many and great deficiencies to be remedied; and the remedy lies, not in the ballot-box, not in the exercise of your political powers, but in the faithful education of yourselves and your children. These truths you have often heard and slept over. Awake! Resolve earnestly on Self-culture. Make yourselves worthy of your free institutions, and strengthen and perpetuate them by your intelligence and your virtues.

Notes

1. The Franklin Lectures were begun in 1831 "to give entertainment and instruction, upon terms so moderate, that everybody might attend them." William E. Channing, *Self-Culture. An Address Introductory to the Franklin Lectures* (Boston: Dutton and Wentworth, 1838), 83. This information is gleaned from a statement by Walter Channing, chairman of the Lectures' Executive Committee. The lectures were presumably aimed at a working-class audience, and they seem to have been a part of the larger milieu which made public oratory a major part of American cultural life in the nineteenth century. The lyceum movement is the best example of this cultural phase.

2. Channing's use of this organic metaphor for human development was a characteristic trope for nineteenth-century Romantic thought in general. Emerson also relied on this metaphor to describe individual human progress.

3. For the centrality of the idea of "disinterestedness" in Channing's thought, see the discussion in the introduction of this volume.

4. Matthew 6:23—"But if thine eye be evil, thy whole body shall be full of darkness, how great *is* that darkness!"

5. Channing probably refers to George Craik, *The Pursuit of Knowledge Under Difficulties* (London, 1830).

6. John 9:5—"As long as I am in the world, I am the light of the world."

7. Horace Mann (1796–1859) gave up a prominent legal and political career to accept an appointment as secretary of the newly created Massachusetts Board of Education in 1837, and went on to transform the school system in Massachusetts.

8. Edmund Dwight (1780–1849) was a prominent Boston manufacturer who led in the establishment of the Massachusetts Board of Education in 1837. He provided financial support for Mann's efforts as secretary of the Board of Education.

9. It should be noted that in 1862, the Morrill Act provided Federal land to the states to establish what are now known as the land-grant universities.

10. Sir Walter Scott (1771–1832) was the author of the popular Waverley novels.

ADDRESS DELIVERED AT LENOX (1842)*

*The original text that follows this introduction is *An Address Delivered at Lenox, on the First of August, 1842, the Anniversary of Emancipation, in the British West Indies* (Lenox, Mass.: J. G. Stanly, 1842).

By 1842, Channing's frail health had become seriously impaired. In 1841, the first five volumes of his Complete Works were published, and on April 7, 1842, he preached his last sermon at the Federal Street Church in Boston. He then set out on a journey to Pennsylvania, which was marred by difficulties in travel and increasing weakness. In July he went to Lenox, Massachusetts, in the Berkshire Mountains, where he began to regain strength during a two-month stay. The sign of that temporary renewal is his anti-slavery address at Lenox, the last public speech he was to make. Channing gave the address at his own initiative, and as John White Chadwick explained, he found the people of the region "forgetful of the slave" and therefore "resolved to stir up their minds."[1] The result is a distillation of his arguments against slavery, which had first been articulated in his longer treatise Slavery (1835). Not only does the work have significance as Channing's final work, it includes some of his most blistering denunciations of the evils of slavery, which had come increasingly to prey on Channing's mind as America's great national evil. His caustic reply to those who defended slavery as an institution which satisfied the material wants of the slave is especially notable: "A man, who thinks food and raiment a compensation for liberty, who would counsel men to sell themselves, to become property, to give up all rights and power over themselves, for a daily mess of pottage, however savory, is a slave in heart." Channing took as his occasion for the speech the anniversary of the emancipation of the slaves in the British West Indies, an event which was accomplished through moral persuasion and law, and without violence. In 1842, he could still hope that a similar end would come of slavery in America. Some two months after de-

---

1. John White Chadwick, *William Ellery Channing: Minister of Religion* (Boston and New York: Houghton Mifflin, 1903), 417.

livering this address, Channing died in Bennington, Vermont. He was spared having to witness the carnage of the Civil War, but also denied the experience of living to see the emancipation for which he so fervently hoped.

AN ADDRESS DELIVERED AT LENOX
ON THE FIRST OF AUGUST, 1842,
THE ANNIVERSARY OF EMANCIPATION,
IN THE BRITISH WEST INDIES

Introductory Remarks.

I have been encouraged to publish the following address by the strong expression of sympathy with which it was received. I do not indeed suppose, that those, who listened to it with interest and who have requested its publication, accorded with me in every opinion which it contains. Such entire agreement is not to be expected among intelligent men, who judge for themselves. But I am sure, that the spirit and substance of the address met a hearty response. Several paragraphs, which I wanted strength to deliver, are now published, and for these of course I am alone responsible.

I dedicate this address to the Men and Women of Berkshire. I have found so much to delight me in the magnificent scenery of this region, in its peaceful and prosperous villages and in the rare intelligence and virtues of the friends whose hospitality I have here enjoyed, that I desire to connect this little work with this spot. I cannot soon forget the beautiful nature and generous spirits, with which I have been privileged to commune in the Valley of the Housatonick.

Lenox, Mass., Aug. 9, 1842

ADDRESS.

This day is the anniversary of one of the great events of modern times, the Emancipation of the Slaves in the British West India islands. This Emancipation began Aug. 1st. 1834, but it was not completed until Aug. 21st. 1838.[1] The event indeed has excited little attention in our country, partly because we are too much absorbed in private interests and local excitements to be alive to the triumphs of humanity at a distance, partly because a moral contagion has spread from the South through the North and deadened our sympathies with the oppressed. But West India emancipation, though received here so coldly, is yet an era in the annals of philanthropy. The greatest events do not always draw most attention at the moment. When the *Mayflower,* in the dead of winter, landed a few pilgrims, on the ice-bound, snow-buried rocks of Plymouth, the occurrence made no noise. Nobody took note of it, and yet how much has that landing done to change the face of the civilized world! Our fathers came to establish a pure church; they little thought of revolutionizing nations. The emancipation in the West Indies, whether viewed in itself, or in its immediate results, or in the spirit from which it grew, or in the light of hope which it sheds on the future, deserves to be commemorated. In some respects it stands alone in human history. I therefore invite to it your serious attention.

Perhaps I ought to begin with some apology for my appearance in this place; for I stand here unasked, uninvited. I can plead no earnest solicitation from few or many for the service I now render. I come to you simply from an impulse in my own breast; and in truth had I been solicited, I probably should not have consented to speak. Had I found here a general desire to celebrate this day, I should have felt, that another speaker might be enlisted in the cause, and I should have held my peace. But finding that no other voice would be raised, I was impelled to lift up my own, though too feeble for any great exertion. I trust you will accept with candor what I have been obliged to prepare in haste, and what may have little merit but that of pure intention.

I have said that I speak only from the impulse of my own mind. I am the organ of no association, the representative of no feelings but my own.[2] But I wish it to be understood, that I speak from no sudden impulse; from no passionate zeal of a new convert; but from deliberate and long cherished conviction. In truth my attention was directed to Slavery fifty years ago, that is, before most of you were born; and the first impulse came from a venerable man, formerly of great reputation in this part of our country and in all our churches, the Rev. Dr. Hopkins, who removed more than a century ago from Great Barrington to my native town, and there bore open and strong testimony against the Slave Trade, a principal branch of the traffic of the place.[3] I am reminded by the spot where I now stand, of another incident which may show how long I have taken an interest in this subject. More than twenty years ago, I had an earnest conversation with that noble-minded man and fervent philanthropist, Henry Sedgwick, so well and honorably known to most who hear me, on which occasion we deplored the insensibility of the North to the evils of Slavery and enquired by what means it might be removed.[4] The circumstance which particularly gave my mind a direction to this subject, was a winter's residence in a West Indian Island more than eleven years ago. I lived there on a plantation. The piazza in which I sat and walked almost from morning to night, overlooked the negro village belonging to the estate. A few steps placed me in the midst of their huts. Here was a volume on Slavery opened always before my eyes, and how could I help learning some of its lessons.[5] The gang on this estate, (for such is the name given to a company of slaves,) was the best on the island, and among the best in the West Indies. The proprietor had laboured to collect the best materials for it. His gang had been his pride and boast. The fine proportions, the graceful and sometimes dignified bearing of these people, could hardly be overlooked. Unhappily misfortune had reduced the owner to bankruptcy. The estate had been mortgaged to a stranger who could not personally superintend it, and I found it under the care of a passionate and licentious manager, in whom the poor slaves found a sad contrast to the kindness of former days. They sometimes came to the house where I resided, with their mournful or indignant complaints; but were told that no redress could be found from the hands of their late master. In this case of a plantation passing into strange hands, I saw that the mildest form of slavery might at any time be changed into the worst. On returning to this country I delivered a discourse on Slavery, giving the main views which I have since communicated; and this was done, before the cry of Abolitionism was heard among us. I seem then to have a peculiar warrant for now addressing you. I am giving you not the ebullitions of new vehement feelings, but the results of long and patient reflection; not the thoughts of others, but my own independent judgments. I stand alone, I speak in the name of no party. I have no connection, but that of friendship and respect, with the opposers of Slavery in this country or abroad. Do not mix me up with other men good or bad; but listen to me as a separate witness, standing on my own ground, and desirous to express with all plainness what seems to be the truth.

On this day a few years ago, Eight Hundred Thousand human beings were set free from slavery; and to comprehend the greatness of the deliverance, a few words must first be said of the evil from which they were rescued. You must know Slavery to know Emancipation. But in a single discourse, how can I set before you the wrongs and abominations of this detestable institution? I must pass over many of its features, and will select one, which is at present vividly impressed on my mind. Different minds are impressed with different evils. Were I asked, what strikes me as the greatest evil inflicted by this system, I should say, it is the outrage offered by slavery to human nature. Slavery does all that lies in human power to unmake men, to rob them of their humanity, to degrade men into brutes; and this it does by declaring them to be Property. Here is the master evil. Declare a man a chattel, something which you may own, and may turn to your use, as a horse or a tool; strip him of all right over himself, of all right to use his own powers, except what you concede to him as a favor and deem consistent with your own profit; and you cease to look on him as a Man. You may call him such; but he is not to you a brother, a fellow being, a partaker of your nature, and your equal in the sight of God. You view him, you treat him, you speak to him, as infinitely beneath you, as belonging to another race. You have a tone and a look towards him, which you never use towards a man. Your relation to him demands that you treat him as an inferior creature. You cannot if you would treat him as a man. That he may answer your end, that he may consent to be a slave, his spirit must be broken, his courage crushed; he must fear you. A feeling of his deep inferiority must be burnt into his soul. The idea of his rights must be quenched in him, by the blood of his lashed and lacerated body. Here is the damning evil of slavery. It destroys the spirit, the consciousness of a man. I care little in comparison for his hard outward lot, his poverty, his unfurnished house, his coarse fare; the terrible thing in slavery is the spirit of a slave, the extinction of the spirit of a man. He feels himself owned, a chattel, a thing bought and sold, and held to sweat for another's pleasure, at another's will, under another's lash, just as an ox or horse. Treated thus as a brute, can he take a place among men? A slave! Is there a name so degraded on earth, a name which so separates a man from his kind?

and to this condition millions of our race are condemned in this land of liberty.

In what is the slave treated as a Man? The great right of a Man is to use, improve, expand his powers, for his own and other's good. The slave's powers belong to another, and are hemmed in, kept down, not cherished, or suffered to unfold. If there be an infernal system, one especially hostile to humanity, it is that which deliberately wars against the expansion of men's faculties; and this enters into the essence of slavery. The slave cannot be kept a slave, if helped or allowed to improve his intellect and higher nature. He must not be taught to read. The benevolent christian, who tries, by giving him the use of letters, to open to him the word of God and other good books, is punished as a criminal. The slave is hedged round, so that philanthropy cannot approach him to awaken in him the intelligence and feelings of a man. Thus his humanity is trodden under foot.

Again, a Man has the right to form and enjoy the relations of domestic life. The tie between the brute and his young endures but a few months. Man was made to have a home, to have a wife and children, to cleave to them for life, to sustain the domestic relations in constancy and purity, and through these holy ties to refine and exalt his nature. Such is the distinction of a man. But slavery violates the sanctity of home. It makes the young woman property, and gives her no protection from licentiousness. It either disallows marriage or makes it a vain show. It sunders husband and wife, sells them into distant regions, and then compels them to break the sacred tie and contract new alliances, in order to stock the plantation with human slaves. Scripture and nature say, "What God hath joined, let not man put asunder;" but slavery scorns God's voice in his word and in the human heart. Even the Christian church dares not remonstrate against the wrong, but sanctions it, and encourages the poor ignorant slave to form a new, adulterous connexion, that he may minister to his master's gain. The slave-holder enters the hut of his bondsman, to do the work which belongs only to death, and to do it with nothing of the consolatory, healing influences, which christianity sheds round death. He goes to tear the wife from the husband, the child from the mother, to exile them from one another, and to convey them to unknown masters. Is this to see a man, in a slave? Is not this to place him beneath humanity?

Again, it is the right, privilege and distinction of a Man, not only to be connected with a family, but with his race. He is made for free communion with his fellow creatures. One of the sorest evils of life is to be cut off from the mass of men, from the social body; to be treated by the multitude of our fellow creatures as outcasts, as Pariahs, as a fallen race, unworthy to be approached, unworthy of the deference due to men; and this infinite wrong is done to the slave. A slave! that name severs all his ties except with beings as degraded as himself. He has no country, no pride or love of nation, no sympathy with the weal or woe of the land which gave him birth, no joy in its triumphs, no generous sorrow for its humiliation, no feeling of that strong unity with those around him which common laws, a common government, and a common history create. He is not allowed to go forth, as other men are, and to connect himself with strangers, to form new alliances by means of trade, business, conversation. Society is every where barred against him. An iron wall forbids his access to his race. The miscellaneous intercourse of man with man, which strengthens the feeling of our common humanity, and perhaps does more than all things to enlarge the intellect, is denied him. The world is nothing to him; he does not hear of it. The plantation is his world. To him the universe is narrowed down almost wholly to the hut where he sleeps, and the fields where he sweats for another's gain. Beyond these he must not step without leave; and even if allowed to wander, who has a respectful look or word for the slave? In that name he carries with him an atmosphere of repulsion. It drives men from him as if he were a leper. However gifted by God, however thirsting for some higher use of his powers, he must hope for no friend beyond the ignorant, half-brutalized caste with which bondage has united him. To him there is no race, as there is no country. In truth, so fallen is he beneath sympathy, that multitudes will smile at hearing him compassionated for being bereft of these ties. Still he suffers great wrong. Just in proportion as you sever a man from his country and race, he ceases to be a man. The rudest savage, who has a tribe with which he sympathises, and for which he is ready to die, is far exalted above the slave. How much more exalted is the poorest freeman, in a civilized land, who feels his relation to a wide community; who lives under equal laws to which the greatest bow; whose social ties change and enlarge with the vicissitudes of life; whose mind and heart are open to the quickening, stirring influences of this various world. Poor slave! humanity's out-cast and orphan! to whom no door is open, but that of the naked hut of thy degraded caste! art thou indeed a man? Dost thou belong to the human brotherhood? What is thy whole life but continued insult? Thou meetest no look, which does not express thy hopeless exclusion from human sympathies. Thou mayest indeed be pitied in sickness and pain, and so is the animal. The deference due to a man, and which keeps alive a man's spirit, is unknown to thee. The intercourse, which makes the humblest individual in other spheres partaker more or less in the improvements of his race, thou must never hope for. May I not say, then, that nothing extinguishes humanity like slavery.

In reply to these and other representations of the wrongs and evils of this institution, we are told that slaves are well fed, well clothed, at least better than the peasantry and operatives in many other countries; and this is gravely adduced as a vindication of slavery. A man capable of offering it, ought, if any one ought, to be reduced to bondage. A man, who thinks food and raiment a compensation for liberty, who would counsel men to sell themselves, to become property, to give up all rights and power over themselves, for a daily mess of pottage, however savory, is a slave in heart. He has lost the spirit of a man, and would be less wronged than other men, if a slave's collar were welded round his neck.

The domestic slave is well fed, we are told, and so are the domestic animals. A nobleman's horse in England is better lodged and more pampered than the operatives in Manchester. The grain which the horse consumes, might support a starving family. How sleek and shining his coat! How gay and rich his caparison! But why is he thus curried, and pampered, and bedecked? To be bitted and curbed; and then to be mounted by his master, who arms himself with whip and spur to put the animal to his speed; and if any accident mar his strength or swiftness, he is sold from his luxuriant stall to be flayed, overworked, and hastened out of life by the merciless draymen. Suppose the nobleman should say to the half-starved, ragged operative of Manchester, "I will give up my horse, and feed and clothe you with like sumptuousness, on condition that I may mount you daily with lash and spurs, and sell you when I can make a profitable bargain." Would you have the operative, for the sake of good fare and clothes, take the lot of the brute? or, in other words, become a slave? What reply would the heart of an Old England or New England laborer make to such a proposal? and yet if there be any soundness in the argument drawn from the slave's comforts, he ought to accept it thankfully and greedily.

Such arguments for slavery are insults. The man capable of using them ought to be rebuked as mean in spirit, hard of heart, and wanting all true sympathy with his race. I might reply, if I thought fit, to this account of the slave's blessings, that there is nothing very enviable in his food and wardrobe, that his comforts make no approach to those of the nobleman's horse, and that a laborer of New England would prefer the fare of many an alms-house at home. But I cannot stoop to such reasoning. Be the comforts of the slave what they may, they are no compensation for the degradation, insolence, indignities, ignorance, servility, scars, and violations of domestic rights to which he is exposed.

I have spoken of what seems to me the grand evil of slavery, the outrage it offers to human nature. It would be easy to enlarge on other fatal tendencies and effects of this institution. But I forbear not only for want of time, but because I feel no need of a minute exposition of its wrongs and miseries to make it odious. I cannot endure to go through a labored proof of its iniquitous and injurious nature. No man wants such proof. He carries the evidence in his own heart. I need nothing but the most general view of slavery, to move my indignation towards it. I am more and more accustomed to throw out of sight its particular evils, its details of wrong and suffering, and to see in it simply an institution which deprives men of Freedom; and when I thus view it, I am taught immediately, by an unerring instinct, that slavery is an intolerable wrong. Nature cries aloud for Freedom as our proper good, or birthright and our end, and resents nothing so much as its loss. It is true, that we are placed at first, in subjection to others' wills; and spend childhood and youth under restraint. But we are governed at first that we may learn to govern ourselves; we begin with leading strings that we may learn to go alone. The discipline of the parent is designed to train up his children to act for themselves, and from a principle of duty in their own breasts. The child is not subjected to his father to be a slave, but to grow up to the energy, responsibility, relations and authority of a man. Freedom, courage, moral force, efficiency, independence, the large, generous action of the soul, these are the blessings in store for us, the grand ends to which the restraints of education, of family, of school and college are directed. Nature knows no such thing as a perpetual yoke. Nature bends no head to the dust, to look forever downward. Nature makes no man a chattel. Nature has implanted in all souls the thirst, the passion for liberty. Nature stirs the heart of the child, and prompts it to throw out its little limbs in restlessness and joy and to struggle against restraint. Nature impels the youth to leap, to run, to put forth all his powers, to look with impatience on prescribed bounds, to climb the steep, to dive into the ocean, to court danger, to spread himself through the new world which he was born to inherit. Nature's life, nature's impulse, nature's joy is Freedom. A greater violence to nature cannot be conceived, than to rob man of liberty.

What is the end and essence of life? It is to expand all our faculties and affections. It is to grow, to gain by exercise new energy, new intellect, new love. It is to hope, to strive, to bring out what is within us, to press towards what is above us. In other words, it is to be Free. Slavery is thus at war with the true life of human nature. Undoubtedly there is a power in the soul, which the loss of freedom cannot always subdue. There have been men, doomed to perpetual bondage, who have still thought and felt nobly, looked up to God with trust, and learned by experience, that even bondage, like all other evils, may be made the occasion of high virtue. But these are exceptions. In the main, our nature is too weak to grow under the weight of chains.

To illustrate the supreme importance of Freedom, I would offer a remark, which may sound like a paradox, but will be found to be true. It is this, that even Despotism is endurable, only because it bestows a degree of freedom. Despotism, bad as it is, supplants a greater evil, and that is anarchy; and anarchy is worse, chiefly because it is more enslaving. In anarchy all restraint is plucked from the strong, who make a prey of the weak; subduing them by terror, seizing on their property, and treading every right under foot. When the laws are prostrated, arbitrary, passionate, lawless will, the will of the strongest, exasperated by opposition, must prevail; and under this the rights of person, as well as property are cast down, and a palsying fear imposes on men's spirits a heavier chain, than was ever forged by an organized despotism. In the whole history of tyranny in France, liberty was never so crushed as in the reign of terror in the revolution; when mobs and lawless combinations usurped the power of the State. A despot to be safe must establish a degree of order, and this implies laws, tribunals, and some administration of justice, however rude; and still more, he has an interest in protecting industry and property to some degree, in order that he may extort the more from his people's earnings under the name of revenue. Thus despotism is an advance toward liberty; and in this its strength very much lies; for the people have a secret consciousness, that their rights suffer less, under one, than under many tyrants, under an organized absolutism, than under wild, lawless, passionate force; and on this conviction, as truly as on armies, rests the despot's throne. Thus freedom and rights are ever cherished goods of human nature. Man keeps them in sight even when most crushed; and just in proportion as civilization and intelligence advance, he secures them more and more. This is infallibly true notwithstanding opposite appearances. The old forms of despotism may indeed continue in a progressive civilization, but their force declines; and public opinion, the will of the community, silently establishes a sway over what seems and is denominated, absolute power. We have a striking example of this truth in Prussia, where the King seems unchecked, but where a code of wise and equal laws ensures to every man his rights to a degree experienced in few other countries, and where the administration of justice cannot safely be obstructed by the will of the sovereign. Thus freedom, man's dearest birthright, is the good towards which civil institutions tend. It is at once the sign and the means, the cause and the effect of human progress. It exists in a measure under tyrannical governments, and gives them their strength. Nowhere is it wholly broken down, but under domestic slavery. Under this, man is made Property. Here lies the damning taint, the accursed blighting power, the infinite evil of bondage.

On this day, four years ago, Eight Hundred Thousand human beings were set free from the terrible evil of which I have given a faint sketch. Eight hundred thousand of our brethren, who had lived in darkness and the shadow of death, were visited with the light of liberty. Instead of the tones of absolute, debasing command, a new voice broke on their ears, calling them to come forth, to be free. They were, undoubtedly, too rude, too ignorant, to comprehend the greatness of the blessing conferred on them this day. Freedom to them undoubtedly seemed much what it is not. Children in intellect, they seized on it as a child on a holiday. But slavery had not wholly stifled in them the instincts, feelings, judgments of men. They felt on this day, that the whip of the brutal overseer was broken; and was that no cause for exulting joy? They felt, that wife and child could no longer be insulted or scourged in their sight, and they be denied the privilege of lifting up a voice in their behalf. Was that no boon? They felt that henceforth they were to work from their own wills, for their own good, that they might earn perhaps a hut, which they might call their own, and which the foot of a master could not profane, nor a master's interest lay waste. Can you not conceive how they stretched out their limbs, and looked on them with a new joy, saying, These are our own. Can you not conceive how they leaped with a new animation, exulting to put forth powers, which were from that day to be "their own?" Can you not conceive how they looked round them on the fields and hills, and said to themselves, We can go now where we will; and how they continued to live in their huts with new content, because they could leave them if they would? Can you not conceive, how dim ideas of a better lot dawned on their long dormant minds; how the future, once a blank, began to brighten before them; how hope began to spread her unused pinions; how the faculties and feelings of men came to a new birth within them? The father and mother took their child to their arms and said, Nobody can sell you from us now. Was not that enough to give them a new life? The husband and wife began to feel, that there was an inviolable sanctity in marriage; and a glimpse, however faint, of a moral, spiritual bond, began to take place of the loose sensual tie, which had held them together. Still more, and what deserves special note, the colored man raised his eyes, on this day, to the white man, and saw the infinite chasm between himself and the white race growing narrower; saw and felt that he too was a Man, that he too had rights; that he belonged to the common father, not to a frail, selfish creature; that under God he was his own master. A rude feeling of dignity, in strange contrast with the abjectness of the slave, gave new courage to that look, gave a firmer tone, a manlier tread. This, had I been there, would have interested me especially. The tumult of joyful feeling bursting forth in the broken language which slavery had taught, I should have sympathized with. But the sight of the slave rising into a man, looking on the white race with a steady eye, with the secret consciousness of a common nature, and beginning to comprehend his heaven-descended, inalienable rights, would have been the crowning joy.

It was natural to expect that the slaves, on the first of August, receiving the vast, incomprehensible gift of freedom, would have rushed into excess. It would not have surprised me, had I heard of intemperance, tumult, violence. Liberty, that mighty boon, for which nations have shed rivers of their best blood, for which they have toiled and suffered for years, perhaps for ages, was given to these poor, ignorant creatures in a day, and given to them after lives of cruel bondage, immeasurably more cruel than any political oppression. Would it have been wonderful, if they had been intoxicated by the sudden, vast transition, if they had put to shame the authors of their freedom, by an immediate abuse of it? Happily, the poor negroes had enjoyed one privilege in their bondage. They had learned something of Christianity, very little indeed, yet enough to teach them that liberty was the gift of God. That mighty power, religion, had begun a work within them. The African nature, seems singularly susceptible of this principle. Benevolent missionaries, whom the anti-slavery spirit of England had sent into the colonies, had for some time been working on the degraded mind of the bondmen, and not wholly in vain. The slaves, whilst denied the rank of men by their race, had caught the idea of their relation to the Infinite Father. That great doctrine of the Universal, Impartial Love of God, embracing the most obscure, dishonored, oppressed, had dawned on them. Their new freedom thus became associated with religion, the mightiest principle on earth, and by this it was not merely saved from excess, but made the spring of immediate elevation.

Little did I imagine, that the emancipation of the Slaves, was to be invested with holiness and moral sublimity. Little did I expect, that my heart was to be touched by it, as by few events in history. But the emotions, with which I first read the narrative of the great gift of liberty in Antigua, are still fresh in my mind. Let me read to you the story; none I think, can hear it unmoved. It is the testimony of trust-worthy men, who visited the West Indies to observe the effects of Emancipation.[6]

"To convey to the reader some account of the way in which the great crisis passed, we here give the substance

of several accounts which were related to us in different
parts of the island, by those who witnessed them.

"The Wesleyans kept watch-night in all their chapels, on the night of the 31st of July. One of the Wesleyan
missionaries gave us an account of the watch meeting at
the chapel in St. Johns. The capacious house was filled
with the candidates for liberty. All was animation and ea-
gerness. A mighty chorus of voices swelled the song of expectation and joy, and as they united in prayer, the voice
of the leader was drowned in the universal acclamation of
thanksgiving, and praise, and blessing, and honor, and
glory to God who had come down for their deliverance. In
such exercises the evening was spent until the hour of
twelve approached. The missionary then proposed, that
when the clock on the cathedral should begin to strike, the
whole congregation should fall upon their knees, and receive the boon of freedom in silence. Accordingly as the
loud bell tolled its first notes, the crowded assembly prostrated themselves on their knees. All was silent, save the
quivering, half stifled breath of the struggling spirit. The
slow notes of the clock fell upon the multitude; peal on
peal, peal on peal, rolled over the prostrate throng, in
tones of angels' voices, thrilling among the desolate
chords and weary heart strings. Scarce had the clock
sounded its last note, when the lightning flashed vividly
around, and a loud peal of thunder roared along the sky;
God's pillar of fire, and trump of jubilee! A moment of
profoundest silence passed; then came the burst; they
broke forth in prayer; they shouted, they sung, "Glory Al-
leluia;" they clapped their hands, leaped up, fell down,
clasped each other in their free arms, cried, laughed, and
went to and fro, tossing upward their unfettered hands; but
high above the whole there was a mighty sound which ever
and anon swelled up; it was the uttering in negro broken
dialect, of gratitude to God.

"After this gush of excitement had spent itself, and
the congregation became calm, the religious exercises
were resumed, and the remainder of the night was occupied in singing and prayer, in reading the Bible, and in ad-

dresses from the missionaries, explaining the nature of the freedom just received, and exhorting the freed people to be industrious, steady, obedient to the laws, and to shew themselves in all things worthy of the high boon which God had conferred upon them.

"The first of August came on Friday, and a release was proclaimed from all work until the next Monday. The day was chiefly spent, by the great mass of negroes, in the churches and chapels. Thither they flocked as clouds, and as doves to their windows. The clergy and missionaries throughout the island were actively engaged, seizing the opportunity, in order to enlighten the people on all the duties and responsibilities of their new situation, and above all, urging them to the attainment of that higher liberty with which Christ maketh his children free. In every quarter we were assured that the day was like a Sabbath. Work had ceased; the hum of business was still, and noise and tumult were unheard in the streets. Tranquility pervaded the towns and country. A Sabbath indeed! when the wicked ceased from troubling, and the weary were at rest, and the slave was freed from the master! The planters informed us, that they went to the chapels where their own people were assembled, greeted them, shook hands with them, and exchanged most hearty good wishes."*

Such is the power of true religion, on the rudest minds. Such, the deep fountain of feeling in the African soul. Such, the race of men, whom we are trampling in the dust. How few of our assemblies, with all our intelligence and refinement, offer to God this overflowing gratitude, this profound, tender, rapturous homage! True, the slaves poured out their joy with a child-like violence; but we see a childhood full of promise. And why do we place this race beneath us? Because nature has burnt on them a darker hue. But does the essence of humanity live in color? Is the black man less a man than the white? Has he not human powers, human rights? Does his color reach his soul? Is reason in him a whit blacker than in us? Have his conscience and affections been dipped in an inky flood? To the

---

*See Emancipation in the West Indies, by Thome and Kimball.

eye of God, are his pure thoughts and kind feelings less fair than our own? We are apt to think this prejudice of color founded in nature. But in the most enlightened countries in Europe, the man of African descent is received into the society of the great and good, as an equal and friend. It is here only that this prejudice reigns; and to this prejudice, strengthened by our subjection to southern influence, must be ascribed our indifference to the progress of liberty in the West Indies. Ought not the emancipation of nearly a million of human beings, so capable of progress as the African race, to have sent a thrill of joy, through a nation of freemen? But this great event was received in our country with indifference. Humanity, justice, Christian sympathy, the love of liberty, found but few voices here. Nearly a million of men, at no great distance from our land, passed from the most degrading bondage into the ranks of freedom, with hardly a welcome, from these shores.

Perhaps you will say, that we are bound to wait for the fruits of emancipation, before we celebrate it as a great event in history. I think not so. We ought to rejoice immediately, without delay, whenever an act of justice is done, especially a grand public act, subverting the oppression of ages. We ought to triumph, when the right prospers, without waiting for consequences. We ought not to doubt about consequences, when men, in obedience to conscience, and in the exercise of their best wisdom, redress a mighty wrong. If God reigns, then the subversion of a vast crime, then the breaking of an unrighteous yoke, must in its final results be good. Undoubtedly an old abuse, which has sent its roots through society, cannot be removed without inconvenience or suffering. Indeed no great social change, however beneficial, can occur without partial, temporary pain. But must abuses be sheltered without end, and human progress, given up in despair, because some, who have fattened on wrongs, will cease to prosper at the expense of their brethren. Undoubtedly Slavery cannot be broken up without deranging in a measure the old social order. Must, therefore, slavery be perpetual! Has the Creator laid on any portion of his children the necessity of everlasting bondage? Must wrong know no end? Has oppression a charter from God, which is never to grow old? What a libel on God, as well as on man, is the supposition, that society cannot subsist without perpetuating the degradation of a large portion of the race! Is this indeed the law of the creation, that multitudes must be oppressed? That states can subsist and prosper only through crime? Then there is no God. Then an evil spirit reigns over the universe. It is an impious error to believe, that injustice is a necessity under the government of the Most High. It is disloyalty to principle, treachery to virtue, to suppose that a righteous, generous work, conceived in a sense of duty and carried on with deliberate forethought, can issue in misery, in ruin. To this want of faith in rectitude, society owes its woes, owes the licensed frauds and crimes of statesmen, the licensed frauds of trade, the continuance of slavery. Once let men put faith in rectitude, let them feel that justice is strength, that disinterestedness is a sun and a shield, that selfishness and crime are weak and miserable, and the face of the earth would be changed. The groans of ages would cease. We ought to shout for joy, not shrink like cowards, when justice and humanity triumph over established wrongs.

The emancipation of the British Islands, ought then to have called forth acclamation at its birth. Much more should we rejoice in it now, when time has taught us the folly of the fears and the suspicions which it awakened, and taught us the safety of doing right. Emancipation has worked well. By this I do not mean, that it has worked miracles. I have no glowing pictures to exhibit to you of the West Indian Islands. An act of the British parliament, declaring them free, has not changed them into a paradise. A few strokes of the pen, cannot reverse the laws of nature, or conquer the almost omnipotent power of early and long continued habit. Even in this country, where we breathe the air of freedom from our birth, and where we have grown up amidst churches and school-houses and under wise and equal laws, even here we find no paradise. Here are crime and poverty and wo; and can you expect a poor ignorant race, born to bondage, scarred with the lash, uneducated, and unused to all the motives which stimulate industry, can you expect these to unlearn in a day the lessons of years, and to furnish all at once themes for eloquent description. Were you to visit those islands, you would find a slovenly agriculture, much ignorance, and more sloth than you see at home; and yet Emancipation works well, far better than could have been anticipated. To me it could hardly have worked otherwise than well. It banished slavery, that wrong and curse not to be borne. It gave freedom, the dear birthright of humanity; and had it done nothing more, I should have found in it cause for joy. Freedom, simple Freedom is "in my estimation just, far prized above all price." I do not stop to ask, if the emancipated are better fed and clothed than formerly. They are Free, and that one word contains a world of good unknown to the most pampered slave.

But emancipation has brought more than naked liberty. The emancipated are making progress in intelligence, comforts, purity; and progress is the great good of life. No matter where men are at any given moment; the great question about them, is, are they going forward? Do they improve? Slavery was immoveable, hopeless degradation. It is the glory of liberty to favor progress, and this great blessing, emancipation has bestowed. We were told indeed, that Emancipation was to turn the green islands of the West Indies into deserts; but they still rise from the tropical sea as blooming and verdant as before. We were told, that the slaves, if set free, would break out in universal massacre; but since that event, not a report has reached us of murder perpetrated by a colored man on the white population. We were told, that crimes would multiply; but they are diminished in every emancipated island, and very greatly in most. We were told that the freed slave, would abandon himself to idleness, and this I did anticipate, to a considerable degree, as the first result. Men, on whom industry had been forced by the lash, and who had been taught to regard sloth as their master's chief good, were strongly tempted to surrender the first days of freedom to indolent indulgence. But in this respect the evil has been so small, as to fill a reflecting man with admiration. In truth, no race but the African could have made the great transition with so little harm to themselves and others. In general, they resumed their work after a short burst of joy. The desire of property, of bettering their lot, at once sprang up within them in sufficient strength to counterbalance the love of ease. Some of them have become proprietors of the soil. New villages have grown up under their hands; their huts are more comfortable; their dress more decent, sometimes too expensive. When I tell you that the price of real estate in these islands has risen, and that the imports from the mother country, especially those for the laborer's use, have increased, you will judge whether the liberated slaves, are living as drones. Undoubtedly the planter has sometimes wanted workmen, and the staple product of the island, sugar, has decreased. But this can be explained without much reproach to the emancipated. The laborer, who in slavery was over-tasked in the cane-field and sugar mill, is anxious to buy or hire land sufficient for his support, and to work for himself, instead of hiring himself to another. A planter from British Guiana, informed me a few weeks ago, that a company of colored men had paid down seventy thousand dollars for a tract of land in the most valuable part of that colony. It is not sloth, so much as a spirit of manly independence, which has withdrawn the laborer from the plantation; and this evil, if so it must be called, has been increased by his unwillingness to subject his wife and daughter to the toils of the field, which they used to bear in the days of Slavery. Undoubtedly the colored population might do more, but they do enough to earn a better lot than they ever enjoyed, and the work of improvement goes on among them.

I pass to a still brighter view. The spirit of education has sprung up among the people to an extent worthy of admiration. We despise them; and yet there is reason to believe, that a more general desire to educate their children is to be found among them, than exists among large portions of the white population in the slave States of the South. They have learned, that their ignorance is the great barrier between them and the white men, and this they are in earnest to prostrate. It has been stated, that in one island, not a child above ten years of age was unable to read. Human history probably furnishes no parallel of an equal progress, in a half civilized community.

To this must be added their interest in religious institutions. Their expenditures for the support of these are such, as should put to shame the backwardness of multitudes in countries calling themselves civilized. They do more than we, in proportion to their means. Some of them have even subscribed funds for the diffusion of the gospel in Africa, an instance of their zeal, rather than their wisdom; for they undoubtedly need all they can spare for their own instruction. Their conceptions of religion, are of course narrow and rude, but their hearts have been touched by its simpler truths; and love is the key to higher knowledge.—To this let me add, that marriage is acquiring sanctity in their eyes, that domestic life is putting on a new refinement, and you will see that this people have all the elements of social progress. Property, marriage and religion, have been called the pillars of society, and of these the liberated slave has learned the value.

The result of all these various improvements, is what every wise friend of humanity must rejoice in. Their social position is changed. They have taken rank among men. They are no longer degraded by being looked on as degraded. They no longer live under that withering curse, the contempt of their fellow beings. The tone in which they are spoken to, no longer expresses their infinite and hopeless depression. They are treated as men; some of them engage in lucrative pursuits; all the paths of honor as well as of gain are open to them; they are found in the legislatures; they fill civil offices, they have military appointments, and in all these conditions acquit themselves honorably. Their humanity is recognized, and without this recognition men pine and had better be left to perish.

I have no thought of painting these islands as Edens. That great ignorance prevails among the emancipated people, that they want our energy, that the degradation of slavery has not vanished all at once with the name, this I need not to tell you. No miracle has been wrought on them. But their present lot compared with slavery, is an immense good; and when we consider, that as yet we have seen comparatively nothing of the blessed influences of freedom, we ought to thank God with something of their own fervor for the vast deliverance which he hath vouchsafed them.

We commemorate with transport the redemption of a nation from political bondage; but this is a light burden compared with personal slavery. The oppression which these United States threw off by our revolutionary struggle, was the perfection of freedom, when placed by the side of the galling, crushing, intolerable yoke which bowed the African to the dust. Thank God, it is broken. Thank God, our most injured brethren have risen to the rank of men. Thank God, Eight Hundred Thousand human beings have been made free.

These are the natural topics suggested by this day, but there are still higher views to which I invite your attention. There are other grounds on which this first of August should be hailed with gratitude by the Christian. If I saw in the Emancipation which we celebrate, only the redemption of Eight Hundred Thousand fellow creatures from the greatest wrong on earth, I should indeed rejoice; but I know not that I should commemorate it by public solemnities. This particular result moves me less than other views, which, though less obvious, are far more significant and full of promise.

When I look at West Indian emancipation, what strikes me most forcibly and most joyfully, is the Spirit in which it had its origin. What broke the slaves' chain? Did a foreign invader summon them to his standard, and reward them with freedom for their help in conquering their masters? Or did they owe liberty to their own exasperated valor; to courage maddened by despair; to massacre and unsparing revenge? Or did calculations of the superior profit of free labor, persuade the owner to emancipation as a means of superior gain? No. West Indian emancipation was the fruit of Christian principle acting on the mind and heart of a great people. The liberator of those slaves was Jesus Christ. That voice, which rebuked disease and death and set their victims free, broke the heavier chain of slavery. The conflict against slavery began in England, about fifty years ago. It began with Christians. It was at its birth a christian enterprise. Its power was in the consciences and generous sympathy of men, who had been trained in the school of Christ. It was resisted by prejudice, custom, interest, opulence, pride and the civil power. Almost the whole weight of the commercial class, was at first thrown into the opposite scale. The politician dreaded the effects of abolition on the wealth and revenue of the nation. The King did not disguise his hostility; and I need not tell you that it found little favor with the aristocracy. The titled and proud are not the first to sympathize with the abject. The cause had nothing to rely on, but the spirit of the English people; and that people did respond to the reasonings, pleadings, rebukes of christian philanthropy, as nation never did before. The history of this warfare cannot be read without seeing, that, once at least, a great nation was swayed by high and disinterested principles. Men of the world deride the notion of influencing human affairs by any but selfish motives; and it is a melancholy truth, that the movements of nations have done much to confirm the darkest views of human nature. What a track of crime, desolation, war, we are called by history to travel over! Still history is lighted up by great names, by noble deeds, by patriots and martyrs; and especially in Emancipation we see a great nation, putting forth its power and making great sacrifices, for a distant, degraded race of men, who had no claims but those of wronged and suffering humanity. Some, and not a few, have blamed, as superfluous, the compensation given by England to the planter for the slaves. On one account I rejoice at it. It is a testimony to the disinterested motives of the nation. A people, groaning under a debt which would crush any other people, borrowed Twenty Million pounds sterling, a hundred million of dollars, and paid it as the price of the slaves' freedom. This act stands alone in the page of history, and Emancipation having such an origin, deserves to be singled out for public commemoration.

What gave peculiar interest to this act, was the fallen, abject state of the people, on whom freedom was conferred at such a cost. They were not Englishmen. They had no claim founded on common descent, on common history, or any national bond. There was nothing in their lot to excite the imagination. They had done nothing to draw regard. They weighed nothing in human affairs. They belonged to no nation. They were hardly recognised as men. Humanity could hardly wear a more abject form. But under all this abjectness, under that black skin, under those scars of the lash, under those half naked bodies put up to auction, and sold as cattle, the people of England saw the lineaments of humanity, saw fellow creatures, saw the capacities and rights and immortal destinies of men, and in the spirit of brotherhood, and from reverence for humanity broke their chains.

When I look at this act, I do not stop at its immediate results, at the emancipation of Eight Hundred Thousand human beings, nor do I look at the act as standing alone. I look at the spirit from which it sprung, and see here a grand and most cheering foundation of human hope. I see, that Christianity has not come into the world in vain. I see that the blood of the cross was not shed in vain. I see, that the prophecies in the scriptures of a mighty change in human affairs, were not idle words. It is true, that Christianity has done little compared with these predictions. The corruptions of our age, who is so blind as not to see? But that a new principle, derived from Christianity and destined to renovate the earth, is at work among these various elements; that silently a new spirit of humanity, a new respect for human nature, a new comprehension of human rights, a new feeling of brotherhood, and new ideas of a higher social state, have been and are unfolding themselves, under the influences of christian truth and christian civilization, who can deny? Society is not what it once was. Amidst all the stir of selfish passion, the still voice of Christianity is heard; a diviner spirit mixes however imperfectly, with the workings of worldiness; and we are beginning to learn the mighty revolution which a heavenly faith is to accomplish here on earth.

Christianity is the hope of the world, and we ought to regard every conspicuous manifestation of its spirit and power, as an era in human history. We are dazzled by revolutions of empires; we hope much from the rise or fall of Governments. But nothing but christianity can regenerate the earth; and accordingly we should hail with joy every sign of a clearer comprehension, and a deeper feeling of its truths. Christianity truly understood, has a direct tendency to that renovation of the world which it foretells. It is not an abstract system, secluding the disciple from his kind; but it makes him one with his race, breaks down all barriers between him and his brethren, arms him with a martyr's spirit in the cause of humanity, sends him forth to be a saviour of the lost; and just as far as Christianity is thus viewed and felt by its followers, the redemption of the world draws nigh. These views of religion are making their way. They dawn upon us not only in emancipation, but in many other movements of our age; not that they have ever been wholly obscured; but the rank which they hold in the Christian system, and the vast social changes which they involve, have not, until the present day, been dreamed of.

All the doctrines of Christianity are more and more seen to be bonds of close, spiritual, reverential union between man and man, and this is the most cheering view of our time. Christianity is a revelation of the infinite, universal, parental love of God towards his human family, comprehending the most sinful, descending to the most fallen, and its aim is to breathe the same love into its disciples. It shows us Christ tasting death, for every man, and it summons us to take his cross, or to participate of his sufferings in the same cause. Its doctrine of Immortality gives infinite worth to every human being; for every one is destined to this endless life. The doctrine of the "Word made flesh," shows us God uniting himself most intimately with our nature, manifesting himself in a human form, for the very end of making us partakers of his own perfection. The doctrine of Grace, as it is termed, reveals the Infinite Father imparting his Holy Spirit, the best gift he can impart, to the humblest human being who emplores it. Thus love and reverence for human nature, a love for man stronger than death, is the very spirit of Christianity. Undoubtedly this spirit is faintly comprehended by the best of us. Some of its most striking expressions, are still derided in society. Society still rests on selfish principles. Men sympathise still with the prosperous and great, not the abject and down-trodden. But amidst this degradation, brighter glimpses of Christianity are caught than before. There are deeper, wider sympathies with mankind. The idea of raising up the mass of human beings to intellectual, moral, and spiritual dignity, is penetrating many minds. Among the signs of a brighter day, perhaps the West Indian emancipation is the most conspicuous; for in this the rights of the most despised men have been revered.

There are some among us at the present moment, who are waiting for the speedy coming of Christ. They expect, before another year closes, to see him in the clouds, to hear his voice, to stand before his judgement seat. These illusions spring from misinterpretation of Scripture language. Christ in the New Testament, is said to *come,* whenever his religion breaks out in new glory, or gains new triumphs. He came in the Holy Spirit in the day of Pentecost. He came in the destruction of Jerusalem, which, by subverting the old ritual law, and breaking the power of the worst enemies of his religion, ensured to it new victories. He came in the Reformation of the church. He came on this day four years ago, when, through his religion, Eight Hundred Thousand men were raised from the lowest degradation, to the rights, and dignity, and fellowship of men. Christ's outward appearance is of little moment, compared with the brighter manifestation of his spirit. The Christian, whose inward eyes and ears are touched by God, discerns the coming of Christ, hears the sound of his chariot wheels and the voice of his trumpet, when no other perceives them. He discerns the Saviour's advent in the dawning of higher truth on the world, in new aspirations of the church after perfection, in the prostration of prejudice and error, in brighter expressions of Christian love, in more enlightened and intense consecration of the Christian to the cause of humanity, freedom, and religion. Christ comes in the conversion, the regeneration, the emancipation of the world.

You here see, why it is that I rejoice in the great event which this day commemorates. To me this event does not stand alone. It is a sign of the triumph of Christianity, and a presage and herald of grander victories of truth and humanity. Christianity did not do its last work when it broke the slave's chain. No; this was but a type of what it is to achieve. Since the African was emancipated, the drunkard has been set free. We may count the disenthralled from intemperance by hundreds of thousands, almost by millions, and this work has been achieved by Christian truth and Christian love. In this, we have a new proof of the coming of Christ in his kingdom; and the grand result of these and other kindred movements of our times, should be, to give us a new faith in what Christianity is to accomplish. We need this faith. We are miserably wanting in it. We scarcely believe what we see of the triumphs of the cross. This is the most disastrous unbelief of our times. I am pointed now and then to an infidel, as he is called, a man who denies Christianity. But there is a sadder sight. It is that of thousands and millions who profess Christianity, but have no faith in its power to accomplish the work to which it is ordained, no faith in the power of Christ over the passions, prejudices, and corrupt institutions of men, no faith in the end of his mission, in the regenerating energy of his spirit and truth. Let this day, my friends, breathe into all our souls a new trust in the destinies of our race. Let us look on the future with new hope. I see indeed numberless obstructions to the regeneration of the world. But is not a deep feeling of the corruptions of the world fermenting in many breasts? Is there not a new thirst for an individual and social life more in harmony with Jesus Christ, than has yet existed? Can great truths, after having been once developed, die? Is not the human soul opening itself more and more to the divine perfection and beauty of Christ's character? And who can foretell what this mighty agency is to accomplish in the world? The present day is indeed a day of distrust, complaint, and anxious forebodings. On every side, voices of fear and despondency reach us. Let us respond to them, with a voice of faith and hope. Let us not shut our eyes ungratefully on the good already wrought in our times; and seeing in this the pledge of higher blessings, let us arm ourselves with manly resolution to do or suffer, each in his own sphere, whatever may serve to prepare the way for a holier and happier age. It may be, as some believe, that this age is to be preceded by fearful judgments, by "days of vengeance," by purifying fire; but the triumphs of Christianity, however deferred, are not the less surely announced by what it has already achieved.

I have now given the more general views which belong to this occasion; but I cannot close this address without coming nearer home, and touching, however slightly, some topics of a more personal character, and in which we have a more particular interest.

I am a stranger among you; but when I look round, I feel as if the subject of this address peculiarly befitted this spot. Where am I now pleading the cause and speaking the praises of liberty? Not in crowded cities, where, amidst men's works and luxuries, and wild speculations, and eager competitions for gain, the spirit of liberty often languishes; but amidst towering mountains, embosoming peaceful vales. Amidst these vast works of God, the soul naturally goes forth and cannot endure the thought of a chain. Your free air, which we come to inhale for health, breathes into us something better than health, even a freer spirit. Mountains have always been famed for nourishing brave souls and the love of liberty. At Thermopylae, in many a fastness of Switzerland, in the gorges of mountains, the grand battles of liberty have been fought. Even in this country, slavery hardly sets foot on the mountains. She curses the plain; but as soon as you begin to ascend the highlands of the South, slavery begins to disappear. West Virginia and East Tennessee are cultivated chiefly by the muscles of freemen; and could these districts be erected into States, they would soon clear themselves of the guilt and shame of enslaving their brethren. Men of Berkshire! whose nerves and souls the mountain air has braced, *You* surely will respond to him, who speaks of the blessings of freedom and the misery of bondage. I feel, as if the feeble voice, which now addresses you, must find an echo amidst these forest-crowned heights. Do they not impart something of their own power and loftiness to men's souls? Should our Commonwealth ever be invaded by victorious armies, freedom's last asylum would be here. Here may a free spirit, may reverence for all human rights, may sympathy for all the oppressed, may a stern, solemn purpose to give no sanction to oppression, take stronger and stronger possession of men's minds, and from these mountains may generous impulses spread far and wide.

The joy of this occasion is damped by one thought. Our own country is in part the land of slavery; and slavery becomes more hideous here than any where else, by its contrast with our free institutions. It is deformity married to beauty. It is, as if a flame from Hell were to burst forth in the regions of the blessed. No other evil in our country, but this, should alarm us. Our other difficulties are the mists dimming our prospects for a moment. This is a dark cloud, scowling over our whole land; and within it the prophetic ear hear the low muttering of the angry thunder. We in the free States, try to escape the reproach which falls on America, by saying, that this institution is not ours, that the foot of the slave never pressed our soil;

but we cannot fly from the shame or guilt of the institution, as long as we give it any support. Most unhappily, there are provisions of the Constitution binding us to give it support. Let us resolve to free ourselves from these. Let us say to the South, "we shall use no force to subvert your slavery; neither will we use it to uphold the evil." Let no temptations, no love of gain, seduce us to abet or sanction this wrong. There is something worse than to be a slave. It is to make other men slaves. Better be trampled in the dust, than trample on a fellow creature. Much as I shrink from the evils inflicted by bondage on the millions who bear it, I would sooner endure them than inflict them on a brother. Freemen of the mountains! as far as you have power, remove from yourselves, from our dear and venerable mother, the Commonwealth of Massachusetts, and from all the Free States, the baseness and guilt of ministering to slavery, of acting as the Slaveholder's police, of lending him arms and strength to secure his victim. I deprecate all political action on slavery, except for one end, and this end is, to release the free states from all connection with this oppressive institution, to sever slavery wholly from the National Government, to make it exclusively the concern of the States in which it exists. For this end, memorials should be poured in upon Congress, to obtain from that body such modifications of the laws, and such propositions to amend the constitution, as well set us free from obligation to sanction slavery. This done, political action on the subject ought to cease. We shall then have no warrant to name slavery in Congress, or to it, except by that moral influence which every man is bound to exert against every form of evil.

There are some people here, more kind than wise, who are unwilling that any action or sensibility on the subject of slavery should spring up at the North, from their apprehensions of the danger of Emancipation. The danger of Emancipation! this parrot-phrase, caught from the South, is thought by many a sufficient answer to all the pleas that can be urged in favor of the slave. But the lesson of this day, is the safety of Emancipation. The West Indian Islands teach us this lesson with a thousand tongues. Emancipation can hardly take place under more unfavorable circumstances than it encountered in those islands. The master abhorred it, repelled it as long as possible, submitted to it only from force, and consequently did little to mitigate its evils, or to conciliate the freed bondman. In those islands, the slaves were eight or ten times more numerous than the whites.

Yet perfect order has followed emancipation. Since this event, the military force has been reduced, and the colored men instead of breaking into riot, are among the soldiers by whom it is to be oppressed. In this country, the white population of the South exceeds in number the colored; and who that knows the two classes, can apprehend danger from the former, in case of emancipation? Holding all the property, all the intellectual, the civil, the military power, and distinguished by courage, it seems incredible, that the white race should tremble before the colored, should be withheld by fear from setting them free. If the alarm be real, it can be explained only by the old observation, that the injurious are prone to fear, that men naturally suspect and dread those whom they wrong. All tyrants are jealous, and persuade themselves, that were they to loosen the reins, lawlessness, pillage, murder, would disorganise society. But emancipation, conferred deliberately, and conscientiously, is safe. So say facts, and reason says the same. Chains are not the necessary bonds of society. Oppression is not the rock on which States rest. To keep the peace, you need not make the earth a province of Satan; in other words, you need not establish wrong and outrage by law. The way to keep men from cutting your throats, is not to put them under the lash, to extort their labor by force, to spoil them of their earnings, to pamper yourselves out of their compelled toil, and to keep them in brutal ignorance. Do not, do not believe this. Believe, if you will, that seeds of thistles will yield luxuriant crops of wheat; believe that drought will fertilize your fields. But do not believe that you must rob and crush your fellow creatures, to make them harmless, to keep the State in order and peace. Oh! do not imagine that God has laid on any one the necessity of doing wrong; that He, who secures the blessed harmony of the universe, by wise and beneficent laws, has created a world, in which all pure and righteous laws must be broken to perserve the show of peace. I honor free enquiry, and willingly hear my cherished opinions questioned; but there are certain truths which I can no more doubt than my own existence. That God is just and good, and that justice and goodness are his laws, and are at once the safety and glory of his creatures, I can as little question, as that the whole is greater than the part. When I am told, that society can only subsist by robbing men of their dearest rights, my reason is as much insulted, as if I were gravely taught that effects require no cause, or that it is the nature of yonder beautiful stream to ascend these mountains, or to return to its source. The doctrine, that violence, oppression, inhumanity, is an essential element of society, is so revolting, that did I believe it, I would say, let society perish, let man and his works be swept away and the earth be abandoned to the brutes. Better that the globe should be tenanted by brutes, than brutalised men. No: it is safe to be just, to respect men's rights, to treat our neighbors as ourselves; and any doctrine hostile to this, is born of the Evil One. Men do not need to be crushed. A wise kindness avails with them more than force. Even the insane are disarmed by kindness. Once, the mad-house, with its dens, fetters, straight-waistcoats, whips, horrible punishments, at which humanity now shudders and the blood boils with indignation, was thought just as necessary as slavery is now deemed at the South. But we have learned at last, that human nature, even when robbed of reason, can be ruled, calmed, restored by wise kindness; that it was only maddened and made more desperate by the chains imposed to keep it from outrage and murder. Treat men as men, and they will not prove wild beasts. We first rob them of their humanity and then chain them because they are not human. What a picture of slavery is given by the common argument for its continuance! The slaves, we are told must be kept under the lash, or they will turn murderers. Two millions and a half of our fellow creatures at the South, we are assured, have the seeds of murder in their hearts, and must be stripped of all human rights, for the safety of their neighbors. If such be a slave country, the sooner it is depopulated the better. But it is not true. A more innocent race than the African does not exist on the earth. They are less given to violence and murder, than we Anglo-Saxons. But when did wrong ever want excuse? When did oppression ever fail to make out a good cause in its own eyes?

The truth is, that slavery is perpetuated at the South not from the fear of massacre, but from a stronger principle. A respected slaveholder said to me not long ago, ''The question of slavery is a question of Property, and Property is dearer to a man than life.'' The master holds fast his slave, because he sees in him, not a wild beast, but a profitable chattel. Mr. Clay has told us, that the slaves are worth in the market, I think, twelve hundred millions of dollars, and smiles at the thought of calling men to surrender such a mass of property.[7] It is not because they are so fierce, but so profitable, that they are kept in chains. Were they meek angels from God's throne, imprisoned for a while in human frames, and were they at the same time worth Twelve Hundred Millions of dollars in the market, comparatively few, I fear, would be suffered to return to their native skies, as long as the chain could fetter them to the plantation. I know, that there are generous exceptions to the spirit of slavery as now portrayed; but this spirit in the main is mercenary. I know, that other considerations than this of property, that considerations of prudence and benevolence, help to confirm the slaveholder in his aversion to emancipation. There are mixed motives for perpetuating slavery, as for almost all human actions. But the grand motive is Gain, the love of Money, the unwillingness to part with Property, and were this to yield to justice and humanity, the dread of massacre would not long retard emancipation.

My friends, your compassion is often called forth by predictions of massacre, of butchered children, of violated women, in case of emancipation. But do not waste your sympathies on possible evils, which wisdom and kindness may avert. Keep some of your tears and tenderness for what exists; for the poor girl whose innocence has no protection; for the wife and mother who may be widowed and made childless before night by a stroke of the auctioneer's hammer, for the man subjected to the whip of a brutal overseer, and hunted, if he flies, by blood-hounds, and shot down if he outstrips his pursuers. For the universe, I would not let loose massacre on the Southern states, or on any population. Sooner would I have all the slaves perish, than achieve their freedom by promiscuous carnage. But I see no necessity of carnage. I am sure, that to treat men with justice and humanity is not the way to turn them into robbers or assassins. Undoubtedly wisdom is to be used in conferring this great good. We ask no precipitate action at the South; we dictate no mode of conferring freedom. We ask only a settled purpose to bring slavery to an end, and we are sure that this will devise a safe and happy way of exercising justice and love.

Am I asked what is the duty of the North in regard to slavery? On this subject I have lately written; I will only say, I recommend no crusade against slavery, no use of physical or legislative power for its destruction, no irruption into the South to tamper with the slave, or to repeal or resist the laws.[8] Our duties on this subject are plain. First, we must free ourselves, as I have said, from all constitutional or legal obligations to uphold slavery. In the next place, we must give free and strong expression to our reprobation of slavery. The North has but one weapon, moral force, the utterance of moral judgment, moral feeling and religious conviction. I do not say that this alone is to subvert slavery. Providence never accomplishes its ends by a single instrument. All social changes come from mixed motives, from various impulses, and slavery is to fall through various causes. But among these, a high place will belong to the general conviction of its evils and wrongs. Opinion is stronger than kings, mobs, lynch laws, or any other laws for repressing thought and speech. Whoever spreads through his circle, be it wide or narrow, just opinions and feelings in regard to slavery, hastens its fall. There is one point on which your moral influence may be exerted with immediate effect. Should a slave-hunter ever profane these mountainous retreats by seeking here a flying bondman, regard him as a legalized robber. Oppose no force to him; you need not do it. Your contempt and indignation will be enough to disarm the "man-stealer" of the unholy power conferred on him by unrighteous laws.

I began this subject in hope, and in hope I end. I have turned aside to speak of the great stain on our country, which makes us the bye-word and scorn of the nations; but I do not despair. Mighty powers are at work in the world. Who can stay them? God's word has gone forth and "it cannot return to him void."[9] A new comprehension of the Christian spirit, a new reverence for humanity, a new feeling of brotherhood and of all men's relation to the common Father—this is among the signs of our times. We see it; do we not feel it? Before this, all oppressions are to fall. Society silently pervaded by this, is to change its aspect of universal warfare for peace. The power of selfishness, all-grasping and seemingly invincible, is to yield to this diviner energy. The song of angels, "On Earth Peace," will not always sound as fiction. O come thou kingdom of Heaven, for which we daily pray! Come, Friend and Saviour of the race, who didst shed thy blood on the cross to reconcile man to man, and Earth to Heaven! Come, ye predicted ages of righteousness and love, for which the faithful have so long yearned. Come, Father Almighty, and crown with thine omnipotence the humble strivings of thy children to subvert oppression and wrong, to spread light and freedom, peace and joy, the truth and spirit of thy Son, through the whole earth.

Notes

1. The emancipation of slaves in the British West Indies was the culmination of a long history of organization and legislation which began with opposition to the slave trade in the eighteenth century. Under legislation enacted by the House of Commons in 1833, slaves were to be freed, but subjected to a seven-year apprenticeship in which they were bound to their masters. This apprenticeship period was cut short, and all slaves were freed in August, 1838.

2. Channing had refused to join abolitionist organizations despite his opposition to slavery, fearing that his independence of thought and his influence might be thereby compromised.

3. Samuel Hopkins (1721–1805) was the influential Calvinist clergyman who founded the Hopkinsian system of Calvinism (see the discussion in the introduction). He was an early anti-slavery spokesman, influential in the prohibition of slavery in Rhode Island. He is the author of *A Dialogue Concerning the Slavery of the Africans, Shewing it to be the Duty and Interest of the American Colonies to Emancipate all Their African Slaves* (Norwich, CT, 1776), and *A Discourse Upon the Slave Trade, and the Slavery of the Africans* (Providence, R.I., 1793).

4. Henry Dwight Sedgwick (1784–1831) was a New York attorney and legal scholar, contributor to the *North American Review,* and opponent of slavery.

5. Channing went to St. Croix for health reasons in 1830, staying six months. The "volume on Slavery" which opened to him there was his influential *Slavery* (Boston, 1835).

6. James A. Thome and J. Horace Kimball, *Emancipation in the West Indies; or Six Months Tour in Antigua, Barbadoes, and Jamaica in the Year 1837* (New York, 1838).

7. In a speech to the United States Senate on February 7, 1839, Henry Clay (1777–1852) estimated a slave population of 2 to 3 million, valued at $400 each to arrive at his figure. In the same speech, Clay referred to "a visionary dogma, which holds that negro slaves can not be the subject of property." Channing's *Slavery* (1835) is one possible object of his reference. See *Works of Henry Clay,* ed. Calvin Colton, 7 vols. (New York, 1897), 6:139–59.

8. Channing refers to his *The Duty of the Free States* (1842) in *Works,* 6:231–372.

9. Isaiah 55:11—"So shall my word be that goeth forth out of my mouth: it shall not return unto me void, but it shall accomplish that which I please, and it shall prosper *in the thing* whereto I sent it."

Textual Corrections ("Address at Lenox")

On p. 268, line 11, a period has been substituted for a comma after "received".

On p. 269, line 23, a comma between "I" and "should" has been deleted.

On p. 269, line 32, a period has been added after "own".

On p. 273, line 22, "he" has been inserted before "sleeps".

On p. 274, line 34, a double quotation mark replaces the single quotation mark in the original text.

On p. 275, line 12, a comma has been added after "degradation".

On p. 278, line 16, spacing has been added between the words "with new".

On p. 281, in footnote, "Thome" has replaced "Thorne".

On p. 282, line 25, "unrightous" has been changed to "unrighteous".

On p. 283, line 13, "shout" has been substituted for "shont".

On p. 283, line 25, "breathe" has been substituted for "breath".

On p. 284, line 17, a period has been added after "most".

On p. 285, line 4, a period has been added after "colony".

On p. 287, line 11, a comma has been excised before "enterprise".

On p. 288, lines 6–7, "common descent" has replaced "commond escent".

On p. 288, line 7, a period has been added after "bond".

On p. 289, line 39, "than" has replaced "then".

On p. 291, line 29, "holier" has replaced "holilier".

On p. 291, line 29, "is" has replaced "s".

On p. 293, line 2, a period has been added after "support".

On p. 293, line 23, a comma after "action" has been excised.

On p. 295, line 15, "even" has been substituted for "ever".

On p. 296, line 21, "and" has been substituted for "aud" after "wife".

A SELECTED BIBLIOGRAPHY

I. BIBLIOGRAPHICAL STUDIES

Myerson, Joel. "William Ellery Channing." In *First Printings of American Authors,* edited by Matthew J. Bruccoli et al., 3:319–20. Detroit: Gale Research, 1977–79.

Robinson, David. "William Ellery Channing." In *The Transcendentalists: A Review of Research and Criticism,* edited by Joel Myerson, 310–16. Modern Language Association, 1984.

Wright, Conrad. "A Channing Bibliography: 1929–1959." *Proceedings of the Unitarian Historical Society* 12 (1959):22–24.

II. WORKS BY CHANNING

The Works of William E. Channing, D.D. 6 vols. Boston: James Munroe, 1841–43.

The Works of William E. Channing, D.D., rev. ed. Boston: American Unitarian Association, 1886.

III. BIOGRAPHY AND CRITICISM

Ahlstrom, Sydney. "The Interpretation of Channing." *New England Quarterly,* 30 (1957):99–105.

Brooks, Van Wyck. *The Flowering of New England 1815–1865.* New York: E. P. Dutton, 1956.

Brown, Arthur W. *Always Young for Liberty: A Biography of William Ellery Channing.* Syracuse: Syracuse University Press, 1956.

Brownson, Orestes Augustus. "The Laboring Classes." *Boston Quarterly Review,* 3 (1840):358–95, 420–512.

Buell, Lawrence. *Literary Transcendentalism: Style and Vision in the American Renaissance.* Ithaca: Cornell University Press, 1973.

Chadwick, John White. *William Ellery Channing: Minister of Religion.* Boston: Houghton, Mifflin, 1903.

Channing, William Henry. *Memoir of William Ellery Channing.* 3 vols. Boston: William Crosby and H.P. Nichols, 1848. Reprinted in one volume as *The Life of William Ellery Channing.* Boston: American Unitarian Association, 1880.

Delbanco, Andrew. *William Ellery Channing: An Essay on the Liberal Spirit in America.* Cambridge: Harvard University Press, 1981.

Edgell, David P. *William Ellery Channing: An Intellectual Portrait.* Boston: Beacon Press, 1955.

Hedge, Frederic Henry. "Address of Rev. Frederic H. Hedge." In *Services in Memory of Rev. William E. Channing, D.D., at the Arlington-Street Church, Boston, on Sunday Evening, October 6, 1867,* 26–31. Boston: John Wilson and Son, 1867.

Howe, Daniel Walker. *The Unitarian Conscience: Harvard Moral Philosophy, 1805–1861.* Cambridge: Harvard University Press, 1970.

Hutchison, William R. *The Transcendentalist Ministers: Church Reform in the New England Renaissance.* New Haven: Yale University Press, 1959.

Mendelsohn, Jack. *Channing: The Reluctant Radical.* Boston: Little, Brown, 1971.

Parrington, Vernon Lewis. *The Romantic Revolution in America 1800–1860.* New York: Harcourt, Brace, 1927.

Patterson, Robert Leet. *The Philosophy of William Ellery Channing.* New York: Bookman Associates, 1952.

Peabody, Elizabeth Palmer. *Reminiscences of Rev. Wm. Ellery Channing, D. D.* Boston: Roberts Brothers, 1880.

Rice, Madeline Hook. *Federal Street Pastor: The Life of William Ellery Channing.* New York: Bookman Associates, 1961.

Robinson, David. "The Legacy of Channing: Culture as a Religious Category in New England Thought." *Harvard Theological Review,* 74 (1981): 221–39.

Schneider, Herbert W. *A History of American Philosophy.* New York: Columbia University Press, 1946.

Spiller, Robert E. "A Case for W. E. Channing." *New England Quarterly,* 3 (1930):55–81.

Stange, Douglas C. *Patterns of Antislavery among American Unitarians, 1831–1860.* Rutherford, N.J.: Fairleigh Dickinson University Press, 1977.

Wright, Conrad. *The Liberal Christians: Essays on American Unitarian History.* Boston: Beacon Press, 1970.

INDEX TO INTRODUCTION

INDEX TO TEXTS

305

201 · Religious Right   1980's   Self-imposed
                                    slavery.
                                    Impotence